KIERKEGAARD'S INFLUENCE ON LITERATURE, CRITICISM AND ART

TOME II: DENMARK

Kierkegaard Research: Sources, Reception and Resources
Volume 12, Tome II

Kierkegaard Research: Sources, Reception and Resources
is a publication of the Søren Kierkegaard Research Centre

Kierkegaard's Influence on Literature, Criticism and Art

Tome II: Denmark

Edited by
JON STEWART

ASHGATE

Published by
Ashgate Publishing Limited
Wey Court East
Union Road
Farnham
Surrey, GU9 7PT
England

Ashgate Publishing Company
110 Cherry Street
Suite 3-1
Burlington, VT 05401-3818
USA

www.ashgate.com

British Library Cataloguing in Publication Data
A catalogue record for this book is available from the British Library.

The Library of Congress has cataloged the printed edition as follows:
Kierkegaard's influence on literature, criticism, and art : Denmark / edited by Jon Stewart.
    p. cm.—(Kierkegaard research ; v. 12, t. 2)
  Includes index.
  ISBN 978-1-4724-1201-0 (hardcover) 1. Kierkegaard, Søren, 1813–1855—Influence.
2. Kierkegaard, Søren, 1813–1855—Literary art. 3. Criticism. I. Stewart, Jon (Jon Bartley)
  B4377.K5124 2012
  198'.9—dc23

                                                                                    2012026885

ISBN 9781472412010 (hbk)

Cover design by Katalin Nun

Printed in the United Kingdom by Henry Ling Limited, at the Dorset Press, Dorchester, DT1 1HD

Contents

List of Contributors

Julie K. Allen, University of Wisconsin-Madison, Department of Scandinavian Studies, 1302 Van Hise Hall, 1220 Linden Drive, Madison, WI 53706, USA.

William Banks, University of Wisconsin-Madison, Department of Scandinavian Studies, 1306 Van Hise Hall, 1220 Linden Drive, Madison, WI 53705, USA.

Poul Houe, Department of German, Scandinavian and Dutch, University of Minnesota, 205 Folwell Hall, 9 Pleasant Street S.E., Minneapolis, MN 55455-0124, USA.

Søren Landkildehus, c/o Hong Kierkegaard Library, St. Olaf College, 1510 St. Olaf Avenue, Northfield, MN 55057-1097, USA.

Esben Lindemann, c/o Søren Kierkegaard Research Centre, Farvergade 27 D, 1463 Copenhagen K, Denmark.

Peter Tudvad, Reichenbergerstr. 157, D-10999 Berlin, Germany.

Steen Tullberg, Grundtvig Centre, Aarhus University, Vartov Department, Farvergade 27 D, 1463 Copenhagen K, Denmark.

List of Abbreviations

BA   *The Book on Adler*, trans. by Howard V. Hong and Edna H. Hong, Princeton: Princeton University Press 1998.

C   *The Crisis and a Crisis in the Life of an Actress*, trans. by Howard V. Hong and Edna H. Hong, Princeton: Princeton University Press 1997.

CA   *The Concept of Anxiety*, trans. by Reidar Thomte in collaboration with Albert B. Anderson, Princeton: Princeton University Press 1980.

CD   *Christian Discourses*, trans. by Howard V. Hong and Edna H. Hong, Princeton: Princeton University Press 1997.

CI   *The Concept of Irony*, trans. by Howard V. Hong and Edna H. Hong, Princeton: Princeton University Press 1989.

CIC   *The Concept of Irony*, trans. with an Introduction and Notes by Lee M. Capel, London: Collins 1966.

COR   *The Corsair Affair; Articles Related to the Writings*, trans. by Howard V. Hong and Edna H. Hong, Princeton: Princeton University Press 1982.

CUP1   *Concluding Unscientific Postscript*, vol. 1, trans. by Howard V. Hong and Edna H. Hong, Princeton: Princeton University Press 1982.

CUP2   *Concluding Unscientific Postscript*, vol. 2, trans. by Howard V. Hong and Edna H. Hong, Princeton: Princeton University Press 1982.

CUPH   *Concluding Unscientific Postscript*, trans. by Alastair Hannay, Cambridge and New York: Cambridge University Press 2009.

EO1   *Either/Or*, Part I, trans. by Howard V. Hong and Edna H. Hong, Princeton: Princeton University Press 1987.

EO2   *Either/Or*, Part II, trans. by Howard V. Hong and Edna H. Hong, Princeton: Princeton University Press 1987.

EOP   *Either/Or*, trans. by Alastair Hannay, Harmondsworth: Penguin Books 1992.

EPW   *Early Polemical Writings*, among others: *From the Papers of One Still Living*; *Articles from Student Days*; *The Battle Between the Old and the New Soap-Cellars*, trans. by Julia Watkin, Princeton: Princeton University Press 1990.

EUD   *Eighteen Upbuilding Discourses*, trans. by Howard V. Hong and Edna H. Hong, Princeton: Princeton University Press 1990.

FSE   *For Self-Examination*, trans. by Howard V. Hong and Edna H. Hong, Princeton: Princeton University Press 1990.

FT   *Fear and Trembling*, trans. by Howard V. Hong and Edna H. Hong, Princeton: Princeton University Press 1983.

FTP   *Fear and Trembling*, trans. by Alastair Hannay, Harmondsworth: Penguin Books 1985.

JC   *Johannes Climacus, or De omnibus dubitandum est*, trans. by Howard V. Hong and Edna H. Hong, Princeton: Princeton University Press 1985.

JFY   *Judge for Yourself!*, trans. by Howard V. Hong and Edna H. Hong, Princeton: Princeton University Press 1990.

JP   *Søren Kierkegaard's Journals and Papers*, vols. 1–6, ed. and trans. by Howard V. Hong and Edna H. Hong, assisted by Gregor Malantschuk (vol. 7, Index and Composite Collation), Bloomington and London: Indiana University Press 1967–78.

KAC   *Kierkegaard's Attack upon "Christendom," 1854–1855*, trans. by Walter Lowrie, Princeton: Princeton University Press 1944.

KJN   *Kierkegaard's Journals and Notebooks*, vols. 1–11, ed. by Niels Jørgen Cappelørn, Alastair Hannay, David Kangas, Bruce H. Kirmmse, George Pattison, Vanessa Rumble, and K. Brian Söderquist, Princeton and Oxford: Princeton University Press 2007ff.

LD   *Letters and Documents*, trans. by Henrik Rosenmeier, Princeton: Princeton University Press 1978.

LR   *A Literary Review*, trans. by Alastair Hannay, Harmondsworth: Penguin Books 2001.

M   *The Moment and Late Writings*, trans. by Howard V. Hong and Edna H. Hong, Princeton: Princeton University Press 1998.

P   *Prefaces / Writing Sampler*, trans. by Todd W. Nichol, Princeton: Princeton University Press 1997.

PC   *Practice in Christianity*, trans. by Howard V. Hong and Edna H. Hong, Princeton: Princeton University Press 1991.

PF   *Philosophical Fragments*, trans. by Howard V. Hong and Edna H. Hong, Princeton: Princeton University Press 1985.

PJ   *Papers and Journals: A Selection*, trans. by Alastair Hannay, Harmonds-worth: Penguin Books 1996.

PLR   *Prefaces: Light Reading for Certain Classes as the Occasion May Require*, trans. by William McDonald, Tallahassee: Florida State University Press 1989.

PLS   *Concluding Unscientific Postscript*, trans. by David F. Swenson and Walter Lowrie, Princeton: Princeton University Press 1941.

PV   *The Point of View* including *On My Work as an Author*, *The Point of View for My Work as an Author*, and *Armed Neutrality*, trans. by Howard V. Hong and Edna H. Hong, Princeton: Princeton University Press 1998.

PVL   *The Point of View for My Work as an Author* including *On My Work as an Author*, trans. by Walter Lowrie, New York and London: Oxford University Press 1939.

R   *Repetition*, trans. by Howard V. Hong and Edna H. Hong, Princeton: Princeton University Press 1983.

SBL   *Notes of Schelling's Berlin Lectures*, trans. by Howard V. Hong and Edna H. Hong, Princeton: Princeton University Press 1989.

SLW   *Stages on Life's Way*, trans. by Howard V. Hong and Edna H. Hong, Princeton: Princeton University Press 1988.

SUD   *The Sickness unto Death*, trans. by Howard V. Hong and Edna H. Hong, Princeton: Princeton University Press 1980.

SUDP   *The Sickness unto Death*, trans. by Alastair Hannay, London and New York: Penguin Books 1989.

TA   *Two Ages: The Age of Revolution and the Present Age. A Literary Review*, trans. by Howard V. Hong and Edna H. Hong, Princeton: Princeton University Press 1978.

TD   *Three Discourses on Imagined Occasions*, trans. by Howard V. Hong and Edna H. Hong, Princeton: Princeton University Press 1993.

UD   *Upbuilding Discourses in Various Spirits*, trans. by Howard V. Hong and Edna H. Hong, Princeton: Princeton University Press 1993.

WA   *Without Authority* including *The Lily in the Field and the Bird of the Air, Two Ethical-Religious Essays, Three Discourses at the Communion on Fridays, An Upbuilding Discourse, Two Discourses at the Communion on Fridays*, trans. by Howard V. Hong and Edna H. Hong, Princeton: Princeton University Press 1997.

WL *Works of Love*, trans. by Howard V. Hong and Edna H. Hong, Princeton: Princeton University Press 1995.

WS *Writing Sampler*, trans. by Todd W. Nichol, Princeton: Princeton University Press 1997.

Karen Blixen:

Kierkegaard, Isak Dinesen, and the Twisted Images of Divinity and Humanity

Søren Landkildehus

> *Elle est retrouvée.*
> *Quoi?—L'Éternité.*
> *C'est la mer allée*
> *Avec le soleil.*
> Rimbaud, *L'Éternité*, 1872[1]

I. Introducing Karen Blixen/Isak Dinesen

Karen Blixen, née Dinesen in 1885, emerged in the 1930s as a distinctive author *hors catégorie*, whose works were and are at a distance from the prevailing literary tendencies of that era, and which continue to provoke readers with their depth and playfulness. Her authorship is popularly known through her autobiographical tale of her life in Kenya, *Out of Africa*, and her anecdote of destiny, *Babette's Feast*, both of which have enjoyed dramatization. Thus, the popular knowledge of Karen Blixen is nowadays due to the dissemination through the medium of film. But in her own time, Karen Blixen was a celebrated storyteller, who moved confidently amongst the intelligentsia in Denmark as well as with other celebrated artists, such as for example Marilyn Monroe and Arthur Miller.

As a writer, Karen Blixen is not first and foremost a Danish writer, since most of her production was initially published in English. Perhaps one might call her a bilingual author, since the Danish versions of her stories were published almost simultaneously.[2] She published most and eventually all of her Danish versions under her own name, but kept publishing the English versions under the pseudonym Isak Dinesen. Her father, Wilhelm Dinesen, who published various writings of varying quality, committed suicide probably due to suffering from syphilis. Karen saw

---

I am grateful to Hugh S. Pyper for excellent conversation on this topic over the years, to Lise Faillettaz for stimulating discussion on an earlier draft, to Kirsten Søltoft Klercke for valuable comments and suggestions, to Antony Aumann for his helpful, insightful and critical remarks, and to the Hong Kierkegaard Library for repeatedly supporting my research.

[1]   Arthur Rimbaud, *Oeuvres des Ardennes au Désert*, Paris: Pocket 2008, p. 169.

[2]   Some stories were translated into Danish and at least one into English by others, see Liselotte Henriksen, *Blixikon*, Copenhagen: Gyldendal 1999, passim.

some repetition of her father's fate in her own life,[3] and so one interpretation of the adoption of the pseudonym is that it signifies the repetition of hereditary sin—from Abraham to Isaac—from the father to the son/heir, and here the "heir" of the writer.

As a woman, Karen married the Swedish Baron Bror von Blixen-Finecke in 1914. They settled in East Africa on a coffee farm, which had been purchased by Bror but funded by Karen's relations. The marriage did not last and ended in divorce in 1925. Each had their affairs, with Karen's well-known relationship to Denys Finch Hatton, who tragically died in an airplane crash, in the foreground. Yet, it was probably because of Bror's promiscuity that Karen contracted syphilis in 1914. Eventually, she had to give up the farm in 1931, and with ruined health and financially destitute she returned to live with her mother in Denmark. Karen—as a ruined woman—is symbolized in her retaining of her name by marriage: Blixen is the African destiny, her frail embodiment, and paradoxically the distinction of nobility. Blixen is thus as a female writer's name a continual reminder that she is not what she says she is—her name is a story.

There are, I think, at least three figures that need to be distinguished: *Karen*, the individual whose life and knowledge is expressed in her writings; *Blixen*, the official persona of the ruined woman whose destiny is as frightening as it is intriguing; and *Isak Dinesen*, the writer whose works have made a lasting contribution to global literature. In assessing the influence of Kierkegaard on the latter's production, we shall converse with the two former figures in the following. Of course, the three are somewhat similar to Fernando Pessoa's heteronyms of one single individual, rather than three individual identities: they each accentuate something distinctive, and as such I use the three appellations with a view to accentuate when this elusive and vanishing writer is the individual, Karen, the historic/histrionic woman, Blixen, and the storyteller, Dinesen.

II. Introducing the Connection: Karen, Blixen, Dinesen, and Kierkegaard

Karen read Kierkegaard.[4] Scholars have been quick to notice that *Ehrengard* is Blixen's answer to "The Seducer's Diary."[5] Perhaps there are other answers to the Kierkegaardian *opus* one might detect in Dinesen's. What influences, what thoughts and circumstances might we not compare in the lives of two literary giants? What might we care to know?

---

[3]   Judith Thurman, *Isak Dinesen: The Life of a Storyteller*, New York: Picador 1982, p. 48.
[4]   Evidence of Karen Blixen as reader of Kierkegaard can be seen in her letters from Africa in Karen Blixen, *Breve fra Afrika 1914–24*, ed. by Frans Lasson, Copenhagen: Gyldendal 1978, p. 280, and Karen Blixen, *Breve fra Afrika 1925–31*, ed. by Frans Lasson, Copenhagen: Gyldendal 1978, p. 133, p. 146. Her knowledge of Kierkegaard can be estimated from her post-Africa letters in *Karen Blixen i Danmark, breve 1931–1962*, vols. 1–2, ed. by Frans Lasson and Tom Engelbrecht, Copenhagen: Gyldendal 1996, vol. 1, p. 31, p. 117, p. 121; vol. 2, p. 141, pp. 147–51, p. 173, p. 236, pp. 244–5, p. 247, pp. 250–1, p. 451. However, Blixen is not an explicit reader of Kierkegaard, and often her mentioning Kierkegaard is *en passant*. An example of this is her citing of the seducer's diary in her essay on marriage. Thanks to Kirsten Søltoft Klercke for alerting me to this example.
[5]   Thurman, *Isak Dinesen*, p. 439.

What intrigues me is not what might be called "answers" to the questions posed by another's authorship, but, in our case, the cor*responding* (*sic*) themes that are shared by two great Danes of literature. This sort of ambition could inspire a writing frenzy of tomes, but my *quest* is regulated by the *request* of reviewing the reception of Kierkegaard in Dinesen's authorship, which in turn could open for a lengthy dissertation. So, for the purpose of sketching the reception without exhausting the topic, I found it curious that the sole volume Karen had of Kierkegaard's was *The Lily in the Field and the Bird of the Air*, as recorded by Pia Bondesson.[6] In her letters from Africa, Karen revealed that she was familiar with *Either/Or* and *The Concept of Anxiety*. In her letters from the period 1931–62, she is "introduced" to Kierkegaard through the efforts of Aage Henriksen, who became a sort of distinguished *Caliban* to her *Prospero*.[7] Henriksen urged her to read his dissertation on Kierkegaard's novels, and he attempted to compare her to Kierkegaard, which she did not receive favorably, according to Thurman.[8] However, she had a "strange feeling of personal relationship" with Kierkegaard.[9] Blixen felt that this relationship had to be measured and distant, since she would throw herself on Shakespeare and kiss Heine, but would make a bad impression on Kierkegaard figuratively as well as literally.[10] In the same exchange, Blixen mused over the theme of what to do when the devil is laughing, to which Blixen prescribed "laughing back at him."[11] Taken as a key to her authorship, "laughing back" may be usefully applied as a way to respond to Kierkegaard's dire and demanding view of the image of the divine and the human in his discourses on the lilies and the birds. It is also, as a curious aside, a telling translation of the name "Isak" which Blixen used with her maiden surname of Dinesen as a pseudonym signing most of her major works.[12]

---

[6]   *Karen Blixens Bogsamling på Rungstedlund*, ed. by Pia Bondesson, Copenhagen: Gyldendal 1982.

[7]   In *Budbringersken*, Copenhagen: Gyldendal 2008, pp. 182–239, Aage Henriksen narrates his account of the court Blixen kept at Rungstedlund. Many of the young male writers and artists of the day were willingly attending her there. Henriksen has also a tale to tell about a physical ailment of his, the origin of which he dates back to a long drawn out scene with Blixen on a premature and staged deathbed, ibid. pp. 228–39. In this sense, Henriksen is *marked* by Blixen personally in the "deformity" of the "pain" she gave him, and professionally as one of our foremost connoisseurs of Blixen's authorship. Figuratively, through her *kind cruelty* Blixen gave Henriksen a voice and yet maltreated him, which is not unlike the *cruel kindness* of Prospero towards Caliban. Note that I am treating the exchange between Blixen and Henriksen in virtue of the latter's narration of it as in a large measure *literary*, and so I do not presume any actual determination of their private relationship, which for all purposes is just that.

[8]   Thurman, *Isak Dinesen*, p. 384.

[9]   *Karen Blixen i Danmark, breve 1931–1962*, vol. 2, p. 147.

[10]   Ibid., p. 150.

[11]   Ibid., Blixen also accounts for her "alliance with the devil," since she determines that she is enduring the experience of the "demonic paradox" which theoretically places the individual as higher than the ordinary, yet is secretly outside of the ordinary sphere.

[12]   Blixen continued to use the pseudonym when publishing abroad, which was where she had had her breakthrough. After her translation of *Seven Gothic Tales* into Danish Karen *came out* as an authoress in Denmark using Karen Blixen as her signing name. This peculiarity ought not disturb our continued referral to her technique of "laughing back" at us.

In this article, I am going to focus on Dinesen's *Last Tales* and in particular the fragments of the novel *Albondocani*.[13] Kierkegaard is here chiefly represented by the book on the lilies and the birds and snippets from *Philosophical Fragments*. What I am interested in showing is that Kierkegaard employs a technique of twisted images to provoke the reader to make a specific response. Dinesen, I aim to show, uses a similar kind of technique. However, I interpret her usage as a means of "laughing back"—perhaps at Kierkegaard. As a consequence, the devil is in the detail of Kierkegaard's writings which Dinesen is quick to pick up on, and which she does not pass over in silence.[14] If the divine is supposed to teach us how to be human by means of the incarnation, the *devil laughs at* us when we face the insurmountable task of the *imitatio*, and again when we admit we cannot fulfill the requirements of reduplicating a Christian faith in a human life. In short, how can we learn to be human from the divine?[15]

III. Twisted Takes on the Images of God and Man

If someone were to say that God is absent in the writings of Kierkegaard, others would be justified in requiring a clarification of this. One way of allowing a predication of absence is to consider the vast distance between human supplicant and the divine

---

[13]   In this way I am disclosing a concrete Kierkegaardian influence, and thus "digging" the influence out of the "mine" of Dinesen's work. No doubt there are many more "ores" to exploit, but that is a testament to future research and not a description of a "state of the art" research which has not tended to the Dinesen/Kierkegaard connection in any sustained manner.

[14]   Kirsten Søltoft Klercke has called my attention to a crucial difference between Kierkegaard and Karen Blixen, which, according to Klercke, is the essential humanity of Kierkegaard's care when addressing the single individual who reads his texts as opposed to Karen Blixen's inhumanity. The latter often comes across as cold and superhumanly above the ordinary in virtue of her faith in fate. But in a different sense the two differ in their narrative prowess: Kierkegaard is not a storyteller as such, but Blixen is.

[15]   It would be difficult to make sense of a generalized overview of what influence Kierkegaard had on Karen Blixen, and it is even more of a task to explicate points of "contact" in Dinesen's stories—the influence can be seen as pervasive and thus as a matter of fact must be shown in concrete examples (as is done here). Such a pervasive influence might suffer from a certain anxiety on the part of the author that any specific mention of the influence in the artwork is avoided; hence the painstaking work is to limit the scope of one's reading. On the contrary, the influence can be seen as sporadic and generally unimportant to understanding Dinesen's stories, and for this reason the few and in this regard interesting examples will exhaust the treatment of the influence. Such a sporadic influence might suffer from a nonchalance on the part of the author that mention of the influence is not even made; hence the painstaking work is to find enough material to support one's reading. In this article, the reading of Dinesen's stories as influenced by Kierkegaard is limited in light of intelligibility and availability of space. It occurs to me that most of Dinesen's stories can be read as influenced from having read Kierkegaard, and as such I would argue that the influence is pervasive. However, it does not follow from holding that view that one would be able to or should give a generalized overview of what that influence is. In this case, a uniform whole does not emerge from adding up all the various instances of influence.

invoked in the prayers of the "right-handed" authorship: God is the "Father" who is in "heaven." When God is to teach us how to be human, Kierkegaard prays that we may learn it from the birds and the lilies—and again if we forget it. Forgetting it, of course, in light of the (now) 2,000 years since Christ walked the earth, and forgetting it because of all the crowds of people with whom we are bound to interact both presently and historically. Yet, although there is forgetfulness, God teaches through the Gospel, which, however, introduces the indirectness of the allegories and the elusiveness of Christ's example, of which *noli me tangere* is intangible by the fact of the divine nature of Christ. So, the God that teaches is distant in these terms, even if he has once been close to his disciples and even if he might be close to us again through what Kierkegaard calls *contemporaneity*. Nevertheless, the presence of the believer with his savior in contemporaneity functions by calling to attention the presence of the divine in human life in spite of time and generations. Although God can be present but in an absent way, so God can be absent in a present way: God is "there" in our prayers, in our loving actions, in our turning ourselves to God, and in a twisted fashion God is "here" as the ever-present possibility of salvation when we are not praying, not loving, not turned towards him.[16]

God is *always* teaching in disguise, a statement which I shall elaborate shortly. Nevertheless, Kierkegaard's aim is not to make available the teaching of Christ, and thus he does not function as an intermediary between God and individual. Rather, as readers we experience the intimacy between God and Kierkegaard, while the latter is engaged in a specific sort of talking to himself—divine monologues with a hint of the demonic.[17] Kierkegaard's technique of employing a rhetorical "you" functions in a similar fashion to the "you" of the love command: as it is said from the sphere of religious categories the "you" designates any supplicant and therefore also the writer of the religious discourse. Whenever "you" appears in the text we should include the writer in that "you," as we should include the writer as co-extensive with the appellation "that single individual whom I call my reader."[18] What this reading accomplishes is a view of Kierkegaard teaching us Christianity *maieutically* by way of showing us how he is being taught through his personal relationship to the divine.[19] This way God is disguised in the clothing (hair and hide) of someone we might know, which is similar to the thought expressed by Grundtvig in his hymn "To Bid the World rightly Goodbye" when Grundtvig sings: "Come in the last watch of the night, come wearing the clothes of one of my beloved."[20]

In *Philosophical Fragments*, Kierkegaard offers the similes of two kings: one who in all his splendor approaches a lowly girl with whom he has fallen in love; the other who hides all his splendor under the guise of just as lowly a boy as the girl

---

[16]   Cf. *Guds Uforanderlighed*, *SKS* 13, 319–39 / *M*, 263–81.

[17]   *SKS* 4, 428–9 / *CA*, 127–8.

[18]   *SKS* 11, 9 / *WA*, 3.

[19]   Compare this reading with Kierkegaard's programmatic first upbuilding discourse in which he sketches how one ought to teach faith by way of showing how one has been taught by the divine, and not by pushing doctrinal matters onto someone whom one wishes had faith. *SKS* 5, 15–25 / *EUD*, 7–29.

[20]   *Den Danske Salmebog*, Copenhagen: Kgl. Vajsenhus' Forlag 1990, no. 609; my translation.

with whom the king has fallen in love.[21] Kierkegaard is anxious to show that God had to be incarnate as a carpenter's son and not as a king, since the full splendor of God would not achieve the object of the coming of Christ as an act of love.[22] The girl would in the first simile accept the king as her suitor, but doing so in fear and in the awareness of the gulf between her and the king. Whereas in the second simile the girl would not have the same concern. The problem for the girl in the second simile would be to recognize the king in his disguise. The thematic of this second simile is played out masterly by Charles Dickens in his *Our Mutual Friend*, where the main character John Harmon, the inheritor to a large fortune on condition he marries Bella Wilfer who is described as a spoiled and money-fixated girl, finds himself forced to hide under a false identity as John Rokesmith. As circumstances would have it, John Rokesmith ends up married to Bella Wilfer who is oblivious to the fact that her husband is really John Harmon, but reconciled to a lowly existence. In the final chapters, the denouement of revelation discloses Rokesmith's long-entertained worries of whether she could handle the revelation, and that he kept quiet to test her love. Bella Wilfer reacts somewhat uncommonly, perhaps, since she merely resigns to her fate without questioning the deception. Whether it be Dickens' or Kierkegaard's rendition, the disguised is distinguished as such paradoxically, since there must be a denouement through which one comes face to face with what was hidden.[23] With tragic irony this implication may be acknowledged by the deceived beloved only after the revelation, but from the outset by audiences who are let in on the secret. In this sense, knowing Christ through the narratives of tradition continually twists the expectation of whom Christ is, since to some extent the deal—as it were—is done: Christ has already resurrected himself, and the *noli me tangere* Christ is thus essentially absent.[24]

Kierkegaard wrote extensively on the theme of the lily and the bird in *Upbuilding Discourses in Various Spirits* and *Christian Discourses*, where in the former the topic is about how glorious it is to be human and in the latter how one may distinguish a Christian from a pagan. As pointed out above, Kierkegaard is *merely* relating his own edification in the Christian virtues, which in the book *The Lily in the Field and the Bird of the Air* are silence, obedience, and joy. Now Kierkegaard is famously without authority, and so Christ is not teaching through him. Through whom is Christ teaching in his absence? Through the divinely appointed teachers: the lily and the bird. This introduces the technique of the grotesque: *what is required of the human being is taught by what is not human.* As if the problem of the divine teaching humanity is not pertinent

---

[21]   *SKS* 4, 230–42 / *PF*, 23–36.

[22]   Compare John 3:16.

[23]   Compare 1 Corinthians 13:12–13, which presumably would explain the acceptance of the deception, since love, as is well known, abides and endures all things (1 Corinthians 13:7). However, Kierkegaard does note that the God in the figure of the lowly servant is in fact the *true* figure of God. Nevertheless, the paradox is apt to reoccur when we consider that the reason for the true figure of God as servant is, according to Kierkegaard, a wish to be equal with the human being. There must be a denouement through which we realize that the true figure of God is of a different meaning than the one we might aspire to embody as "equal" servants. I am thankful to Leonardo Lisi for discussion on this point.

[24]   As opposed to his carnal state in which touching Christ led to miraculous cures.

enough, the grotesque twists the inhuman origin of the teaching into focus.[25] Through the lily and the bird the human is supposed to learn how to be human, and to take their lessons seriously.[26] Kierkegaard is well aware that there is a barrier to accomplishing this by the allegorical set-up. The poet, he claims, may laud the presentation of the virtues of the teachers, but would in equal measure bemoan the inability to become a bird or a lily, since it seems the very nature of the creature is a necessary condition to enable the lauded behavior. However, scolding the poet Kierkegaard points to the divine demand which does not allow evasion by poetizing. The deeper problem of whether what is taught is essentially inappropriate for humanity is never questioned, given the standard is set from a divine standpoint, whereas the teaching is no doubt appropriate for the God-man. The paradox of God teaching humans humanity through his incarnate example would in defense of the poet be the point of admitting—perhaps tearfully—that what the lilies and the birds teach about virtues divinely determined as humanly appropriate is befitting a God-man but not merely man.[27]

By insisting on the appropriateness of the divine humanity, the God that has been twisted into man, bird, and plant is also through the incarnation twisting the image of humanity to a degree that with the *ecce homo*, we ought to be horrified not just at the fact of the suffering, but *a fortiori* in the acknowledgment that humanity has acquired an exemplar in the divine. In this way, being created in the image of the divine the human is perpetually re-created ethically in the twisted image of the dying God whose *disguise* is a particular human being. The upshot is that humanity has no business thinking that it could auto-determine the content of "humanity," since we have already been imaged as physical beings through creation proper and as mental beings through Christ's re-creation.[28] In this sense, paraphrasing Kierkegaard, we learn from the lily and the bird to be silent in order to still our own wants and desires (that is, to seek God's realm *first*), to be obedient to God's will and to suffice in resigning to it, and to be happy in the quotidian life being present in our embodiment. Nevertheless, what the lilies and the birds teach us is a twisted (divine) image of the human by force

---

[25]   Thanks to Antony Aumann for alerting me to explicate my use of "grotesque" such that I am arguing for divine teaching as bizarre and unnerving.

[26]   *SKS* 11, 10 / *WA*, 3. *SKS* 11, 14–15 / *WA*, 8–9.

[27]   Antony Aumann scolds me for being silent about the fact that the bird and the lily are "metaphors," and thus the twist I am arguing for sounds far too close to the poet's lament: would that one were a bird, etc. We are, according to Aumann, not called on to take on the examples of the lily and the bird literally, but see in their examples the ideal human responses which we ought to embody. I have no quarrel with this. My insistence on the image of the twisted is taking serious that the poet in a non-biased way may have a very good and, for Kierkegaard, excellent point about the difficulty of embodying the ideality which is exemplified in the lily and the bird. The figure of the poet in Kierkegaard is never just a strawman that neatly serves a function to facilitate Kierkegaard's more "Christian" project: the poet is everywhere a real (and sane) alternative to the "Christian."

[28]   In a somewhat different line of inquiry, Augustine examines the mental image of man as replicating the triad which the Trinity exemplifies. See Augustine, *The Trinity*, trans. by Edmund Hill and ed. by John E. Rotelle, Brooklyn, New York: New City Press 1991. In any case, the central idea is that humanity ought to be disillusioned regarding the ambition of self-creative autonomy.

of the twisted (absent) divinity which in its twisted (human) form has twisted itself (indirect communication) into appointing the *twisted* (grotesque) teachers. The story God tells of humanity is as short as his story of himself: as much as God is absent so is humanity essentially absent, since *noli me tangere* its *image* has absconded.

IV. The Divine Art

Karen would laud Kierkegaard for being true to the story.[29] "Where there is no story and never has been, or where someone has betrayed the story, there silence is emptiness," writes Dinesen in the last chapter of *Albondocani* and continues "but when that storyteller, who unto death has been faithful to the story, *quietens*, then quietude speaks."[30] The last chapter is the story of the storyteller for storytellers. It is the story of the blank page that speaks more poignantly than all the stories in the world because it speaks out of silence. For Dinesen, quietude is a consequence of being faithful to the story; silence allows an appropriation of the story that engages the audience as it actively considers the story.

Kierkegaard is retelling God's offensive demand on humanity.[31] As a storyteller, Kierkegaard is careful not to disturb the original silence with the sort of mindless chatter which tries to make it easier to understand why God is incarnated as a lowly servant. The ideality of God as absent in the way I developed above echoes the comment Georges Bataille offered when he wrote: "The absence of God is no longer a closure: it is the opening up to the infinite. The absence of God is greater, and more divine, than God."[32] Without further comparison, the comment I take Bataille to be

---

[29]   In his critical assessment of *Two Ages*, see *A Literary Review*, in *SKS* 8, 17–20 / *TA*, 13–16, Kierkegaard lauded Thomasine Gyllembourg for being true to herself as an author, because she is seen to have a life-view. Perhaps with a slightly different tone, then, Kierkegaard's claim about what makes a good author is resounded in Blixen's admonishing remarks on what makes a good storyteller. For a discussion of the importance of life-view in Kierkegaard's thinking see my "The Technique of Critique," in *The Book on Adler*, ed. by Robert L. Perkins, Macon, Georgia: Mercer University Press 2008 (*International Kierkegaard Commentary*, vol. 24), pp. 9–34.

[30]   Karen Blixen, *Sidste Fortællinger*, Copenhagen: Gyldendal 1957, p. 90 (my translation); compare Isak Dinesen's version in *Last Tales*, London: Putnam 1957, p. 126, where there is no mention of whether there could be a lack of story as in the Danish version, but only whether a story could be betrayed. This discrepancy between the versions on the level of detail is itself worthy of study: is Blixen addressing a specific Danish readership, whereas Dinesen is telling stories to a global audience? Or is the absence in the English version an instance of the blank page, which according to both versions is the most vital technique of any author? It may, with caution, be suggested that the absence points to an originality which is not encompassed by the pseudonym, yet it also points to a conversationalism by which the versions are complementary in virtue of the authors (*sic*) being one writer.

[31]   For a different take on God as a storyteller and the writer as retelling God's story, see Johannes Sløk, "Da Gud fortalte en historie," in *Guds Fortælling—Menneskets Historie*, ed. by Kjeld Holm, Aarhus: Centrum 1999, pp. 413–526.

[32]   Georges Bataille, *The Absence of Myth: Writings on Surrealism*, trans. by Michael Richardson, New York: Verso 1994, p. 48.

making is to the effect that, understood correctly, the absence of God is the kind of quietude which opens for retelling the divine story, however, with the twist that this possibility is not God and yet more divine than God. There is in this comment a French *laugh* (worry), which, however, speaks volumes on the twentieth-century despair about *missing* (*sic*) God.[33] Nevertheless, the idea that God is a storyteller by whose absence quietude speaks, is transferable to the retelling of the story, now with the *str(i/u)cture*[34] of remaining faithful to the story.[35]

To tell a story is a divine art,[36] according to the protagonist of the first chapter of *Albondocani*, Cardinal Salviati, who is the survivor of twin brothers, one destined to be inculcated in spiritual learning, the other in the arts; which one Salviati is, is perhaps by mere chance the persona he embodies.[37] This character tells a "first" and a "third" story, in between which there are four stories, one of which we know is told by a Spanish ambassador. Does the cardinal tell a second story, or is it absent as an instance of the blank page? Regardless, the art of storytelling is exclusively divine, whereas what humans may do is writing novels that bring us all too close to the reality of individual human beings whose "bodily warmth" invites the reader to "make them, in all situations of his life, his companions, friends, and advisors."[38] Humanity may advise, divinity directs. Thus, it is only the art of storytelling that has the power to answer the question "who am I?"[39] In the second person, this is incidentally a question the cardinal is asked at the beginning of his "first" story by an elderly lady. She is the *first* person to ask whether the cardinal has "an identity of [his] own to confess to."[40] So, for the *first* story in Dinesen's *Last Tales*, it is for the *first* time a question for the *cardinal* (which is most important) whether he has a "who" to confess. In perspective of Dinesen's authorship, it is not the first time a cardinal plays a crucial role, since in *The Deluge at Norderney* in *Seven Gothic Tales*, the role of Cardinal von Sehestedt is usurped by the cardinal's valet, Kasperson, who is acknowledged as a great actor at the

---

[33] For this sort of twist, see Lawrence Raab, "Supernatural Forces" in his *The History of Forgetting*, London: Penguin 2009, p. 43.

[34] The point of *str(i/u)cture* is to indicate the dialectic of storytelling, which for the storyteller implies the strictures of technique and obligation in the face of the structure provided by the fact of an audience and therefore ultimately communication, thus for any story, there is an "I" (stricture) of message and a "You" (structure) of receivable language. One way of pointing to a Kierkegaardian equivalent would be to talk of reduplication as the storyteller's *str(i/u)cture* of remaining faithful to the story. Antony Aumann questions the rationale behind this artifice, since it looks as if the words are used ordinarily. The artifice, I think, is meant to convey the simultaneity of both the I/You and the stricture/structure, and thus it serves a function beyond the mere reproduction of the words themselves.

[35] Georges Bataille continues the above quoted sentence with a telling parenthesis: "(in the process I am no longer myself, but an absence of self; I am awaiting the sleight of hand that renders me immeasurably joyful.)" *The Absence of Myth: Writings on Surrealism*, p. 48. Thus, with Bataille we can advance the thought that the quietude of the absence of God, is *mutatis mutandis* the quietude of the absence of self, viz. humanity is *in absentia*.

[36] Blixen, *Sidste Fortællinger*, p. 27; Dinesen, *Last Tales*, p. 33.

[37] Blixen, *Sidste Fortællinger*, pp. 15–20.

[38] Dinesen, *Last Tales*, p. 32.

[39] Blixen, *Sidste Fortællinger*, p. 29; Dinesen, *Last Tales*, p. 35.

[40] Dinesen, *Last Tales*, p. 9.

point of denouement.[41] But whereas the story of the deluge is one of the insubstantiality of character by virtue of "cardinality" (*sic*)—that is, answering the question *what am I?*, the story of Cardinal Salviati is an account of *who am I?* The questions are both *cardinal* (*sic*) in the stories, in the sense that identity can be something to which one confesses (*who I am*) and something one professes (*what I am*), thus from two different spheres of enquiry what matters most in telling a story is either a *con*fession of identity or *pro*fession of identity, that is, either we are fashioned through the story, or we fashion ourselves by telling stories. In view of the divine art, a confessional story has divinity outside the storyteller, whereas a professional story assumes divinity all of its own. In other words, a confessional story has a blank page (God is absent), which a professional story will be wont to have (God is absent). Hence, the way in which God is absent in the two spheres of enquiry is significantly different. In the professional story, God is absent because the author assumes the divine role, which is why in the story of the deluge death as the final curtain call marks the end and limit of the powers of the author. In a confessional story, the absence of God is the very possibility of the story being infinite, which is why on the basis of his "confession" Cardinal Salviati can end the story with a reply that whether he serves God or not is a risk every artist and priest has to run.[42] Therefore, to connect briefly to Kierkegaard, how to seek God's realm *first* would for Blixen be something that is as infinitely entertaining as it is infinitely impossible. Nevertheless, with that reply Salviati makes the answer of who he is open-ended: infinity only can provide an answer, that is, an infinity of silence and reflection as much on the part of the audience as it is part and parcel of the "existence" of the identity in question. Let us keep guessing.

There is in Dinesen's writing evidence that with *Anecdotes of Destiny* (and perhaps even as early as *Winter's Tales*) Dinesen makes a turn from being an author who is pulling the strings of the marionettes of her stories, to a storyteller whose stories show the strings of the infinite.[43] This is especially evident in *Albondocani*, to such a degree that we may characterize what Dinesen does as a *twisted laugh*. Whereas a writer of plays for marionettes is laughing at *the what* and plays at making her audience laugh at what is intended as laughable, a storyteller *laughs* at the infinite. This means that the storyteller not only laughs at the blank page, but also at the audience who is captivated by the infinity. By drawing people close by being true to the story, the storyteller distances herself infinitely in letting her audience be left to their own devices in the contact of their own confessional stance towards the story. And—she laughs at the thought that divinely appointed teachers might teach us *a silence* of the "who,"[44] *that silence* of the blank page where we reveal ourselves, and *the silence* of not knowing the answer, because *such silence* is

---

[41]   Dinesen, *Seven Gothic Tales*, p. 267.
[42]   Dinesen, *Last Tales*, p. 35.
[43]   This seems to be supported by the fact that Pino, the marionette-theater owner, no longer can operate his marionettes, because three (!) fingers on his right hand have withered, Dinesen, *Last Tales*, pp. 60–1.
[44]   A "who" which in Kierkegaard's idea of the self before God is transparent, resigned, and silent.

neither divine nor human, but all too close to the demonic monologue: silence will come out with it.[45]

Salviati's third story relates the fate of Flora, a Scottish noblewoman, who in her manner "would remind her partner that the motto of her country is *Noli me tangere*."[46] Flora is described as a woman who would be loath to touch others, a giantess, who is impressive in stature, and thus in physique imposingly present yet untouchable. Flora is untouched both in a spiritual and a physical way. Thus, on the one hand, Flora is withdrawn in the demonic despair in the face of spiritual redemption which is offered her by a monk, Father Jacopo, who subjects himself to her blasphemy. And, on the other hand, Flora is physically frigid as a result of having been the confidant of her mother, and thus the bearer of a great misfortune. Flora befriends Jacopo while staying in Rome, and in the course of their strained friendship, she comes to fancy the sculpture of St. Peter. As a means to drive Jacopo to extremes, she attempts to partake in a holy act as a means to ridicule it. In the end Jacopo seeks advice from Salviati and is reassured that the almighty will answer Flora appropriately. Months later, after the parting of Flora and Jacopo, Salviati meets Flora. She is transformed; she explains that this happened on the night of her departure from Rome. She had gone to see St. Peter once more, and while she gazed at him, a young man cloaked, lithe, and with a rank smell passed her. He kissed the foot of St. Peter for an extended period of time. For some reason, Flora was compelled to follow suit, and kissed the foot too for an equal amount of time. Four weeks later she found a sore on her lips—(herpes)—ending the story Blixen puts the following words in Flora's mouth: "I stood, Your Eminence, before the glass and looked at my mouth. Then I bethought myself of Father Jacopo. To what, I thought, does this bear a likeness? To a rose?—or to a seal?"[47]

Notice the almost sardonic irony with which the untouched lady relates her catching a venereal disease from kissing the foot of St. Peter, the rock of the church. Learning how to be touched by another human being through the medium of the inanimate bronze of St. Peter's foot is something grotesque that equals what is grotesque in learning how to be human from birds and lilies. *Noli me tangere* is in Flora shattered by kissing the representation of the holy. Whereas *noli me tangere* in the divine sphere is the spiritually poignant distance to humanity, the *noli me tangere* of Flora is the physically poignant paradox of the bodily inevitability of humanity which is nonetheless *somewhat* divine. What Christ can do, humans cannot, thus Christ may distance himself from embodiment, but humans—as long as they live—perpetually revert to it in spite of all efforts to the contrary.[48] Hence, to live *today*, to be joyous in the fact of being bodily alive, is a lesson in accepting human embodiment as a sublation of distance. However, according to Dinesen, the

---

[45]   Compare *SKS* 4, 424–30 / *CA*, 124–9.

[46]   Dinesen, *Last Tales*, p. 97.

[47]   Dinesen, *Last Tales*, p. 123.

[48]   Compare Pan Nalin's motion picture *Samsara* (2001), where a Buddhist monk, after a prolonged retreat into a meditative state, is reintroduced to ordinary life with all its many desires and wants. The subtle, if tragic, humor of such scenario is to some extent related in *The Concept of Anxiety*, *SKS* 4, 456 / *CA*, 158, where Kierkegaard tells the anecdote of an Indian solitary who endured two years surviving on dew alone, went to the city, tasted wine, and became an alcoholic.

teacher of that lesson is the human being itself, and the holy is a piece of bronze as rigid and illusory as the delusion that humans can remain distant from one another. The permanence of each is upheld by human willfulness, the efficaciousness of each is the fact of their conductivity, and taken together we are presented with humans, who go through life teaching themselves how to approximate something remotely like the *str(i/u)cture* of humanity by enduring events of which they have no control.

As a second *cardinal* story there is some choice for the audience, since between the *first* and the *third* there are three stories beside the story told by the Spanish Ambassador. So, between silence and joy, I, of course, want to find a story about obedience. My choice for a second cardinal story is *Night Walk*, which is neatly the second of the three stories that all relate to the sculptor Angelo Santasilia living in a not further disclosed post-Renaissance period.[49] In *Night Walk*, Angelo cannot sleep for reasons explained in *The Cloak*, in which the story of the execution of Angelo's master has been told. Angelo wanders one night to the door of a small tavern, where at one table an ugly man is counting money. Angelo tells the man that he cannot sleep, to which the stranger replies: "I never sleep."[50] The man's following remarks are worth quoting in full:

> "I never sleep."
> "Only dolts and drudges sleep," he took up his theme after awhile. "Fishermen, peasants and artisans must have their hours of snoring at any cost. Their heavy nature cries out for sleep even in the greatest hour of life. Drowsiness settles on their eyelids, their lower jaw drops, and the tongue lies dead within it, their limbs sprawl at random, and animal sounds come from them. Divine agony sweats blood at a stone's throw, but they cannot keep awake, and the whizzing of an angel's wings will not wake them up. Those living dead will never know what happened, or what was said, while they themselves lay huddled and gaping. I alone know. For I never sleep."
> Suddenly he turned round in his chair, towards his guest.
> "He said so Himself," he remarked, "and had He not been so hard driven, with what high disdain would he not have spoken! Now it was a moan, like the sea breaking against the shore for the very last time before doomsday. He himself told them so, the fools: 'What, could ye not watch with Me one hour?'"
> For a minute he looked Angelo straight in the face.
> "But no one," he concluded slowly, in indescribable pride, "no one in the world could ever seriously believe that I myself did sleep—on that Thursday night, in the Garden."[51]

If we had a chuckle at silence, a wry smile at Flora's joy, our laugh at the *Night Walker* (*sic*) must be of the surprised kind, which is uttered involuntarily in the sheer horror of the implications hinted at here. Long before the current re-establishing of Judas Iscariot, Dinesen lets this haunting figure enter from another age to teach obedience. But Dinesen is wise; she sees no positivity. The one who obeyed, the one who betrayed, is the simple tool of the divine. Of course, he did not sleep in

---

[49]   As such it is worth studying the "infinity" of the "missing" second story in the triad of the three stories about Angelo.
[50]   Dinesen, *Last Tales*, p. 67.
[51]   Ibid.

the garden, he watched with his master, and watched his master. The real betrayal is the love that is not human. It is the love of a master who is unable to reciprocate on a level which is appropriate between human beings—a master who is described by the "betrayer" in terms so tender and intimate that we ought to see the insane sanity of the "kiss" (referring to the biblical narrative) which gives away the identity of the master as a peculiar act of love. Afterwards, the human being who tried to love the divine in perfect obedience is an outcast, and the ones we readily single out as exemplars (such as Simon Peter) did not obey.[52]

God is wont to twist and does it in ways humans cannot understand. In *Night Walk*, Dinesen is unconcerned with the real drama of Judas; there should be no sense of sympathy with his act. Rather, Dinesen is concerned with Angelo—the human being who may still become human. Too close to divinity and the sacrifice is complete: one will become neither human nor divine. Harking back to Kierkegaard's simile from *Philosophical Fragments*, whether disguised or not, the divine cannot make what is not divine independently equal to it. Divine love is cruel because it demands everything, and so it will consume completely the devotion offered. If there is a lesson here, and there just might be, it would be to be wary of unconditional obedience.

V. The Blank Page

How can we learn to be human from the divine? Reading Dinesen, I should think the answer is clear: we learn to be human in spite of what God sends our way. We battle with God, always being ignorant of whether we serve a divine purpose, and why would we want to know anyway?

But of course, Kierkegaard's concern is not whether we learn to be human, but that we learn what the divine demand is. As such, Kierkegaard would have been delighted with Dinesen—but he would have detected the laugh. Perhaps he would have been frightened? Or would he have recognized an Isaac who lost the faith, there on Mount Moriah, in the background the father who drew a knife…

---

[52]   Antony Aumann challenges me to "come out" and say that Jesus is the betrayer, and that Judas' act was one of obedience and love. Would that it were so easy. Dinesen's continual adherence to a faith in destiny is at stake here: Judas and the divine are betraying one another; what is twisted here is the very "love" which Judas takes himself to be offering. I see no need to defend Judas, but I do want to note that the divine twist is tragic-comic, and so Judas is humanly speaking to be pitied, but divinely speaking to be a subject for laughter.

Bibliography

I. Works by Blixen that Make Use of Kierkegaard

Breve fra Afrika 1914–24, ed. by Frans Lasson, Copenhagen: Gyldendal 1978, p. 280.

Breve fra Afrika 1925–31, ed. by Frans Lasson, Copenhagen: Gyldendal 1978, p. 133; p. 146.

Karen Blixen i Danmark, breve 1931–1962, vols. 1–2, ed. by Frans Lasson and Tom Engelbrecht, Copenhagen: Gyldendal 1996, vol. 1, p. 31; p. 117; p. 121; vol. 2, p. 141; pp. 147–51; p. 173; p. 236; pp. 244–5; p. 247; pp. 250–1; p. 451.

Moderne Ægteskab og andre Betragtninger, preface by Frans Lasson, Copenhagen: Gyldendal, 1981 (Originally published in *Blixeniana 1977*, Copenhagen: Karen Blixen Selskabet 1977.)

II. Sources of Blixen's Knowledge of Kierkegaard[53]

Bruun Andersen, K., *Søren Kierkegaard og kritikeren P.L. Møller*, Copenhagen: Munksgaard 1950.

Hansen, P. Emanuel, *Dagbogsoptegnelser. Omkring Søren Kierkegaard*, Sønderborg [n.p.] 1950.

Heiberg, Johan Ludvig, "Litterær Vintersæd," *Intelligensblade*, vol. 2, no. 24, 1 March 1843, pp. 285–92.

Henriksen, Aage, *Søren Kierkegaards romaner*, Copenhagen: Gyldendal 1954.

Kierkegaard, Søren, *Enten—Eller: et Livs-Fragment*, vols. 1–2, 3rd ed., Copenhagen: C.A. Reitzel 1865.

— *Synspunktet for min Forfatter-Virksomhed. En ligefrem Meddelelse, Rapport til Historien*, ed. by A.B. Drachmann, 2nd ed., Copenhagen: Gyldendal 1906.

— *Lilien paa Marken og Fuglen under Himlen. Tre gudelige Taler*, Copenhagen: Hasse 1922.

— *Søren Kierkegaards dagbøger i udvalg*, ed. by Peter P. Rohde, Copenhagen: Gyldendal 1953.

---

[53] A useful resource for determining the sources of Blixen's knowledge of Kierkegaard is Pia Bondesson, *Karen Blixens bogsamling på Rundstedlund*, Copenhagen: Gyldendal 1982.

III. *Secondary Literature on Blixen's Relation to Kierkegaard*

Anz, Heinrich "'Hiobs Gemeinde'. Überlegungen zur Poetologie des Dichters bei S. Kierkegaard, H. Ibsen, A. Strindberg und K. Blixen," *Text & Kontext*, vol. 21, no. 1, 1998, pp. 7–25.

— " 'Seinerzeit eine Art makabre Modefigur.' Aspekte der Wirkungsgeschichte Søren Kierkegaards in der skandinavischen Literatur," in *Kierkegaard Studies Yearbook*, 1999, pp. 208–14.

Bertung, Birgit, "Har Søren Kierkegaard foregrebet Karen Blixens og Suzanne Brøggers kvindesyn?" *Kierkegaardiana*, vol. 13, 1984, pp. 72–83.

— *Om Kierkegaard, kvinder og kærlighed—en studie i Søren Kierkegaards kvindesyn*, Copenhagen: C.A . Reitzel 1987, pp. 79–91.

Brahde, Per, *Magt og afmagt. Kierkegaard og Nietzsche spejlet i Karen Blixens forfatterskab*, Aalborg: Aalborg Universitet 2004 (*Arbejdspapirer om filosofi og videnskabsteori*, no. 5).

Henriksen, Aage, "Det ubevidste," in his *De ubændige. Om Ibsen—Blixen— hverdagens virkelighed—det ubevidste*, Copenhagen: Gyldendal 1984, pp. 212–20.

Johannesson, Eric O., "Isak Dinesen, Søren Kierkegaard, and the Present Age," *Books Abroad*, vol. 36, 1962, pp. 20–4.

Kleinman, Jackie, "Two Ages. A Story of Søren Kierkegaard and Isak Dinesen," in *Two Ages*, ed. by Robert L. Perkins, Macon, Georgia: Mercer University Press 1984 (*International Kierkegaard Commentary*, vol. 14), pp. 175–87.

Maiorani, Arianna, "Blixen e Kierkegaard: dialogo sul seduttore," *Intersezioni*, vol. 20, no. 1, 2000, pp. 43–57.

Makarushka, Irena "Reflections on the 'Other' in Dinesen, Kierkegaard, and Nietzsche," in *Kierkegaard on Art and Communication*, ed. by George Pattison, New York: Macmillan and London: St. Martin's 1992, pp. 150–9.

Pelensky, Olga Anastasia, "Isak Dinesen and Kierkegaard: The Aesthetics of 'Ehrengard,' " in *Karen Blixen/Isak Dinesen: Tradition, Modernity, and Other Ambiguities*, ed. by Poul Houe and Donna Dacus, Minneapolis: University of Minnesota Press 1985, pp. 46–53.

— "Isak Dinesen and Kierkegaard: The Aesthetics of Paradox in 'Ehrengard,' " in *Isak Dinesen. Critical Views*, Olga Anastasia Pelensky, Athens, Ohio: Ohio University Press 1993, pp. 322–32.

Rasmussen, Inge Lise, "La maschera del seduttore in 'Ehrengard' di Karen Blixen a confronto con il 'Diario del seduttore' di Søren Kierkegaard," in *Kierkegaard e la letteratura*, ed. by Massimo Iiritano and Inge Lise Rasmussen, Rome: Città Nuova 2002 (*NotaBene, Quaderni di studi Kierkegaardiani*, vol. 2), pp. 65–74.

— "Echi kierkegaardiani ni 'Il pranzo di Babette' [di Karen Blixen]," in *L'arte dello sguardo. Kierkegaard e il cinema*, ed. by Isabella Adinolfi, Rome: Città Nuova 2003 (*NotaBene, Quaderni di studi kierkegaardiani*, vol. 3), pp. 71–9.

Roed, Susan, "Vejen fra kaos til kosmos—tre eks.: Grundtvig, Kierkegaard og Blixen," in *Pamves træ. Om krise, kunst og religiøsitet*, Århus: Forlaget Philosophia 1988, pp. 53–74.

Schuler, Jean, "Kierkegaard at 'Babette's Feast': The Return to the Finite," *Journal of Religion and Film*, vol. 1, no. 2, 1997, pp. 9–13.

Smyth, John Vignaux, "Art, Eroticism, and Sadomasochistic Sacrifice in Søren Kierkegaard and Isak Dinesen," in *The New Kierkegaard*, ed. by Elsebet Jegstrup, Bloomington and Indianapolis: Indiana University Press 2004 (*Studies in Continental Thought*), pp. 179–98.

Georg Brandes:

Kierkegaard's Most Influential Mis-Representative

Julie K. Allen

The role of Georg Brandes (1842–1927) as the first prominent international interpreter and promoter of the works of Søren Kierkegaard is surely one of the most ironic twists in the history of Danish literature and philosophy. With the 1877 publication in Danish and Swedish of his monograph *Søren Kierkegaard: A Critical Exposition in Outline*, followed by a German edition in 1879, Brandes emerged as the definitive authority on Kierkegaard in Europe. Jørgen Bonde Jensen asserts, "both in Denmark and in Germany, it [Brandes' monograph] has been definitive for the left-wing intellectuals' understanding of Kierkegaard."[1] Aage Henriksen agrees that "the book fell weightily on the minds of his [Brandes'] contemporaries, and the later literature on Søren Kierkegaard spreads in circles from it....Its value as an incitement can hardly be over-rated, whereas its scientific quality is disputable—and has been disputed."[2]

But although Brandes promoted Kierkegaard widely in his far-flung circle of acquaintances, advising the English literary critic Edmund Gosse in August 1877 that "no one who is interested in Nordic literature should fail to read *Either/Or*," he was also deeply conflicted about Kierkegaard, telling Gosse in a letter in November 1911 that Kierkegaard was "most likely, unfortunately, our greatest man."[3] Brandes' ambivalence toward Kierkegaard can be explained by the fact that, in many ways, Brandes, a Jewish-born atheist who proudly claimed an international reputation as the defender of free, scientifically-based rationality, represents the ideologically opposite pole from Kierkegaard, whom he regarded as "the dangerous spokesman of unfree thought—Christianity."[4] Yet at the same time, Brandes was too aware of Kierkegaard's genius and eloquence to ignore him, a situation that confronted him with the conundrum of how to maximize the utility of Kierkegaard's literary

---

[1]   Jørgen Bonde Jensen, "Vel desværre vor største Mand. Georg Brandes om Søren Kierkegaard," in his *Jeg er kun en Digter. Om Søren Kierkegaard som skribent*, Copenhagen: Babette 1996, p. 169.

[2]   Aage Henriksen, *Methods and Results of Kierkegaard Studies in Scandinavia*, Copenhagen: Munksgaard 1951, p. 23.

[3]   *Correspondance de Georg Brandes*, vols. 1–3, ed. by Paul Krüger, Copenhagen: Rosenkilde and Bagger 1956, vol. 2, p. 64; p. 110.

[4]   Bonde Jensen, *Jeg er kun en Digter. Om Søren Kierkegaard som skribent*, p. 156.

and philosophical strategies while simultaneously minimizing the influence of his religious ideas.

In the mid-1870s, in light of Kierkegaard's increasing influence and "deification in spiritually-obsessed circles," Brandes took it upon himself to separate "the enduring" elements of Kierkegaard's work from "the transitory."[5] He considered himself qualified for such a task for two reasons: first, that he had once been utterly fascinated by him and knew his works backwards and forwards; and second, that he had long since freed himself of Kierkegaard's influence.[6] Brandes acknowledged Kierkegaard's genius, but made it plain that he believed his focus on Christianity to have been a misconception, just as Columbus believed he found a sea route to India when in fact he had discovered America. Similarly, in Brandes' view, when Kierkegaard "abandoned the old, naïve road to faith," he discovered "the America of the great personality, great passion, and great independence," but continued, "with incurable madness," to call it India.[7] Brandes regarded Kierkegaard's new world, his greatest, enduring discovery, to be that of "the individual," while his mistake lay in equating "the individual" with "the Christian," for Brandes regarded "faith in general and Christianity in particular" as transitory and therefore unnecessary.[8]

Rather than debating Kierkegaard's ideas directly, therefore, Brandes focused on redefining and thereby appropriating them for secular humanism. Brandes challenged Kierkegaard's insistence on the centrality of religion on human life by promoting a secular interpretation of his works, stripped of their religious context. Anne Mette Lundtofte suggests that Brandes' target was not Kierkegaard himself, but rather the theologians who "had taken him into exegetic custody,"[9] but in order to undermine his relevance for the religious camp, Brandes first had to demonstrate the fallacy of Kierkegaard's religious convictions. In a letter to Paul Heyse in December 1876, Brandes calls Kierkegaard "Denmark's and certainly also Scandinavia's greatest prose writer of this [the nineteenth] century," as well as "the most difficult Nordic author," but, he claims, "my interpretation of him is entirely original and new; bold, because I depicted his orthodoxy, which has gained him the most admirers here [in Denmark], as precisely his weakest side."[10] In Brandes' view, Kierkegaard's religious writings are the product of a diseased mind and body, while his true genius becomes visible in his aesthetic works and in his final attack on Christendom, which Brandes interprets as evidence that Kierkegaard was on the cusp of breaking free of religion at the time of his premature death.

Although he was just one among many Kierkegaard scholars in Denmark, Brandes' controversial interpretation of Kierkegaard gained additional traction through its wide international circulation. Brandes laments Kierkegaard's fate of

---

[5]   Georg Brandes, *Levned*, vols. 1–3, Copenhagen: Gyldendal 1905–1908, vol. 2, p. 203.
[6]   Brandes, *Levned*, vol. 2, p. 203.
[7]   Georg Brandes, *Søren Kierkegaard. En kritisk Fremstilling i Grundrids*, Copenhagen: Gyldendal 1877, p. 107.
[8]   Bonde Jensen, *Jeg er kun en Digter. Om Søren Kierkegaard som skribent*, p. 149.
[9]   Anne Mette Lundtofte, "Pointing Fingers at the Genius: Reading Brandes Reading Kierkegaard," *Tijdschrift voor Skandinavistiek*, vol. 21, 2000, p. 149.
[10]   *Correspondance de Georg Brandes*, vol. 3, pp. 165–6.

having been born in a small country, writing in a minor language, noting that if his works had been "written in one of Europe's main languages, they would have made their author world famous,"[11] but he uses these circumstances to his own advantage, utilizing his contacts in Germany to ensure that his representation of Kierkegaard's ideas crowded out the more theological interpretations of his work, such as those published by Albert Bärthold throughout the 1870s. As one of the first to publish a critical, biographically-grounded analysis of Kierkegaard in German, Brandes placed himself in a position to influence the way in which Kierkegaard was received by German intellectuals. In his famous letter to Nietzsche in January 1888 in which he suggests that Nietzsche read Kierkegaard, Brandes admits, "The little book I wrote about him (translated Leipzig 1879) does not provide an adequate conception of his genius, for that book is a type of polemic, written to hinder his influence."[12] Brandes' strategy for curbing Kierkegaard's influence, both in Denmark and abroad, was to denigrate his religious works as outdated and deranged, while praising his aesthetic and socially critical works as innovative and ingenious. According to Bonde Jensen, Brandes "gave Kierkegaard redress by putting him down...[but] he also puts him down, in the sense that he shows him his contempt by elevating him."[13]

The results of Brandes' efforts to manipulate Kierkegaard's European reception were manifold and varied. His misrepresentation of Kierkegaard as a primarily secular thinker, with an unfortunate but ignorable tendency toward religious melancholy, was certainly influential, but it was not ultimately definitive, nor did it go unchallenged. His anti-religious stance and bold-faced disparagement of Kierkegaard's religiosity earned him augmented opposition and enmity in his homeland, which ultimately drove him into temporary exile in Germany, where his own international reputation took root. His positivistic interpretation of Kierkegaard's ideas paved the way for the early to mid-twentieth century appropriation of Kierkegaard as the father of existentialism, but it was also provocative enough to arouse defenders of the religious viewpoint. The controversy over Brandes' book sparked a wave of general interest in Kierkegaard's works, both aesthetic and religious, that eventually spread throughout continental Europe, England, and the United States. Brandes' unintended accomplishment of generating additional interest in Kierkegaard serves to reinforce the original irony of his decision to appoint himself Kierkegaard's spokesman, as Habib C. Malik summarizes:

> Two related ironies characterize the Brandes–Kierkegaard connection: that the posthumous intellectual and spiritual legacy of the one thinker, whose fundamental orientation ran counter to the pervading positivism of his century, should, at a critical moment, fall into the hands of a true child and representative of that very positivism; and that this latter, the pure product of the new "liberated" age, should end up serving, in spite of himself, as popularizer of the very same thinker he had intended to suppress.[14]

---

[11] Brandes, *Kierkegaard*, p. 156.

[12] *Correspondance de Georg Brandes*, vol. 3, p. 450.

[13] Bonde Jensen, *Jeg er kun en Digter. Om Søren Kierkegaard som skribent*, p. 163.

[14] Habib C. Malik, "The Biographical-Psychological Approach and Its Perils: Georg Brandes and Criticism as Suppression," in his *Receiving Søren Kierkegaard: The Early Impact and Transmission of His Thought*, Washington, DC: Catholic University of America Press 1997, p. 279.

Despite his own intentions, Brandes' lasting contribution to the reception of Kierkegaard's works is not the image of Kierkegaard as a brilliant aesthetician and secular humanist that he marketed to the world. Instead, Brandes deserves credit for increasing the horizons of Kierkegaard scholarship in both breadth and depth, illustrating the potential of biographical criticism for textual interpretation, and demonstrating the resilience and relevance of Kierkegaard's work to the modern world.

I. Brandes' Biography and Significance

Born on February 4, 1842, during the reign of Denmark's last absolute monarch, Georg Morris Cohen Brandes embodied many of the paradoxes that characterized Denmark's entry into the twentieth century. Brandes was a man of stark contrasts and contradictions, in terms of social class, religion, national identity, personal beliefs, and political orientation. He promoted women's rights but had a reputation as a callous philanderer. He advocated the rights of the underclass and oppressed minorities, but admired "great men" like Nietzsche and Bismarck. He was supremely confident to all external appearances, but plagued by self-doubt in the privacy of his own mind. He was skeptical of all religion, including his own Jewishness, but he was fascinated by Kierkegaard and Jesus. He had a larger-than-life personality which ensured that the causes he espoused and the ideas he promoted received disproportionate attention.

Born as the oldest child of Herman and Emilie Brandes, Brandes was raised as a non-practicing Jew in Copenhagen. The Brandes household was as completely assimilated as was possible for a Jewish family at that place and time. Aside from circumcision as an infant and *pro forma* confirmation at the Copenhagen Synagogue on May 17, 1857,[15] Brandes never identified himself as a Jew, but his Jewish heritage played a major role in his self-perception and reception by his countrymen nonetheless. From an early age, Brandes was aware of a sense of isolation from mainstream Danish society as a result of being Jewish. One of the anecdotes he liked to tell about the issue involved asking his mother, as a young boy, what a Jew looked like, and having her hold him up to a mirror, causing him to scream.[16] Brandes biographer Jørgen Knudsen explains the significance of this moment for Brandes, as articulated in a passage in his biography of British Prime Minister Benjamin Disraeli's childhood that he later admitted was largely autobiographical:[17]

> He learnt for the first time that he was a Jew, and all that the name implies.
>
> He discovered that he was not reckoned as one of the people among whom he lived, had no part in the deeds of their forefathers or in their history, but was an isolated being: and yet was constantly thrown with others, whom he did not know and had never seen before; who regarded him as ugly, nay, even repulsive; to whom his mode of speaking

---

[15]   Henry J. Gibbons, "Georg Brandes: The Reluctant Jew," *The Activist Critic*, Copenhagen: Munksgaard 1980 (*Orbis Litterarum*, Supplement, no. 5), p. 57.

[16]   Brandes, *Levned*, vol. 1, p. 20.

[17]   Jørgen Knudsen, *GB. En Georg Brandes-biografi*, Copenhagen: Gyldendal 2008, p. 22.

was ridiculous, nay, even repugnant, and who pointed at him the finger of scorn. In the reading lessons, a Jew was inevitably a ridiculous, vulgar, or mean and avaricious person, a cheat, a usurer, or a coward.[18]

Though the adult Brandes often said that he would have completely forgotten that he was a Jew if he had not been continually reminded of it,[19] the perception of Brandes as a Jew by those around him ensured that his Jewish identity played a significant role in both the development of his ideas and the reaction his ideas elicited.

Although his family home and upbringing were not Jewish in any meaningful way, as Brandes often insisted,[20] he was only two generations removed from a tradition of observant Judaism and grew up defining himself in opposition to it. He explains the process of inverse identity formation in his autobiography:

> At home there was never any discussion of religious faith. Neither of my parents had any relation to the Jewish religion; neither of them attended synagogue. Since the Jewish dietary laws were observed in my grandmother's home, where they had different dishes for meat and dairy, and a special set for Passover, Orthodox Judaism came to represent for me a collection of strange old, superstitious prejudices, with particular reference to food. Its poetry was a closed book to me.[21]

In his discussion of Brandes' reluctant acknowledgement of his Jewish heritage, Henry J. Gibbons suggests that Brandes learned this attitude from his mother, Emilie, who was "fiercely intelligent, coldly rational, and defiantly anticlerical, [and who] lumped Christianity and Judaism together and despised both."[22]

Brandes had an extremely close relationship with his mother, whose personality and preferences shaped Brandes' own. Brandes' friend Edmund Gosse, an English literary critic, described her after a visit in 1874 as an "irreconcilable opponent of all conservative institutions, bitterly disposed toward the monarchy, sharply anticlerical, politically a red republican."[23] Brandes himself reflected, many years later, that "I gradually realized that there was no one who was more difficult to please than mother. No one was stingier with praise than she, and she loathed all sensitivity. She appeared to me as the superior mind, corrected and raised me through satire."[24] Throughout his mother's life, Brandes visited her every day when he was in Copenhagen and wrote her copious letters when abroad.

Not least because of his mother's high expectations and sparing praise, Brandes' intellectual development was a lonely path. He was an exceptionally gifted child, always the youngest and smartest student in the class. Knudsen explains that Brandes was terribly bored in school, because of the disconnect between him and his circumstances, describing him as "a religiously indifferent Jewish boy in a Christian

---

[18]   Georg Brandes, *Lord Beaconsfield: A Study*, trans. by Mrs. George Sturge, New York: Scribner 1880, p. 23.

[19]   Gibbons, "Georg Brandes: The Reluctant Jew," p. 55.

[20]   Ibid., p. 56.

[21]   Brandes, *Levned*, vol. 1, pp. 55–6.

[22]   Gibbons, "Georg Brandes: The Reluctant Jew," p. 56.

[23]   Knudsen, *GB*, p. 23.

[24]   Brandes, *Levned*, vol. 1, pp. 47–8.

society, an overly gifted student among mediocre classmates, an independent little person in a school environment which inculcated obedience above all, a tremendously bright, sensitive, critical and cheerfully observant spirit in a pompous world."[25] After he became a university student in 1859, Brandes dove into his studies whole-heartedly. Rubow explains that Brandes' life at the university until he went to Paris in 1866, was an "ascetic and exhausting life of duty and study," in which he divided his days between the legal studies he dared not neglect for fear of incurring his parents' disapproval and the frantic study of philosophy and literature either alone or with classmates.[26] He lived in the world of books, devouring in particular the works of the German Romantics, such as Novalis.

One of the most seminal moments in Brandes' intellectual life took place during his student years, when he underwent a roughly four-year period of religious searching. He had long felt social pressure to embrace Christianity from close friends such as Julius Lange (1838–96), as Brandes describes in his edition of Lange's letters (1898),[27] but he had never given it much serious thought before 1859, when he began studying Christianity in earnest. He read the Bible cover to cover, as well as Jakob Peter Mynster's (1775–1854) autobiography, Hans Lassen Martensen's (1808–84) book on Meister Eckhart, Rasmus Nielsen's (1809–84) *Evangelietroen og den moderne Bevidsthed*, as well as several of Kierkegaard's works.[28] For the better part of two years, Brandes read, thought, and vacillated between Christianity and Hegelian rationalism. His diaries contain heartfelt accounts of his desire to live a moral life and his search for spiritual truth, in both religious and philosophical texts. Finally, in the fall of 1861, Brandes felt that he had achieved certainty. In his diary on October 27, 1861, Brandes exclaims, "I am happy. In the last approx. 14 days a change has taken place in my soul. I have learned to pray to God, learned to kneel down and stretch out my arms to the star-filled sky....First and last I have received peace and quiet in my soul; I have become a Christian."[29] His euphoric certainty did not last, however, and Brandes became increasingly disillusioned with Christianity over the course of the following two years. By March 1863, he had begun to distance himself from religion entirely, though he did not make the decision lightly, as his diary entry from January 3, 1865 makes clear: "It is a terrible condition when one's heart unceasingly desires what one's head unceasingly denies."[30] Ultimately, his head won out, and, over the course of the 1860s, Brandes developed a decisively atheistic viewpoint, which he maintained for the rest of his life.

[25]   Knudsen, *GB*, p. 24.
[26]   Paul V. Rubow, *Georg Brandes' Briller*, Copenhagen: Levin and Munksgaard 1932, p. 102.
[27]   Georg Brandes, *Julius Lange. Breve fra hans Ungdom*, Copenhagen: Det Nordiske Forlag 1898.
[28]   Johnny Kondrup, "Kierkegaard og Brandes," *Kierkegaard inspiration. En antologi*, ed. by Birgit Bertung et al., Copenhagen: C.A. Reitzel 1991, p. 71.
[29]   Georg Brandes, *Dagbog 21. juli 1861 – 22. juli 1863*, Manuscript Department, Danish Royal Library, Copenhagen, p. 137.
[30]   Brandes, *Dagbog juli 1863 – 4. august 1867*, Manuscript Department, Danish Royal Library, Copenhagen, p. 95.

Brandes' religious crisis and its outcome had a profound effect on the evolution of his personal and professional world-view toward scientific rationalism and ethical humanism. Malik explains, "as a consequence of this experience, Brandes permanently lost all feeling for religion, discarded any lingering attachments to the romantic school in literature, and paved the way for 'the Modern Breakthrough,' that was founded on a new secular realism and a radical positivism."[31] As Brandes explained in a letter to Marie Pingel in June 1870, "I believe in *thought*, I believe that *reason* and freedom, because they are the strongest in their essence, will always make their way to the light, and I believe in the irresistibility, unconquerability, and truth of these forces. This is my simple faith."[32] He remained deeply affected by his study of Kierkegaard, but he oriented himself as diametrically opposed to religion as possible.

Under the guidance of his philosophy professor at the University of Copenhagen, Hans Brøchner (1820–75), a second cousin of Kierkegaard's and a dedicated Hegelian, Brandes supplanted Kierkegaard with the works of thinkers such as Hegel, Heiberg, Strauss, Spinoza, and Feuerbach. In particular, Brandes turned against Brøchner's longtime competitor and Kierkegaard's erstwhile devotee Rasmus Nielsen, who had been instrumental in disseminating Kierkegaard's ideas among the younger generation of Danish scholars. In his polemic, *Dualism in our Recent Philosophy*,[33] Brandes denounced Nielsen's position that faith and knowledge can be unified and attacked the concept of "the paradox" as "anti-rational,"[34] a charge he would later repeat in his Kierkegaard monograph.

Throughout the late 1860s, Brandes searched for a new philosophical role model. He traveled to Paris in 1866 and 1870, immersing himself in the study of French positivists, including Hippolyte Taine (1828–93), Charles Sainte-Beuve (1804–69), and Ernst Renan (1823–92), whose agenda of secular, scientific, and social realism captivated him and became the subject of his doctoral dissertation, *Contemporary French Aesthetics*, in 1870. However, the person who made the deepest impression on Brandes in France was the Englishman John Stuart Mill, whose book *On the Subjugation of Women* Brandes had translated in 1869. Mill seemed to Brandes to embody his ideal of a "man of action...whose energy, both the revolutionary and the persistent, was placed completely in the service of the new social thinkers."[35] Precisely because of the differences between them, Brandes found himself drawn to Mill. In his autobiography, Brandes describes his determination to turn from abstract thoughts to concrete action:

> Our desire is no longer flight from society and reality with our longings and our thoughts. Just the reverse: we want to realize our ideas in society, in life. In order not to become a nation of bad poets, we want to strive for the real, the defined goal, the useful, which the previous generation despised. Who would not be happy to be able to do even a little good?[36]

---

[31]   Malik, *Receiving Søren Kierkegaard*, p. 232.
[32]   Henning Fenger, *Georg Brandes' læreår*, Copenhagen: Gyldendal 1955, p. 171.
[33]   Georg Brandes, *Dualismen i vor nyeste Philosophie*, Copenhagen: Gyldendal 1866.
[34]   Rubow, *Georg Brandes' Briller*, p. 121.
[35]   Brandes, *Levned*, vol. 2, pp. 310–11.
[36]   Brandes, *Levned*, vol. 1, p. 315.

In Mill, Brandes felt that he had found a new model for how to live an active intellectual life. In a letter to his mother from England in July 1870, he explains his new perspective on his professional calling: "I feel that my conversation with him at last forms a kind of turning point in my inner intellectual history."[37] Although Mill had never read Hegel, Brandes believed that Mill's life and works demonstrated the Hegelian unity of idea and reality,[38] and resolved to emulate him by acting on his own intellectual convictions.

Upon his return to Denmark, Brandes made good on this resolve with his polemical lectures entitled "Main Currents in 19th-Century Literature," the first installment of which he delivered at the University of Copenhagen on November 3, 1871. Brandes' account of the revolutionary literary developments across Europe during the preceding decades, in explicit contrast to the stagnant state of Danish literature, challenged the conservative intellectual establishment and set in motion Denmark's transformation from a literary backwater to a cultural hub. The subsequent literary movement, as well as concurrent revolts against cultural, political, moral, and social norms, became known as the "Modern Breakthrough," and Brandes was widely acknowledged as its instigator. F.J. Billeskov Jansen (1907–2002) explains that Brandes "was concerned with liberating scholarship from the Church and other authorities and with liberating women from male hegemony. Brandes fought for free thought and free love."[39]

As a result, Brandes rapidly became the most polemical figure in Danish literary and cultural life of the time. His life and works provoked both ardent admiration and undisguised loathing among his contemporaries. Henry Gibbons concludes that "most of what was written about him during his lifetime was partisan and polemical, and falls into two neatly divided categories: the hagiographies by convinced Brandesians and the denunciations by Brandes' numerous enemies."[40] Repeatedly denied the professorship in aesthetics at the University of Copenhagen to which he believed himself entitled, he made his living by writing newspaper articles and giving lectures throughout Scandinavia. When he found himself blacklisted by the leading newspapers in Copenhagen, he and his brother Edvard founded their own journal, *The Nineteenth Century.* The antagonism Brandes faced in Denmark finally drove him to self-imposed exile in Germany. Together with his German wife, Gerda, Brandes lived in Berlin from 1877 to 1883, working as a freelance writer and contributing to a wide range of culturally progressive publications, including Julius Rodenberg's *Deutsche Rundschau*. He mingled with the brightest stars in Berlin's cultural firmament, but remained deeply invested in the Danish intellectual scene.

By the time Brandes returned to Copenhagen in 1883, enticed by a privately-financed professorship, his interests had begun to shift from liberal democracy and

---

[37]   *Georg Brandes' Breve til Forældrene*, ed. by Morten Borup, vols. 1–3, Copenhagen: Reitzel 1978, vol. 1, p. 279.

[38]   Rubow, *Georg Brandes' Briller*, p. 127.

[39]   F.J. Billeskov Jansen, "Brandes," in *Kierkegaard and Human Values*, ed. by Niels Thulstrup and Marie Mikulová Thulstrup, Copenhagen: C.A. Reitzel 1980 (*Bibliotheca Kierkegaardiana*, vol. 7), p. 206.

[40]   Gibbons, "Georg Brandes: The Reluctant Jew," p. 55.

realistic literature to the theory of the great man. He is credited with being the first critic to publicize the importance of Friedrich Nietzsche's work, through a series of articles on Nietzsche's "Aristocratic Radicalism" published in the Danish newspaper *Tilskueren* in 1888 and the *Deutsche Rundschau* in 1890. Between 1890 and 1927, Brandes wrote monographs on great men from across the spectrum of world history, including Shakespeare (1895), Goethe (1914), Voltaire (1916), Julius Caesar (1918), Michelangelo (1921), and Jesus (1925).

The final decades of Brandes' life were marked by his increasing advocacy for politically disadvantaged minorities. He lectured widely on the Armenian genocide and worked tirelessly on behalf of the Danish-speaking population in German-controlled Schleswig-Holstein. His outspoken opposition to World War I not only earned him the enmity of politicians on both sides of the conflict, including his erstwhile good friend French Prime Minister Georges Clemenceau, but also destroyed much of his popularity in Europe. When he died on February 19, 1927, his once-towering international reputation was in eclipse, while the rise of German fascism and the anti-Semitic policies of the Nazis ensured that his name disappeared from German literary histories, except as the man who introduced Nietzsche and Kierkegaard to the world.

II. Brandes' Relationship to Kierkegaard

In an intellectual sense, Brandes grew up in the shadow of Kierkegaard, whose period of greatest notoriety in Denmark coincided with Brandes' formative years. His 1877 monograph on Kierkegaard begins with his childhood memories of being told by his nanny to straighten his stockings so as not to look like the infamously ill-dressed Kierkegaard, recently caricatured in *The Corsair*. As he played in the streets of Copenhagen with his friends, Brandes saw the windows of Kierkegaard's apartment illuminated with both candles and genius.[41] His first reading of *Either/Or* at age 17 made an overwhelming impression on Brandes, who later recalled, "Never before in Danish literature had I encountered such a superiority of spirit, such a strength of thought, and (as it seemed to be then) such experience of the world."[42] A.B. Drachmann (1860–1935) highlights Kierkegaard's influence, both attributed and unacknowledged, on the methods and ideas of Brandes' early publications, in particular *Aesthetic Studies* and *Criticisms and Portraits*.[43] Paul V. Rubow describes Brandes' relationship to Kierkegaard as "the most serious in his entire spiritual life,"[44] but the nature of that relationship was competitive, not unlike a sibling rivalry in which a younger child struggles to define his own identity in opposition to an older sibling.

The posthumous publication of Kierkegaard's papers, beginning in 1869, perpetuated the tendency inaugurated by *The Corsair* of focusing on Kierkegaard's

---

41   Brandes, *Kierkegaard*, p. 1.
42   Ibid., p. 120.
43   A.B. Drachmann, "Brandes og Søren Kierkegaard," *Tilskuerens Festskrift til Georg Brandes*, Copenhagen: Gyldendal 1912, p. 38.
44   Rubow, *Georg Brandes' Briller*, p. 101.

biography rather than the content and implications of his writings. Malik explains that such a "biographical-psychological approach" to Kierkegaard, which focuses on the "sensational aspects of Kierkegaard's personal life and the inner workings of his mind, as delineated in his journals, became [a] convenient tool in the hands of those who wished to deflect attention from the substantive significance of his works, thereby undermining their potential intellectual and spiritual influence."[45] Making generous use of Kierkegaard's posthumously published personal papers, Brandes became the most prominent practitioner of this approach with respect to Kierkegaard, starting a trend that has continued for more than a hundred years. Yet although Kierkegaard's life does offer valuable insights into his work, Brandes' approach was calculating and highly subjective, cherry-picking material to support his predetermined condemnation of Kierkegaard's religious views. Henriksen objects to Brandes' application of the biographical-psychological approach to Kierkegaard, since "for the sake of clarity, Søren Kierkegaard's tremendously complicated psychic mechanism was to be reduced to a quantity that could be handled conveniently, and out of the mass of his experiences the few were to be selected which must be supposed to have dominated the history of his life."[46]

Brandes' ambivalence toward Kierkegaard throughout his career derived from his intensive engagement with Kierkegaard's work during his youthful exploration of Christianity. According to Fenger, "from 1861 to 1864, Kierkegaard stood for him [Brandes] as the incarnation of faith and religion."[47] He read *Either/Or* in the summer of 1860, followed in quick succession during the fall of 1860 by *The Moment, Fear and Trembling, From the Papers of One Still Living, On My Work as an Author, For Self-Examination*, as well as *Stages on Life's Way*.[48] In the course of his studies in the summer of 1861, he turned to Hegel and Goethe, but returned to Kierkegaard in the fall, working through the *Concluding Unscientific Postscript, The Sickness unto Death, Philosophical Fragments, The Concept of Anxiety*, and *Repetition* over the course of the following year.[49] He identified with the tension between Kierkegaard's spheres of existence and wrestled with Kierkegaard's conception of sin, as he noted in his diary in October 1861: "Kierkegaard is for me...qualitatively different from all others....I have felt inexpressible exhilaration, knelt and prayed, but there is a duplicity in me, the deepest cleft in my soul...."[50] Even at the peak of his enthusiasm for Christianity, Brandes remained deeply ambivalent toward Kierkegaard, as he expressed in his diary on November 18, 1861: "Søren Kierkegaard's *Concluding Unscientific Postscript* has torn down most of my defenses all at once. Is he not the greatest man in Denmark or in the world? And yet, may God protect me from him, or else I will never live my own life."[51] The man Brandes most admired was also the man he perceived as the most significant challenge to the development of his own

[45] Malik, *Receiving Søren Kierkegaard*, p. 217.
[46] Henriksen, *Methods and Results of Kierkegaard Studies in Scandinavia*, p. 26.
[47] Fenger, *Georg Brandes' læreår*, p. 134.
[48] Rubow, *Georg Brandes' Briller*, p. 106.
[49] Ibid., p. 107.
[50] Brandes, *Dagbog 21. juli 1861– 22. juli 1863*, p. 139.
[51] Ibid., p. 157.

ideas. It was perhaps inevitable that Brandes would challenge Kierkegaard, if only to counter his influence on his thinking.

In turning away from Kierkegaard, Brandes perceived himself as blazing his own path and finding his own identity, though in conscious reaction to Kierkegaard. Several scholars have attempted to explain the connection between Brandes' rejection of Kierkegaard and Christianity. Johnny Kondrup suggests that Kierkegaard's work made Brandes aware of the impossibility of becoming a Christian,[52] while Henning Fenger posits that Brandes' rejection of Christianity was based on his rejection of Kierkegaard: "If this, the whole Kierkegaard gospel, was the true Christianity, *he*, Brandes, chose deliberately not to be a Christian."[53] Yet any equation Brandes might have made of Kierkegaard's work with conventional Danish Christianity deliberately misrepresents Kierkegaard's main point, as Bonde Jensen argues:

> When Kierkegaard says that one must not believe that Christianity excludes or destroys the sensual—if it did, then even health itself would become suspicious—then Brandes objects that this is an unfortunate proof, since health has always been suspicious precisely for Christianity. But that is the not the case for Kierkegaard. So what? It makes no difference.[54]

In his eagerness to condemn religion, particularly the Christianity of Grundtvig and Martensen, as bankrupt, Brandes essentially ignored Kierkegaard's own objections and lumped him in with those whose views of Christianity he himself objected to. He went so far as to equate the Grundtvigian views of Rasmus Nielsen on the relationship of science to religion and knowledge to faith with Kierkegaard's legacy.[55] In his monograph Brandes placed the blame on Kierkegaard more explicitly, explaining that "with Kierkegaard, the spiritual life in Denmark has been driven to the extremity where a leap has to be made, a leap into the depths of black Catholicism or the jump to the cape from which liberty awaits you."[56] For his own part, Brandes made the leap into atheism and gave Kierkegaard the credit for having driven him to the brink.

Yet once he had rejected Kierkegaard's premises, Brandes could not leave his works alone. In order to defend his own position, Brandes felt it necessary to discredit Kierkegaard, but he did not want to attack him openly, especially since he still admired his literary skills, wit, irony, and persuasive style. He recognized both the potency of Kierkegaard's work, as well as its value, stripped of the religious content he found so offensive and archaic, in the service of his own intellectual agenda. For these reasons, Brandes pursued his goal of re-interpreting Kierkegaard by guiding the reception of Kierkegaard's works toward a more secular interpretation that discounted the theological aspects of his authorship. With the monograph, Brandes introduces a strategy, which Malik describes as "criticism as suppression"[57]

---

52   Kondrup, "Kierkegaard og Brandes," p. 74.
53   Fenger, *Georg Brandes' læreår*, p. 51.
54   Bonde Jensen, *Jeg er kun en Digter. Om Søren Kierkegaard som skribent*, p. 163.
55   Malik, *Receiving Søren Kierkegaard*, p. 235.
56   Brandes, *Kierkegaard*, p. 271.
57   Malik, *Receiving Søren Kierkegaard*, p. 254.

and Kondrup as "negative reception,"[58] that eventually became a hallmark of his literary-critical involvement in European cultural politics.

During the 1870s, Brandes inaugurated this approach by becoming a prominent representative of Kierkegaard both in Denmark and abroad. The first three volumes of *Main Currents* (1872–74), which established Brandes' credibility as a literary critic throughout Europe, are preoccupied with Kierkegaard on the level of both content and tone. Billeskov Jansen explains, "in this long showdown with Danish idealism, SK is present as the representative of the Christian, anti-rationalistic reaction; he stands as an absolutist and orthodox fanatic. But the militant spirit of this controversial work on literary history is in fact that of SK."[59] In the first volume of *Main Currents*, subtitled *Emigrant Literature*, Brandes attacks all forms of idealism and religious conviction, and, perfecting the strategy of biographical-psychological criticism, depicts Kierkegaard "as an irrepressible aesthetic genius, longing to break out into freedom, yet hopelessly shackled by the gloomy religious upbringing he had received at home."[60] Rubow points out the structural similarities between *Emigrant Literature* and volume one of *Either/Or*, and identifies Kierkegaard's attack on Christendom as the "deepest foundation" for Brandes' book:

> It is the Kierkegaardian attitude, the single man with unique spiritual gifts and a great mission, that is Brandes' focus in this book. Even the situation of the individual facing the crowd with his demand for truth and justice at any price, must have been borrowed from Kierkegaard and not the practical Stuart Mill.[61]

In the second volume of *Main Currents*, *The Romantic School in Germany*, Brandes links Kierkegaard closely to such prominent, religious-conservative German Romantics as Friedrich Schlegel, Novalis, and Tieck. He depicts him as "representative of the darkest reaction…to which the backlash against the rationalism of the eighteenth century drove Danish thinking" and condemns him for having supplanted "the passion for thinking with the passion for believing."[62] He attacks Kierkegaard's concern with subjective issues as evidence of his refusal to "draw any external or social consequences from his teachings,"[63] and he makes no mention of the high price Kierkegaard paid for his very personal involvement with the external, social consequences of his ideas.

In 1874, Brandes found an opportunity to present his views on Kierkegaard to a German audience through his German translator Adolf Strodtmann's (1829–79) discussion of Kierkegaard in his book, *Das geistige Leben in Dänemark.*[64]

[58]   Johnny Kondrup, "Keine hinreichende Vorstellung von seinem Genie. Strategien in der negativen Kierkegaardrezeption von Georg Brandes," *Kierkegaardiana*, vol. 18, 1996, p. 150.
[59]   Billeskov Jansen, "Brandes," p. 206.
[60]   Malik, *Receiving Søren Kierkegaard*, p. 238.
[61]   Rubow, *Georg Brandes' Briller*, p. 129.
[62]   Ibid., p. 130.
[63]   Georges Brandes, *Den romantiske Skole i Tyskland*, Copenhagen: Gyldendal 1873, p. 17.
[64]   Adolf Strodtmann, *Das geistige Leben in Dänemark. Streifzüge auf den Gebieten der Kunst, Literatur, Politik und Journalistik des skandinavischen Nordens*, Berlin: Paetel 1873.

Strodtmann's book was a pioneering effort to awaken German interest in modern Dano-Norwegian artists and writers, including Carl Bloch, Henrik Ibsen, Frederik Paludan-Müller, Søren Kierkegaard, and Brandes himself. While a prisoner of war in Copenhagen in 1848, Strodtmann acquired a superficial familiarity with Denmark's cultural and intellectual life, but his published account of Danish politics, literature, religion, and society reflects a much deeper and more partisan engagement with Danish culture than Strodtmann had cause or occasion to develop. Although his name does not appear on the title page of Strodtmann's book, there can be little doubt about Brandes' influence on its depiction of modern Danish culture. Brandes had made Strodtmann's acquaintance in Berlin in 1871 and introduced him to the works of Ibsen and Kierkegaard. Brandes' letters to his family from an extended stay in Strodtmann's home in Steglitz during the fall of 1872 reveal both the extent of his involvement and his determination to use Strodtmann's book as a vehicle for conveying his particular opinions about Danish high culture to a German audience. On October 3, he asked his brother Edvard to send Strodtmann copies of three articles on Danish art written by Holger Drachmann (1846–1908), as well as a copy of Julius Lange's (1838–96) history of Danish art, with the explanation that Strodtmann "needs these for what he is writing about Denmark, with which I must help him, if it is not to be terribly wrong."[65] The secrecy implicit in their collaboration is revealed in his letter from October 13, 1872, in which he exhorts his parents not to mention to anyone that he was staying with Strodtmann, "as I have written out 5–6 pages of notes for his descriptions of Denmark and I want no one to say that they are from me."[66] The book's Danish debut was disastrous, in large part because of Strodtmann's sympathy with the German nationalists in Schleswig-Holstein, but Brandes defended his decision to assist Strodtmann, explaining that "the irony is that it is my accomplishment alone that the book has turned out as positive about Denmark as it has. Everything that is written correctly about our art and our literature is my contribution."[67] Although Brandes had tried to keep his contributions anonymous, Strodtmann lavished such extravagant praise on Brandes and relied so heavily on his opinions that Brandes' involvement was unmistakable to Danish critics, who dubbed Strodtmann as "the German apostle of 'free-thinking' "[68] and his book "a faithful and willing echo of Mr. Brandes' well-known judgments."[69]

With regard to Kierkegaard, Strodtmann's echo of Brandes' judgment is that Kierkegaard is a genius, but ultimately misguided. Strodtmann quotes from an article by Brandes in *Dagbladet*, in which he compares Kierkegaard to the pioneering Danish astronomer Tycho Brahe, who made great contributions to the field of astronomy but failed to ascribe to heliocentrism. Like Brahe, Brandes suggests,

[65]   *Georg Brandes. Breve til Forældrene 1872–1879*, ed. by Torben Nielsen, vols. 1–3, Copenhagen: C.A. Reitzel 1994, vol. 1, p. 34.
[66]   Ibid., vol. 1, p. 40.
[67]   Ibid., vol. 1, p. 51.
[68]   Anonymous, "*Das geistige Leben in Dänemark* von Adolf Strodtmann," *Dagens Nyheder*, March 31, 1873.
[69]   Anonymous, "Literatur: A. Strodtmann, *Das geistige Leben in Dänemark*," *Dagbladet*, March 25, 1873.

Kierkegaard made important contributions to philosophy but continued to adhere to an outmoded and flawed world-view, namely, a religious one. Strodtmann, echoing Brandes' assessment in *Main Currents*, categorizes Kierkegaard as the last of the early ninetenth-century Romantics, and quotes extensively from the first volume of *Either/Or*. His analysis of Kierkegaard's theological position parrots Brandes' views precisely, arguing that Kierkegaard's genius is hampered by his indefensible Christian spiritual components and interpreting his attack on Christendom as "an admission of the practical impossibility of Christianity, and his entire life's work… as a demonstration of the ultimate untenability of Christian faith."[70] At the end of the 30 pages devoted to Kierkegaard, Strodtmann declares, "The authentic intellectual heir to Søren Kierkegaard is Georg Brandes…the shrewdest and most sensible critic [since the days of Lessing]."[71]

Many scholars since Strodtmann have also described Brandes as Kierkegaard's student and successor. Rubow identifies Kierkegaard as Brandes' most significant spiritual teacher, explaining that "the shape of his spirit is Kierkegaardian."[72] Fenger describes him as Kierkegaard's apprentice, even as he altered Kierkegaard's message, because of his loyalty to his own credo of humanism and liberalism.[73] Using the quotation from Hamann about Tarquinius Superbus and the poppies that Kierkegaard placed at the beginning of *Fear and Trembling*, and which Brandes appropriated for his Kierkegaard monograph, Bonde Jensen demonstrates how Brandes regarded himself as occupying the position of Tarquinius' son in relation to Kierkegaard, namely the intended recipient of Kierkegaard's indirect communication.[74]

In keeping with time-tested tactics of medieval succession, Brandes honored his spiritual father by attempting to supplant him. His major treatment of Kierkegaard, in his 1877 monograph, *Søren Kierkegaard. En kritisk Fremstilling i Grundrids*, is a devastatingly skillful evisceration of Kierkegaard's work, with ample references to Kierkegaard's biography. It does not merely attack Kierkegaard's premises and conclusions, but offers instead a radical revision of his ideas, so as to render them palatable and useful to Brandes and his followers. As the most definitive book on Kierkegaard ever to emerge from Denmark, Brandes' monograph has shaped the reception of Kierkegaard's work throughout the world. Rubow praises the book as "by far the most competent and objectively penetrating [book] Brandes wrote, but also the most intimate of all of his works. It is with this book that the actual scholarly study of Kierkegaard in Denmark begins."[75] Kondrup agrees with Rubow about the book's seminal influence on the study of Kierkegaard, but he also points

---

[70]   Strodtmann, p. 123; Malik, *Receiving Søren Kierkegaard*, p. 231.
[71]   Strodtmann, *Leben*, pp. 125–6.
[72]   Rubow, *Georg Brandes' Briller*, p. 128.
[73]   Fenger, *Georg Brandes' læreår*, p. 172.
[74]   Bonde Jensen, *Jeg er kun en Digter. Om Søren Kierkegaard som skribent*, p. 149. In the original story, the son of Tarquinius Superbus, the King of Rome in 600 BC, had conquered the town of Gabii and sent a messenger to his father for advice on how to deal with dissenters. Unsure of the messenger's reliability, Tarquinius took him out into his garden, lopped off the heads of his poppies with his cane, and sent the messenger back to his son, whereupon his son ordered the beheading of the dissenting citizens of Gabii.
[75]   Rubow, *Georg Brandes' Briller*, p. 140.

out the Kierkegaard monograph's relevance as "an important element in the author's inner history, more precisely a self-accounting, and, as such, an indirect testament to Kierkegaard's tremendous significance for Georg Brandes."[76] Brandes does not directly acknowledge his own indebtedness to Kierkegaard anywhere in the book, but he believed it to be his finest, subtlest piece of work.[77]

With the Kierkegaard monograph, in which he attempts to explain Kierkegaard's work as a result of his life experiences, Brandes pioneered the genre of the author biography in Denmark, drawing heavily on Taine's belief that "literary works were simply the outer manifestations of the inner lives of poets"[78] and his theory that each individual can be understood with reference to three causes: race, milieu, and historical moment. The monograph is derived from four controversial lectures on Kierkegaard that Brandes delivered in Copenhagen, Stockholm, and Oslo in the fall of 1876. The book preserves both the conversational tone and the four-part structure of the lectures, subdivided into a total of 28 short chapters. The first section, up to chapter 9, deals with Kierkegaard's youth and upbringing, in particular his relationship to his father, which Brandes regards as sickly and unnatural, poisoning Kierkegaard's mind and spirit from the outset.[79] Brandes negatively contrasts Kierkegaard's highly intellectual childhood, in particular his imaginary promenades through the streets of Copenhagen with his father, with John Stuart Mill's vigorous excursions in nature with his own father. He explains:

> While the relatively happy young Mill was led by his father's hand into sciences, which albeit required a man's intellectual force to master, but sciences nonetheless, this dark and fantastic Puritan of the lowest class [Michael Pedersen Kierkegaard] initiated his poor child into all of the fears and worries, with which the Christian orthodoxy, preached by an uneducated man who passed his time with scruples and religious constraints, can envelop a childish mind.[80]

Brandes goes on to describe how Kierkegaard's school days under the tutelage of the tyrannical Michael Nielsen (1776–1846) reinforced his respect for authority, his spirit of subjugation, and his spiteful arrogance. He pans Kierkegaard's treatise on Hans Christian Andersen (1805–75) as a failed beginner's attempt and dismisses the young Kierkegaard as a pampered dilettante.[81]

The second part of the book, comprising chapters 10–15, deals primarily with Kierkegaard's engagement to Regine Olsen, which Brandes regarded as one of only two central experiences in Kierkegaard's life, on which he drew for many of his works, for Kierkegaard is the type of writer, he notes, "whose nature is so fertile, whose inner climate is so tropical, that [he] could produce shelves of important works from very simple conditions of everyday life, which [he] experienced with the most intensive

---

[76]   Kondrup, "Kierkegaard og Brandes," p. 70.

[77]   *Correspondance de Georg Brandes*, vol. 3, p. 450.

[78]   Lundtofte, "Pointing Fingers at the Genius: Reading Brandes Reading Kierkegaard," p. 151.

[79]   Brandes, *Kierkegaard*, p. 11.

[80]   Ibid., p. 13.

[81]   Ibid., pp. 46–7.

energy."[82] Brandes postulates that Kierkegaard only needed the idea of Regine for inspiration, rather than an actual relationship with her, and attributes the breaking of the engagement to both her superfluity and Kierkegaard's presumed physical defects. The real impact of the broken engagement for Kierkegaard, according to Brandes, was its humiliating aftermath in the gossip-circles of Copenhagen, particularly because, as Brandes hypothesizes, Kierkegaard's relationship with Regine was a metaphor for his relationship to contemporary Danish society: "From the beginning, he approached with the best intentions. He amused, captivated, interested it to the highest degree, and it enjoyed his wit, but did not understand his suffering and his melancholy."[83] The second experience in this category, according to Brandes, was the *Corsair* affair, which he deals with in the final section (chapters 23–28) of the book, along with the attack on Christendom. He describes the final decade of Kierkegaard's life as a journey along a continuum of consciousness, ever further from Christian orthodoxy and closer to free thinking, which, as Kondrup underscores, allows Brandes to represent Kierkegaard as a path breaker toward his own "Modern Breakthrough," and himself as Kierkegaard's rightful heir.[84]

In the third part of the monograph, encompassing chapters 16–22, Brandes offers a critical overview of Kierkegaard's *oeuvre* and philosophy of the stages of life, but even this analysis is permeated with biographical concerns. Brandes explains Kierkegaard's concept of the three spheres of existence, but, as Lundtofte notes, uses them as a guide to constructing Kierkegaard's own character "as three different 'types,' translating the Kierkegaardian triad of the aesthetic, the ethical, and the religious into three stages of Kierkegaard's own development from…'the Genius' to 'the Pervert' and finally 'the Agitator.' "[85] He points out what he regards as inconsistencies in Kierkegaard's work, particularly with regard to Judge William's defense of marriage in *Either/Or* and *Stages on Life's Way*, and explains them as the result of Kierkegaard's cripplingly oppressive experiences in life, in particular his misfortune of having been born in a time period when Christianity had come under attack from Hegelianism. He argues that Kierkegaard was born with an oppositional nature, but that the momentary supremacy of Hegelianism during Kierkegaard's student days caused him to misdirect his sympathies toward the Christian theology he would otherwise have annihilated.[86] Brandes' interpretation of Kierkegaard's religious views, which he attributes primarily to Kierkegaard's father's influence is condescending and simplistic, disregarding the complexity and nuance inherent in both Kierkegaard's understanding of Christianity and his individual faith. He fails to acknowledge the keen intellectual struggles involved in Kierkegaard's own conversion to Christianity, but assumes a blind obedience to the same Danish theocracy which Kierkegaard later confronted.

---

[82]   Ibid., p. 77.
[83]   Ibid., p. 75.
[84]   Kondrup, "Kierkegaard og Brandes," p. 76.
[85]   Lundtofte, "Pointing Fingers at the Genius: Reading Brandes Reading Kierkegaard," p. 150.
[86]   Brandes, *Kierkegaard*, pp. 23–4.

Brandes' primary intent with this section seems to be to discredit Kierkegaard's work by denying the critical thought behind his positions. He laments Kierkegaard's youthful imprisonment in Christian orthodoxy, "as in a monastery,"[87] and asserts that Kierkegaard has never acquired intellectual autonomy because of this excessively heavy ballast.[88] Brandes accuses Kierkegaard of sacrificing his critical faculties to his reverence, defined as "the voluntary surrender of criticism out of awe for something venerable":

> Reverence is something completely different from piety, although these words literally denote the same thing: piety is an expression of immediacy, trustingly folding one's arms; reverence does not *want* to apply critical thinking, it deliberately destroys its critical instruments. Kierkegaard had little piety, but much reverence.[89]

Bonde Jensen asserts that Brandes cannot respect Kierkegaard, that he has a complete lack of sympathy for him, and regards his entire project as "*only* harmful."[90] He exhibits no desire to debate Kierkegaard's views on their merits, but only to point out his errors, his incorrect approach, and explain them with reference to his character, his psyche, his upbringing, and his time. He accuses him of "incurable mental derangement"[91] and blames Kierkegaard for the common misreadings of his early texts, due to the duplicity of both his literary style and his personality. On the whole, Brandes' critique of Kierkegaard relies on irresolvable contradictions. He accuses him of both servility and arrogance, humility and self-satisfaction, reverence and contempt, of which he identifies the latter two qualities as Kierkegaard's fundamental passions.[92]

Projecting his own priorities onto Kierkegaard and finding him wanting, Brandes argues that Kierkegaard was too critical of contemporary Danish society and not critical enough of religious belief. Brandes seems to suggest that, given different parents and a healthier childhood, Kierkegaard would have produced an entirely different philosophy, much closer to Mills' or Brandes' own. He dismisses Kierkegaard's premises about the individual, asserting that the idea of free will "has long ago been abandoned by every scientific psychology, but which he, in his capacity as a theologian, takes as a given,"[93] labels his aesthetic approach outdated, and decries his unfamiliarity with various academic disciplines, including "all of modern theology, comparative mythology, [and] historical studies of the ancient Christian period."[94] One of his repeated criticisms of Kierkegaard is his lack of a sophisticated appreciation for nature, music, and art,[95] which Bonde Jensen interprets as an expression of Brandes' feeling of being personally misunderstood

---

87   Ibid., p. 14.
88   Ibid., p. 19.
89   Ibid., p. 33. The Danish word for reverence was *pietet*, while piety is *fromhed*.
90   Bonde Jensen, *Jeg er kun en Digter. Om Søren Kierkegaard som skribent*, p. 156.
91   Brandes, *Kierkegaard*, p. 107.
92   Ibid., pp. 21–2; p. 35.
93   Ibid., p. 198.
94   Ibid., pp. 143–4.
95   Ibid., p. 2.

by Kierkegaard.[96] He also denies Kierkegaard any true appreciation for music, based largely on Kierkegaard's choice to analyze Mozart, whose "carefree and bubbling" style does not suit Brandes' image of Kierkegaard, rather than Beethoven, whose melancholy nature more closely expresses Brandes' conception of Kierkegaard's innermost being, characterized by his "heavy blood and heavy mind."[97]

On one level, then, Brandes' treatment of Kierkegaard is, in keeping with the spirit of *The Corsair* attacks, an analysis of Kierkegaard the man, rather than Kierkegaardian philosophy. Throughout his study of Kierkegaard's work, Brandes tends to disregard Kierkegaard's carefully constructed system of pseudonyms, tearing down the "doubled row of erected palisades" by which Kierkegaard has attempted to distance himself from his work,[98] and attributing every utterance to Kierkegaard himself. He regards the pseudonyms as Kierkegaard's strategy for concealing himself and misleading his readers, rather than tools of a literary or philosophical strategy.[99] Brandes' approach is to reveal the man behind the masks, but once he has done so, he complains of the gaps between Kierkegaard's life and the experiences of his characters. In one breath, he asserts that Kierkegaard's texts can only be understood by recourse to Kierkegaard's biography;[100] in the next, he disparages as "inauthentic" Kierkegaard's fictional characters, such as the married Judge William, whose experiences do not correspond to Kierkegaard's own, such that it is "pure poetical excitement that underlies the discussion of marriage in *Either/Or*."[101]

On another level, however, Brandes reveals that still he reveres Kierkegaard's genius and is deeply concerned with rehabilitating Kierkegaard's rhetorical and literary strategies for his own use. According to Lundtofte, Brandes saw "Kierkegaard's great contribution, not only to Danish literature, but also to Danish civilization," as his " 'passionate style'…of building his 'argument' as a string of linguistic images rather than grounding them in scientific observations."[102] Passages, such as most of chapter 19, in which he effuses over Kierkegaard's accomplishment, in his aesthetic works, of liberating Danish literature from conventional genres and language norms evoke the suspicion that Brandes' apparent contempt for Kierkegaard could, in fact, be just a blind attempt to conceal his actual intent of

> exposing the misconception that Kierkegaard has suffered—a misconception which Brandes saw manifested not only in public gossip but also in the way theologians had read and positioned Kierkegaard in their own camp. If the public had soiled Kierkegaard's name by dragging him through the mud of gossip, the theologians had soiled his intellectual reputation by claiming him to be nothing but a religious thinker,

---

[96]   Bonde Jensen, *Jeg er kun en Digter. Om Søren Kierkegaard som skribent*, p. 153.

[97]   Brandes, *Kierkegaard*, p. 137; p. 5.

[98]   Ibid., p. 80.

[99]   Ibid., p. 44; p. 89.

[100]   Ibid., p. 100.

[101]   Ibid., p. 169; p. 170.

[102]   Lundtofte, "Pointing Fingers at the Genius: Reading Brandes Reading Kierkegaard," p. 156.

according to Brandes, and his biography is an attempt to release Kierkegaard from the chatter of the public as well as from the grip of the theologians by grounding his study in psychological analysis, not in religion nor any other uncritically received ideas.[103]

As untenable as he found Kierkegaard's theological views, Brandes admired his literary style, which had been overlooked in the tumult over his person and his theology. Lundtofte suggests that although Brandes rejects the content of much of Kierkegaard's work, he mastered Kierkegaard's style of combining "theoretical reflections with persuasive rhetoric in an impressive double Dutch that goes beyond the traditional limits of critical investigation and exposition."[104] Brandes rejects Kierkegaard in order to reclaim him, tears him down in order to build him up again, but he does so in order to serve his own intellectual agenda.

The construction of Kierkegaard that Brandes endorses is that of the free-thinking radical of the "Attack on Christendom." Calling him an "agitator," Brandes identifies with Kierkegaard's activism in a social and political cause, his use of literature as a weapon of "cultural warfare against unenlightened tradition,"[105] and their common goal of exposing Christian morality as hollow ideology. Rather than regarding Kierkegaard's final works as the culmination of his entire authorship, Brandes interprets them as evidence of Kierkegaard's belated recognition of his earlier error in opposing Hegelian rationalism. He ignores the deep divide separating Kierkegaard's Christian views from Danish Lutheranism that is evident throughout his authorship and chooses instead to interpret Kierkegaard's attack on the Danish State Church as equivalent to early Saxon converts taking the ax to their former idols.[106] Brandes praises *The Sickness unto Death* and *Practice in Christianity* for Kierkegaard's energetic critique of mainstream Christianity and reviews each of his objections to Christian practice in detail. At this point, Brandes' biography of Kierkegaard becomes an exposé of their common culture, a condemnation of the intellectual cowardice and religious superstition of Danish society, which both Kierkegaard and Brandes recognized and against which they rebelled, though Kierkegaard spent much of his time fighting the wrong enemies: "He paid no attention to the fact that, while he stood on the fortifications and defended the castle against harmless speculators, the free-thinkers forced their way in behind his back and conquered the courtyard."[107] Brandes no longer positions himself as the earnest seeker of truth kneeling at Kierkegaard's altar, but rather as a leader of the free-thinkers, insisting that Kierkegaard's "burning love of truth" earns him a place by his side on the barricades of social reform.

Despite the irreconcilable differences of opinion documented throughout the book, it is this sense of solidarity with Kierkegaard that wins Brandes over in the end to a more positive assessment of his rival. He concludes by expressing his regret at Kierkegaard's untimely death: "I wish that he could have lived."[108] Throughout the

---

[103]   Ibid., pp. 153–4.
[104]   Ibid., p. 150.
[105]   Ibid., p. 162.
[106]   Brandes, *Kierkegaard*, p. 254; p. 271.
[107]   Ibid., p. 24.
[108]   Ibid., p. 267.

monograph, his caustic critiques of Kierkegaard's outmoded religiosity are tempered by exclamations of admiration for his literary gifts and outbursts of empathy with his frustrated hopes and desires. In his account of the *Corsair* affair, Brandes describes Kierkegaard's reaction in terms that could just as well represent his own feelings in the wake of the controversy and opposition he provoked in the 1870s: "He realized…that, in small societies, a type of conspiracy of mediocrity exists against the independent person, who will not adopt the others' opinions, but is so bold as to want to teach them something."[109] Brandes cites Kierkegaard's argument that the only way to combat the anonymous attacks of the press would be to print one's own paper, as he did in the final years of his life and as Brandes had done, together with his brother Edvard since the mid-1870s, when none of the leading Danish papers would print his articles. Brandes was convinced that a longer life would have given Kierkegaard the time to come around to a position more like his own, to an acknowledgment of the inadequacy and invalidity of religion as a guiding principle for human behavior.

Brandes' intense personal identification with Kierkegaard renders this monograph his finest piece of writing, in the opinion of most scholars. According to Fenger, in asserting that "no author in our literature has penetrated deeper into the abysses of the human heart, that no one has felt more deeply, thought more sharply, or taken a higher flight in his enthusiasm for the ideals of purity and constancy,"[110] Brandes also reveals his own indebtedness to Kierkegaard, to whom he owes many of his rhetorical strategies and with whom he shared an "idealistic, passionate and aristocratic attitude towards this world and its problems."[111] Billeskov Jansen explains that Brandes "had in his mind conquered SK's faith, but he left the battle with SK's weapons as booty. It was SK's fight against the established Church that Brandes transferred to the camp of humanistic individualism."[112]

More than a century later, Brandes' writings about Kierkegaard offer at least as much insight into the mind and heart of their author as their subject, making them doubly valuable to scholars of Danish cultural history. The tides of international Kierkegaard reception have ebbed and flowed, sometimes moving in the secular direction that Brandes indicated, sometimes taking a more theological path, while the reception of Brandes' own work has experienced a minor renaissance in the past few decades, partly in connection with an upsurge of interest in Kierkegaard. The fact that Brandes' own reputation has become inextricably linked to that of the man whose influence he struggled against and sought to suppress adds yet another delightful layer of irony to the ongoing saga of two of Denmark's most passionate and insightful thinkers.

---

[109]   Ibid., p. 234.
[110]   Ibid., pp. 271–2.
[111]   Fenger, *Georg Brandes' læreår*, p. 54.
[112]   Billeskov Jansen, "Brandes," p. 206.

Bibliography

I. Works by Georg Brandes that Make Use of Kierkegaard

Dualismen i vor nyeste Philosophie, Copenhagen: Gyldendal 1866, p. 9; p. 40; p. 57; p. 67; p. 72.

Den franske Æsthetik i vore Dage. En Afhandling om H. Taine, Copenhagen: Gyldendal 1870, p. 57; p. 154; p. 172; p. 262; pp. 274–5.

Kritiker og Portraiter, Copenhagen: Gyldendal 1870, p. 53; pp. 155–6; p. 159; pp. 248–9; p. 329; p. 331; pp. 358–9; p. 391; p. 407.

Hovedstrømninger i det 19. Aarhundredes Litteratur. Emigrantlitteraturen, Den Romantiske Skole i Tydskland, Copenhagen: Gyldendal 1872, p. 25; p. 191; p. 212; pp. 250–1; p. 269. (English translation: *Main Currents in Nineteenth Century Literature: The Emigrant Literature*, London: Heinemann 1901, p. 17; p. 39; p. 129; p. 148; p. 176; p. 180.)

"Literatur." Review of *Søren Kierkegaard: Dømmer selv! Til Selvprøvelse (1876)*, in *Det 19. Aarhundrede*, May–June 1876, pp. 238–9.

Søren Kierkegaard. En kritisk Fremstilling i Grundrids, Copenhagen: Gyldendal 1877. (German translation: *Sören Kierkegaard. Ein literarisches Characterbild*, Leipzig: Barth 1879.)

"Af Søren Kierkegaards Efterladte Papirer 1849," *Morgenbladet*, December 5, 1880, no. 285, and December 12, 1880, no. 291.

"Søren Kierkegaard," *Morgenbladet*, no. 242, October 16, 1880.

"Goethe og Danmark," in his *Mennesker og Værker i nyere europæisk Litteratur*, Copenhagen: Gyldendal 1883, pp. 1–79, see pp. 65–72.

"Søren Kierkegaard," in his *Mennesker og Værker i nyere europæisk Litteratur*, Copenhagen: Gyldendal 1883, pp. 185–205.

Henrik Ibsen, Copenhagen: Gyldendal 1898, p. 29; p. 50; p. 69; p. 82; p. 88; p. 92; pp. 98–9; p. 102; p. 145.

"Weltliteratur," *Das literarische Echo*, vol. 2, 1899–1900, no. 1, p. 4.

"Søren Aabye Kierkegaards Samlede Værker," *Politiken*, October 1, 1900, p. 1.

Skandinavische Persönlichkeiten, vols. 1–3, Munich: Albert Langen 1902, vol. 3, pp. 258–445.

"Viggo Hørup," in *Politiken*, March 3, 1902 (reprinted in *Samlede Skrifter*, vols. 1–18, vol. 15, 1905, pp. 206–10).

Levned, vols. 1–3, Copenhagen: Gyldendal 1905–8, vol. 2, pp. 202–10.

Kierkegaard und andere skandinavische Persönlichkeiten, Dresden: Reissner 1924.

"Søren Kierkegaardske Papirer," *Politiken*, January 12, 1928.

Brandes, Georg and Brandes, Edvard, *Brevveksling med nordiske Forfattere og Videnskabsmænd*, vols. 1–8, Copenhagen: Gyldendal 1942, vol. 1, p. 11; p. 13;

pp. 59–61; p. 67; p. 296; p. 324; p. 338; pp. 352–3; p. 364; p. 372; vol. 2, p. 58; vol. 3, p. 117; p. 176; p. 377; vol. 4, p. 104; p. 270; p. 320; p. 364; p. 391.

II. Sources of Georg Brandes' Knowledge of Kierkegaard

Barfod, Hans Peter, *Af Søren Kierkegaards Efterladte Papirer med indledende Notitser*, vols. 1–7, Copenhagen: C.A. Reitzel 1869–81.

Brøchner, Hans, "Erindringer om Søren Kierkegaard," *Det nittende Aarhundrede*, vol. 5, March 1, 1877, pp. 337–74.

Kierkegaard, Søren, *Af en endnu Levendes Papirer*, Copenhagen: C.A. Reitzel 1838.

— *Enten/Eller*, Copenhagen: C.A. Reitzel 1843.

— *Frygt og Bæven*, Copenhagen: C.A. Reitzel 1843.

— *Gjentagelsen. Et Forsøg i den Experimenterende Psychologi*, Copenhagen: C.A. Reitzel 1843.

— *Begrebet Angest*, Copenhagen: C.A. Reitzel 1844.

— *Philosophiske Smuler eller en Smule Philosophi*, Copenhagen: C.A. Reitzel 1844.

— *Stadier paa Livets Vei*, Copenhagen: C.A. Reitzel 1845.

— *Afsluttende uvidenskabelig Efterskrift til de philosophiske Smuler*, Copenhagen: C.A. Reitzel 1846.

— *Sygdommen til Døden*, Copenhagen: C.A. Reitzel 1849.

— *Om mit Forfatter-Virksomhed*, Copenhagen: C.A. Reitzel 1851.

— *Til Selvprøvelse. Samtiden anbefalet*, Copenhagen: C.A. Reitzel 1851.

— *Øieblikket*, Copenhagen: C.A. Reitzel 1855.

III. Secondary Literature on Georg Brandes' Relation to Kierkegaard

Ahlenius, Holger, "Søren Kierkegaard, en dansk biografi och en svensk diskussion," *Vår lösen*, vol. 20, no. 4, 1929, pp. 82–7.

Ahnfelt, Arvid, "Søren Kierkegaard 1–2," *Ny Illustrerad Tidning*, vol. 12, nos. 48 and 50, 1876, p. 422; pp. 443–4; p. 446.

— "Några ord om Søren Kierkegaard (Med Anledning af dr. Brandes' Föreläsningar)," *Sanningsökaren*, vol. 1, no. 1, 1877, pp. 15–17.

Anonymous, "Dr. G. Brandes' Föreläsningar," *Stockholmska Dagbladet*, November 18, 1876, no. 269, p. 2; no. 271, p. 2; no. 272, p. 2; no. 269, pp. 2–3; no. 275, p. 3; no. 277, p. 3.

Anonymous, "Georg Brandes," *Aftonbladet*, November 18, 1876, p. 3; November 22, 1876, p. 3; November 25, 1876, p. 3; November 28, 1876, p. 3.

Anonymous, "Georg Brandes," *Göteborgs-Posten*, November 20, 1876, no. 270, p. 1; no. 274, p. 1.

Anonymous, "Hr. Dr. Georg Brandes," *Dagbladet*, no. 274, November 23, 1876.

Anonymous, "Søren Kierkegaards Portrait," *Illustreret Tidskrift*, December 3 and 17, 1876.

Anonymous, "Mod det akademiske kollegiums vægring," *Dagbladet*, December 14, 1876.

Anonymous, "Dr. Brandes' Forelæsninger," *Morgenbladet*, Kristiania, December 15 and 24, 1876.

Anonymous, "Dr. G. Brandes," *Fædrelandet*, December 16, 1876, no. 294, p. 1.

Anonymous, "Svar til G," *Dagbladet*, no. 301, December 27, 1876, p. 1.

Anonymous, "Georg Brandes," *Uppsala-Posten*, 1876, no. 142, p. 2; no. 143, p. 2.

Anonymous, "Stockholms-bref," *Göteborg handels och sjöfartstidning*, 1876, no. 272, B; no. 274, p. 2; no. 278, p. 2.

Anonymous, "Dr. Brandes i Norge," *Morgenbladet*, Kristiania, January 9, 1877.

Anonymous, "Dr. G. Brandes," *Dansk Folketidende*, January 14 and 26, 1877.

Anonymous, "Föreläsningar öfver Sören Kierkegaard," *Uppsala*, March 29, 1877.

Anonymous, "Bref om dansk literatur," *Aftonbladet*, May 23, 1877.

Anonymous, "G.B. *Søren Kierkegaard*," *Illustreret Tidende*, June 10, 1877, p. 375.

A.W.A., "Sören Kierkegaard, " *Ny Illustrerad Tidning*, November 25, 1876, p. 422; December 9, 1876, pp. 443–6.

Bärthold, Albert, *Die Bedeutung der ästhetischen Schriften Sören Kierkegaards mit Bezug auf G. Brandes: "Sören Kierkegaard. Ein literarisches Characterbild,"* Halle: Fricke 1879.

Billeskov Jansen, F.J., "Brandes," *Kierkegaard and Human Values*, ed. by Niels Thulstrup and Maria Mikulová Thulstrup, Copenhagen: C.A. Reitzel 1980 (*Bibliotheca Kierkegaardiana*, vol. 7), pp. 204–8.

Bonde Jensen, Jørgen, "Vel desværre vor største Mand. Georg Brandes om Søren Kierkegaard," in his *Jeg er kun en Digter. Om Søren Kierkegaard som skribent*, Copenhagen: Babette 1996, pp. 148–77.

Borchsenius, Otto, "Til Hr. Dr. Georg Brandes," *Morgenbladet*, October 19, 1880, no. 244.

Cain, Geoffrey, "The Truth-Seekers: Ibsen, Strindberg, and Kierkegaard as Seen by Georg Brandes," in *Litteratur og magt. Nordisk-baltisk litterært symposium*, ed. by Leon Nikulin, Viby, Denmark: Diapason 2000, pp. 41–55.

Dingstad, Ståle, "Dr. Brandes' Forelæsninger," *Morgenbladet*, no. 346 A, December 15, 1876.

Drachmann, A.B., "G. Brandes og Søren Kierkegaard," *Tilskueren*, 1912, January–June, pp. 148–53 (reprinted in *Tilskuerens Festskrift til Georg Brandes*, Copenhagen: Gyldendal 1912, pp. 38–43).

Fenger, Henning, "Georg Brandes and Kierkegaard," in *The Activist Critic: A Symposium on the Political Ideas, Literary Methods and International Reception of Georg Brandes*, ed. by Hans Hertel and Sven Møller Kristensen, Copenhagen: Munksgaard, 1980 (*Orbis Litterarum*, Supplement, no. 5), pp. 49–54.

Frederiksen, Emil, "Georg Brandes og Katholicismen," *Credo*, vol. 15, no. 1, 1934, pp. 6–14.

Garborg, Arne, "Dr. G. Brandes," *Aftenbladet*, Kristiania, no. 8738, December 19 and 21, 1876.

— "*Dagbladet* og Kollegiet," *Aftensbladet*, Kristiania, no. 8748, January 5, 1877.

Grau, Gerd-Günther, "Jüdischer Nietzscheanismus. Brandes, Nietzsche und Kierkegaard," in his *Vernunft, Wahrheit, Glaube. Neue Studien zu Nietzsche und Kierkegaard*, Würzburg: Königshausen und Neumann 1997, pp. 64–94.

— "Jüdischer Nietzscheanismus oder Nietzscheanischer Antisemitismus. Brandes, Nietzsche und Kierkegaard," in *Jüdischer Nietzscheanismus*, ed. by Werner Stegmaier and Daniel Krochmalnik, Berlin and New York: Walter de Gruyter 1997 (*Monographien und Texte zur Nietzsche-Forschung*, vol. 36), pp. 127–50.

Hansen, Knud Lundbek, "Hvordan man sætter Kierkegaard på plads." *Tidehverv*, vol. 63, 1989, pp. 152–8; p. 162.

Hansen, Peter, *Noter til Dr. G. Brandes: "Søren Kierkegaard,"* Kristiania: Johan Dahls efterfølger 1877.

Helveg, F., "Søren Kierkegaard og Nutiden," *Nordisk månedskrift for folkelig og kristelig oplysning*, 1877, vol. 2, pp. 290–319.

Henriksen, Aage, *Methods and Results of Kierkegaard Studies in Scandinavia*, Copenhagen: Munksgaard 1951, pp. 12–14; pp. 22–30; pp. 39–40; pp. 44–5; pp. 48–50; pp. 58–9; p. 91; p. 107; p. 131; p. 154.

Heuch, J.C., "I Anledning af Dr. Brandes' Optræden i Kristiania," *Luthersk Ugeskrift*, no. 6, pp. 103–12.

Houe, Poul, "Et eventyr om to genier—med hver sit syn på eventyr—og deres fælles geniale kritiker. Om Andersen, Kierkegaard og Brandes," in his *En anden Andersen—og andres. Artikler og foredrag 1969–2005*, Copenhagen: C.A. Reitzel 2006, pp. 233–45 (English translation in *Danish Culture, Past and Present: The Last Two Hundred Years. Proceedings of an International Conference Sponsored by The Danish American Heritage Society. Des Moines, Iowa, October 13–16, 2005*, ed. by Linda M. Chementi and Birgit Flemming Larsen, Ames, Iowa: The Danish American Heritage Society 2006, pp. 203–14).

Jørgensen, Kirsten, "Georg Brandes' 'Søren Kierkegaard,' " *Fønix*, vol. 16, 1992, pp. 240–48.

Kirmmse, Bruce H. (ed.), *Encounters with Kierkegaard*, Princeton: Princeton University Press 1996, pp. 51–2; pp. 97–8. (In Danish as *Søren Kierkegaard truffet. Et liv set af hans samtidige*, Copenhagen: C.A. Reitzel 1996, pp. 51–2; pp. 97–8.)

Knudsen, Jørgen, "Studieår: Lange, Kierkegaard, tro og tvivl. 1859–64" and "Søren Kierkegaard," in his *Georg Brandes. Frigørelsens vej, 1842–77*, Copenhagen: Gyldendal 1985, pp. 55–67; pp. 413–20.

Kondrup, Johnny, *Livsværker. Studier i dansk litterær biografi*, Valby: Amadeus, 1986, pp. 55–134.

— "Kierkegaard og Brandes," in *Kierkegaard inspiration. En antologi*, ed. by Birgit Bertung, Paul Müller, Fritz Norlan and Julia Watkin, Copenhagen: C.A. Reitzel 1991 (*Søren Kierkegaard Selskabets populære skrifter*, vol. 20), pp. 70–81.

— "Keine hinreichende Vorstellung von seinem Genie. Strategien in der negativen Kierkegaardrezeption von Georg Brandes," *Kierkegaardiana*, vol. 18, 1996, pp. 148–72.

Krarup, Søren, "Brandes og det moderne sammenbrud," *Information*, April 11, 1984.

Lieblein, J. and J.E. Sars, "Dagbog," *Nyt Norsk Tidsskrift*, vol. 1, Kristiania: H. Aschehoug 1877, pp. 69–72; pp. 161–2; pp. 176–80; pp. 317–20.

Lundtofte, Anne Mette, "Pointing Fingers at the Genius: Reading Brandes Reading Kierkegaard," *Tijdschrift voor Skandinavistiek*, vol. 21, 2000, pp. 149–63.

— *The Case of Georg Brandes: Brandes between Taine, Hegel, Kierkegaard, and Goethe, and the Institutions of Literature in 19th-Century Denmark*, Ph.D. Thesis, New York University 2003.

"M.," "S. Kierkegaard og Dr. G. Brandes," *Dansk Kirketidende*, vol. 34, 1879, nos. 32–3; pp. 509–13.

Malik, Habib Charles, "The Biographical-Psychological Approach and Its Perils: Georg Brandes and Criticism as Suppression," in his *Receiving Søren Kierkegaard: The Early Impact and Transmission of His Thought*, Washington, DC: Catholic University of America Press 1997, pp. 211–82.

Nielsen, Jens Viggo, "Georg Brandes' 'Om Læsning,' individ, fællesskab og verdenshistorie. Belyst gennem forholdet til Nietzsche og Kierkegaard," in *Georg Brandes og Europa. Forelæsninger fra 1. internationale Georg Brandes Konference, Firenze, 7–9 november 2002*, ed. by Olav Harsløf, Copenhagen: Museum Tusculanums Forlag 2004 (*Danish Humanist Texts and Studies*, vol. 29), pp. 355–67. (Italian translation in *Georg Brandes e l'Europa*, ed. by Jørgen Stender Clausen, vols. 1–2 (*Studi Nordici*, vols. 9–10, 2002–03), Pisa and Rome: Istituti Editoriali e Poligrafici Internazionali 2004, vol. 2, pp. 113–21.)

Nielsen, Rasmus, "En literær Overraskelse," *For Ide og Virkelighed*, 1870, vol. 1, pp. 193–221.

Nolin, Bertil, *Den gode europén. Studier i Georg Brandes' idéutveckling 1871–1893*, Uppsala: Svenska Bokförlaget 1965, p. 13; pp. 16–17; p. 23; p. 28; pp. 36–7; p. 64; pp. 75–76; p. 79; p. 132; p. 138; p. 140; pp. 156–7; p. 166; pp. 170–1; p. 181; p. 207; p. 211; p. 225; p. 228; p. 250; p. 275; p. 291; p. 325; p. 331–2; p. 355.

Pages, Neil Christian, *On Aristocratic Radicalism: Singularities of Georg Brandes, Friedrich Nietzsche and Søren Kierkegaard*, Ph.D. Thesis, New York University 1999.

Ploug, Carl, "Dr. G. Brandes," *Fædrelandet*, November 22, 1876.

— "En uberettiget Offentliggørelse," *Fædrelandet*, February 16, 1877, no. 40 (cf. February 19, 1877, no. 42).

Poole, Roger C., "The Travels of Kierkegaard," *Raritan*, vol. 4, no. 4, 1985, pp. 78–90.

Poulsen, Andreas Nordkild, "Søren Kierkegaard og Georg Brandes—fragmenter til to uskrevne poetikker," *Horizont*, 1996, no. 5, pp. 53–92.

Rubow, Paul V., *Georg Brandes og hans Lærere*, Copenhagen: V. Pios Boghandel 1927.

— "Søren Kierkegaard," in *Georg Brandes' Briller. Ny forøget Udgave af "Georg Brandes og den kritiske Tradition i det nittende Aarhundrede,"* Copenhagen: Levin & Munksgaard 1932, pp. 101–65.

Stenström, Thure, *Den ensamme. En motivstudie i det moderna genombrottets litteratur*, Stockholm: Natur och Kultur 1961, pp. 75–96; pp. 336–9.

Wegelius, Martin, "Georg Brandes: Sören Kierkegaard," *Finsk Tidskrift för Vitterhet, Vetenskap, Konst och Politik*, no. 2, 1878, pp. 64–7.

Ernesto Dalgas:

Kierkegaard on *The Path of Suffering*

Esben Lindemann

When Ernesto Dalgas (1871–99) died, barely 28 years old, he had only published two books. They were not bestowed with much attention during Dalgas' time and have indeed subsequently been assessed as being insignificant.[1] Dalgas' two principal works, *The Path of Suffering* and *The Book of Doom*, were only published after his death, both in 1903. What we have are two unfinished novels, which also, at the time of publication, were all but ignored, and this was probably subsequently a determining factor in the low level of interest that was given to Dalgas' texts in general. Hence, for a long time after Dalgas' death, there was no tradition for reading his works in the history of Danish literature. With a few exceptions, his works were only sporadically touched upon in a few comparative literature reference works and shorter articles in journals. Several dissertations in the area of history of literature do not even mention Dalgas' name. The only two commentators who gave Dalgas' texts a more thorough treatment were Axel Garde (1876–1958) in 1908[2] and Aage Henriksen (1921–2011) in 1948.[3] It was only in 1965 that Dalgas' authorship found sympathy with a broader audience. This took place in connection with Aage Henriksen and Henrik Schovsbo's rerelease of *The Book of Doom* that same year. The release spawned a number of reviews in the Danish newspapers.[4] In 1993, *The Path of Suffering* was released in a newly revised edition with an

---

[1]   Henry Boisen, "En glemt filosof," in *Kristendom og Humanisme*, Copenhagen: Levin og Munksgaards Forlag 1922, pp. 51–61. Otto Gelsted, "Ernesto Dalgas," in *Sirius, Dansk Litteraturtidende*, no. 3, Copenhagen: P. Haase og Søn 1924, pp. 139–40. Cai M. Woel, "Ernesto Dalgas," in his *Troubadourer, literære Tidsbilleder*, vols. 1–2, Copenhagen: Woels Forlag 1930–34, vol. 1, pp. 35–46. Jørgen Bukdahl, *Det moderne Danmark*, Copenhagen: Aschehoug 1931, pp. 25–6. K.F. Plesner, "Dansk Dommedag," in *Kulturbærere*, Copenhagen: Aschehoug 1938, pp. 19–26. Aage Henriksen, "Forord," in *Noveller og Fragmenter*, ed. by Aage Henriksen, Copenhagen: Steen Hasselbalchs Forlag 1942, pp. 5–12. Mogens Poulsen, "I Kierkegaards skygge—Ernesto Dalgas," in *Kierkegaardske skæbner, fire radioforedrag*, Copenhagen: Petit Forlaget 1955, pp. 33–42. Jacob Paludan, *Litterært Selskab*, Copenhagen: Hasselbalch 1956, pp. 9–15.

[2]   Axel Garde, *Dansk Aand*, Copenhagen: Gjellerups Forlag 1908.

[3]   Aage Henriksen, "Ernesto Dalgas: Lidelsens Vej. En studie i romanens tilblivelses-historie," *Orbis Litterarum*, no. 6, Copenhagen: Gyldendal 1948, pp. 133–50.

[4]   Ernesto Dalgas, *Dommedags Bog*, ed. by Aage Henriksen and Henrik Schovsbo, 2nd ed., Copenhagen: H. Reitzel 1965. See Henrik Schovsbo, "Efterskrift," in Ernesto Dalgas, *Dommedags Bog*, ed. by Henrik Schovsbo, Copenhagen: Det Danske Sprog- og

elaborate commentary apparatus and postscript by Henrik Schovsbo in the series
Danish Classics.[5] In 1995, Dalgas' philosophical collection of essays *The Book of
Knowledge* edited by Leon Jaurnow was released in an edition that also includes a
thorough postscript.[6] And finally in 1996, *The Book of Doom* was rereleased in the
series *Danish Classics* and included an elaborate commentary apparatus and postscript
by Henrik Schovsbo.[7] Thus it took a number of years after Dalgas' death before his
texts were examined in a more systematic and scholarly manner.

With time Dalgas has become a more recognized name in the history of Danish
literature. He has now gained in reputation in scholarly circles and is being read
by a wider audience than when his books were published for the first time a few
years after his death. Yet Dalgas is still no towering figure in the history of Danish
literature. Literary historians continue to mention him only in snippets, even
though there is a general agreement that his authorship is both original and unique
in a Danish context. A significant part of his authorship still lies untouched, and
the papers he left behind can be found only in a not easily accessible handwritten
collection in the Royal Library Archives in Copenhagen. Moreover, it should be
mentioned that his papers have been ordered systematically only to a very limited
extent. These conditions make it difficult to gain a broader view of Dalgas' total
output or to undertake a thorough investigation of the individual elements of his
authorship. This then naturally also holds true for this article, the purpose of which
is to elucidate the relationship between Ernesto Dalgas and Søren Kierkegaard. A
similar attempt has only been made once before in the form of a short radio lecture
in 1955.[8] A few other texts have fleetingly touched upon Dalgas' use of Kierkegaard
in the authorship.

I have chosen to focus on one of the two works, which posterity considers
Dalgas' most important, namely, *The Path of Suffering*, since this exists in an edition
in which the text has been critiqued and commented upon thoroughly. Moreover,
subsequent literary criticism has often pointed to *The Path of Suffering* as essentially
inspired by Kierkegaard,[9] without anyone ever really expounding on what this
meant. This will be the purpose of this article. Unfortunately space will not permit a
more in-depth study of the unedited handwritten papers. These will only to a lesser
extent be used to underpin the analyses of the novel in focus. *The Path of Suffering*,

---

Litteraturselskab/Borgen 1996 (*Danske Klassikere*), p. 362. Henrik Schovsbo, "Mulighedens
disciple," *Den blå port*, no. 17, Copenhagen: Rhodos 1991, p. 8.

[5]   Ernesto Dalgas, *Lidelsens Vej*, ed. by Henrik Schovsbo, Copenhagen: DSL/Borgen
1996 (*Danske Klassikere*).

[6]   Ernesto Dalgas, *Kundskabens Bog*, ed. by Leon Jaurnow, Copenhagen: Hans Reitzels
Forlag 1995.

[7]   Dalgas, *Dommedags Bog*, ed. by Henrik Schovsbo.

[8]   Poulsen, "I Kierkegaards skygge—Ernesto Dalgas," pp. 33–42.

[9]   Henrik Schovsbo, "Efterskrift," in Dalgas, *Lidelsens Vej*, ed. by Henrik Schovsbo,
p. 294. Garde, *Dansk Aand*, p. 59. Boisen, "En glemt filosof," p. 59. Gelsted, "Ernesto
Dalgas," p. 139. Woel, "Ernesto Dalgas," p. 42. Bukdahl, *Det moderne Danmark*, p. 25.
Plesner, "Dansk Dommedag," p. 21. Henriksen, "Forord," in *Noveller og Fragmenter*, p. 8.
Poulsen, "I Kierkegaards skygge—Ernesto Dalgas," p. 39. Leon Jaurnow, "Indledning," in
Dalgas, *Kundskabens Bog*, ed. by Leon Jaurnow, p. 13.

however, contains Kierkegaard-inspired material to such an extent that this novel in and of itself should form a sufficient basis for justifying the link between the two authors and thinkers.

I. Dalgas' Short Life

Ernesto Dalgas was born on July 22, 1871. He was the son of Enrico Dalgas, a pioneer in the Danish business community and a founder of Det Danske Hedeselskab, which started cultivating the Jutland heath, an important event in Danish political and economic history. This meant that Ernesto grew up in a solid and committed bourgeois home, which was dominated by an extroverted and famous father. Contrary to his father, Ernesto was introverted and sickly.[10] Overall, the two of them, father and son, were the antithesis to each other throughout all of Dalgas' life. Their relationship was marked by many conflicts, and when the young Dalgas reached the age of secondary school, he energetically became a follower of the ideas of the Modern Breakthrough, and the implicit clash of generations became an element in the ongoing conflict with his father. After secondary school, Dalgas moved from his birthplace Aarhus to Copenhagen to study at the university. He started off studying medicine, but after an educational crisis, he switched to philosophy, which he continued until his death, but never completed.[11]

One of Dalgas' teachers at the university was the Danish philosopher Harald Høffding (1843–1931), which is evident in Dalgas' philosophical writings. His journal entries bear witness to the fact that he was particularly interested in the new ideas of the times, namely, positivism, which Høffding promoted in a Danish context. In this connection, Dalgas in particular delved into the epistemological issue of whether it is possible to arrive at certainty. Besides noticing his affinity toward positivism, we also see a decided interest in themes of a more religious and existential character. Dalgas may have been seeking answers to such religious and existential questions because he, in his personal life, had very weak nerves, which resulted in him being admitted to a psychiatric ward twice, the first time in 1893 at St. Hans Hospital near Copenhagen, and the second time in 1898 at Risskov Hospital near Aarhus.[12]

In an original manner Dalgas attempts to unite his apparently contradictory interests in his two large-scale novels.[13] With regards to the religious and existential dimension, it is clear that Dalgas was inspired by Kierkegaard. The young Dalgas had probably been supported and encouraged by his teacher Høffding, who in particular is known for incorporating Kierkegaard into a special form for positivism. But Dalgas had undoubtedly also learned and understood about Kierkegaard's life and thinking

---

[10]   Henriksen, "Forord," in *Noveller og Fragmenter*, p. 5.

[11]   Schovsbo, "Efterskrift," in Dalgas, *Dommedags Bog*, p. 341. Woel, "Ernesto Dalgas," p. 35. Poulsen, "I Kierkegaards skygge—Ernesto Dalgas," p. 34. Jaurnow, "Indledning," in *Kundskabens Bog*, p. 9.

[12]   Schovsbo, "Efterskrift," in *Dommedags Bog*, p. 342. Jaurnow, "Indledning," in *Kundskabens Bog*, p. 10.

[13]   Garde, *Dansk Aand*, p. 60, p. 83. Henriksen, "Forord," in *Noveller og Fragmenter*, p. 8.

through Georg Brandes' (1842–1927) extensive Kierkegaard biography from 1877.[14] On his own connection to Kierkegaard, Dalgas writes the following, looking back at his life just a few months prior to his death: "17 years old, as I became acquainted with *Either/Or*, I became influenced by Kierkegaard's way of thinking, and since then, my own thoughts have been ascetic in nature."[15] What is important to note here, is that Dalgas, in his own understanding of his relationship with Kierkegaard, opines that the influence began at the age of approximately 17 and continued presumably until his death.[16] In what manner Dalgas' ascetic mental makeup was influenced by Kierkegaard's thoughts, and whether he in this connection fathomed Kierkegaard can of course be debated, but there is no doubt that Dalgas read Kierkegaard throughout his life, and that he to a certain extent sees himself as a student of Kierkegaard. Hence, Dalgas views Kierkegaard as a person with whom he can identify, a fellow sufferer, so to speak. Dalgas, for example, uses Kierkegaardian arguments when he—like Kierkegaard before him—breaks off his engagement to his fiancée.[17] Similarly, the main character in *The Path of Suffering* has characteristics that clearly have something in common with those of Kierkegaard and represents a persona, whose characteristics are clearly similar to those of Dalgas.[18] Generally, Kierkegaardian motifs are to be found in Dalgas' texts, but as examples of points of identification for Dalgas in relation to Kierkegaard, one could mention the clash with his father and sexual angst.[19]

On July 11, 1899, Ernesto Dalgas took his own life, probably "exhausted and depleted"[20] as a result of his laborious attempts at understanding the intricacies of life.[21] The last thing he wrote in his journal the day before he died was: "And now I have discovered my limitation and cannot get closer to solving the enigma of life."[22]

II. Kierkegaardian Stylistic Characteristics in The Path of Suffering

When Dalgas uses Kierkegaard in his texts, he does not merely deal with specific existential or religious themes true to the spirit of Kierkegaard. In the manner in which he constructs his texts, he also appears to be inspired by Kierkegaard. We see clear examples of this in the novel *The Path of Suffering*.

---

[14]   Schovsbo, "Efterskrift," in *Lidelsens Vej*, p. 283.
[15]   Note on May 9, 1899, private possession, Schovsbo, "Efterskrift," in *Dommedags Bog*, p. 354.
[16]   Henriksen, "Forord," in *Noveller og Fragmenter*, p. 6.
[17]   Schovsbo, "Efterskrift," in *Lidelsens Vej*, p. 292. Woel, "Ernesto Dalgas," p. 42. Bukdahl, *Det moderne Danmark*, p. 25. Plesner, "Dansk Dommedag," p. 23. Henriksen, "Forord," in *Noveller og Fragmenter*, p. 7. Poulsen, "I Kierkegaards skygge—Ernesto Dalgas," p. 36.
[18]   Schovsbo, "Efterskrift," in *Lidelsens Vej*, p. 283. Garde, *Dansk Aand*, p. 58. Poulsen, "I Kierkegaards skygge—Ernesto Dalgas," p. 36. Aage Henriksen, "Kompositionens sprog," in *Gotisk tid*, Copenhagen: Gyldendal 1971, p. 178.
[19]   Schovsbo, "Efterskrift," in *Lidelsens Vej*, p. 283. Garde, *Dansk Aand*, p. 59.
[20]   Dalgas, *Kundskabens Bog*, ed. by Leon Jaurnow, p. 71.
[21]   Garde, *Dansk Aand*, p. 70. Jaurnow, "Indledning," in *Kundskabens Bog*, p. 8.
[22]   Journal on July 10, 1899, NKS 3640,4°, III, Schovsbo, "Efterskrift," in Dalgas, *Dommedags Bog*, p. 344.

Already on the title page we encounter the first sign of Kierkegaard. Here it says: *The Path of Suffering: An Autobiography of Someone Deceased.* As is known, the aesthete A in *Either/Or* pens three of his aesthetic analyses for a certain audience, namely "symparanekromenoi." This is Kierkegaard's own construction and means: "Fellowship of the Dead." A uses the following title for his treatises: "The Tragic in Ancient Drama Reflected in the Tragic in Modern Drama: A Venture in Fragmentary Endeavor. Delivered before the Συμπαρανεκρωμενοι,"[23] Silhouettes. Psychological Diversion. Delivered before the Συμπαρανεκρωμενοι,"[24] and "The Unhappiest One. An Inspired Address to the Συμπαρανεκρωμενοι."[25] Unlike A, Dalgas does not write his novel for an audience of "Fellowship of the Dead," but just like A, he characterizes himself as deceased. A's term "Fellowship of the Dead" does, after all, include himself as deceased. The placement of this autobiographical designation on the title page has the same function as in A's treatises, namely, that it comes to serve as a framework for the novel. Dalgas thereby, like A, creates a situation where the reader of the text at all times is reminded that the author is or views himself as deceased.

This—true to the Kierkegaardian spirit—lends an enigmatic atmosphere to the author–reader relationship. It is indeed a paradox that a deceased narrator can address a "Fellowship of the Dead" or write his own autobiography. But even if the reader does not take it quite literally, one is bound at some point to ponder what it actually means that the narrator is deceased. In Dalgas' novel, the enigma remains suspended. At the end of the novel, it remains unclear whether it literally is a deceased person narrating, or whether he is deceased in a figurative sense. The text, so to speak, dies a slow death as the narrator becomes silent. Like Kierkegaard, Dalgas masters the art of masking, and it would seem obvious to interpret his *mise-en-scène* of a deceased author as an allusion to Kierkegaard's *Either/Or*, which rightly can be seen as a prime example of a poetic disappearing act.

If one continues to read *The Path of Suffering*, then *Either/Or* seems to be an important model for the novel, which begins with a short introduction by the narrator of the text, City Treasurer Salomon Simonsen, who declares that he, in the following, will write his autobiography. He is a narrator who has his youth behind him and who now, from a vantage point of maturity, will scrutinize the life that has passed. But he will do it in a very specific way because it appears to him that the person about whom he will write is not himself, but rather someone deceased, whose life he "knows inside out, and who by coincidence had the same name,"[26] and whom he merely can observe from the vantage point of a third person. With this explanation, Salomon distances himself from the subsequent story in a manner that conjures up memories of Victor Eremita's preface to *Either/Or*, in which Eremita relinquishes any connection to the subsequent manuscripts, which he, according to his account, merely found in an old desk under strange circumstances. Furthermore, one may add that the narrator in *The Path of Suffering* continuously refers to a journal, on the

---

[23]   *SKS* 2, 137–62 / *EO1*, 137–64.
[24]   *SKS* 2, 163–209 / *EO1*, 165–215.
[25]   *SKS* 2, 211–23 / *EO1*, 217–30.
[26]   Dalgas, *Lidelsens Vej*, p. 8.

basis of which he reconstructs the protagonist's life, meaning his life, and thereby establishes a metalayer in the text that corresponds to Victor Eremita's in *Either/ Or.* Furthermore, this narrating voice often comments on the story at times when there are either gaps or uncertainties in the journal, and thereby highlights the text's fictional character in his attempt to create cohesiveness in the narration. This also very much corresponds to the function of Victor Eremita in *Either/Or.*

In this sense, *The Path of Suffering* has narrative similarities not only to *Either/ Or* but also to several of Kierkegaard's other pseudonymous texts. If one adds to this that *The Path of Suffering* is not merely a novel in the normal sense of the term, but concurrently consists of several interposed fragments of a more philosophical or theoretical nature, it is not that far-fetched to juxtapose it with Kierkegaard's pseudonymous authorship. In *The Path of Suffering* we have throughout a fictitious plot, which from time to time is interrupted by shorter philosophical dissertations. It is, then, like Kierkegaard's pseudonymous texts, fragmented in its setup and is, in terms of genre, to be placed somewhere between fiction and philosophy, although it is important to underscore that the poetic element carries more weight in Dalgas' text than in Kierkegaard's pseudonymous texts.

Moreover, *The Path of Suffering* also includes interposed passages of a more lyrical character, just as we find lyrical fragments in the Kierkegaardian style. In general, Dalgas' novel—just like Kierkegaard's pseudonymous texts—seems to consist of epic, lyric, and philosophical passages, which mutually support each other, either because the epic and lyric passages illustrate the philosophical points, or because the philosophical accounts are used to explain the elements in the plot.[27] These genre shifts with the many narrative layers assist in creating polyphony, through which the texts' themes are elucidated from many different angles. In literary criticism it has often been pointed out that Dalgas mastered the Kierkegaardian style without anyone really expounding on what this meant.[28] Most probably, it is this polyphony and compositional diversity that is referred to.

Another characteristic that *The Path of Suffering* has in common with several of Kierkegaard's texts, and not just the pseudonymous ones, is the way in which the texts never seem to end. In this connection I am considering a fact that many Kierkegaard commentators have also noted.[29] This is seen, in among other works, the second part of *Either/Or*, where Judge William seems incapable of bringing his letters to the rambunctious aesthete A to a close. William at the outset writes

---

[27]   Henriksen, "Kompositionens sprog," p. 178.
[28]   Garde, *Dansk Aand*, p. 59. Boisen, "En glemt filosof," p. 59. Gelsted, "Ernesto Dalgas," p. 139. Woel, "Ernesto Dalgas," p. 42. Bukdahl, *Det moderne Danmark*, p. 25. Plesner, "Dansk Dommedag," p. 22. Henriksen, "Forord," in *Noveller og Fragmenter*, p. 8. Poulsen, "I Kierkegaards skygge—Ernesto Dalgas," p. 39. Jaurnow, "Indledning," in *Kundskabens Bog*, p. 13.
[29]   E.g. Joakim Garff, *"Den Søvnløse". Kierkegaard læst æstetisk/biografisk*, Copenhagen: C.A. Reitzel 1995, p. 300. Jacob Bøggild, *Ironiens tænker. Tænkningens ironi. Kierkegaard læst retorisk*, Copenhagen: Museum Tusculanum 2002, p. 222. Isak Winkel Holm, *Tanken i billedet. Søren Kierkegaards poetik*, Copenhagen: Gyldendal 1998, p. 311. Jørgen Dehs, *Kunst og æstetik*, Copenhagen: Det kongelige danske Kunstakademi 1996, p. 244.

two letters, which almost could be seen as long dissertations. During the course of these letters, he alludes several times to his lack of ability in expressing himself in writing, and in his first letter he is compelled to correct himself and adjust some of his initial objections against A in order to communicate on a par with the aesthete, or even to make himself understandable at all. But even after having dispatched these two extensive dissertations, he feels compelled to send A yet another letter. In the introduction to this third letter, he points out that this time he will not compose the letter himself but rather will send him a sermon written by a friend of his, a pastor from Jutland. But at the same time it is noted that William would have been capable of writing another letter himself, and that he possibly would have been able to express something different in this new letter compared to the previous ones, because, as William writes: "Like the flower that comes year after year, the expression, the presentation, the wrappings are the same and yet not the same, but the attitude, the development, the position are unchanged. If I were to write to you now, I perhaps would express myself differently."[30] Hence the expression changes, although the content remains the same; the same thought can be expressed in many different ways, and William's introduction to this third letter even states that at different times and occasions there would be different ways of expressing the same thing. It is not so strange that the Judge has problems finding just the right style.

We see something similar in *Repetition*, where the incongruity between language and reality are thematized in the same way, both explicitly and through the actual shape of the text. *Repetition* consists of three main sections, which all deal with the concept of repetition. In the first section, repetition is rejected as a possibility, with reference to the constant changeability of the world. In the second main section, it is demonstrated how the protagonist of the text, "the young man," finds himself again as a human being after the decisive and irrevocable separation from his fiancée, which, it seems, serves as an example that repetition, after all, is possible at an existential level. This possibility, however, is withdrawn in the final main section of the book, which serves as a small postscript to the book's plot. Here we learn that the repetition that the "young man" has experienced is not a repetition existentially speaking since he has merely reverted to precisely the same life pattern as before and has not moved on to the next existential level. *Repetition* corrects itself twice, and ends with a quite open ending.

The same holds true with the *Concluding Unscientific Postscript*. Here Kierkegaard wrote an addendum to his text, which consists of two shorter sections. The first of these is signed Johannes Climacus, the pseudonymous author of the book. The title of this section is "An Understanding with the Reader."[31] In it Climacus speaks directly to the reader and actually negates the entire content of the book, stating that it is trivial, a mere expression of the author's own literary and philosophical experiments, "an innocent pastime and amusement."[32] In the same addendum a section follows which is signed by S. Kierkegaard himself, titled "A First and Last Explanation." In this short section, Kierkegaard reveals that he is

---

[30]   *SKS* 3, 317 / *EO2*, 337.
[31]   *SKS* 7, 560 / *CUP1*, 617.
[32]   *SKS* 7, 562 / *CUP1*, 619.

the actual author of all the pseudonymous texts, and in a way negates Climacus' negation. As we already have mentioned, a certain kind of enigmatic atmosphere is built up around the text, which corresponds to the text's unclear relation to reality. Here again some biographical circumstances come into play because when the section is titled "A First and Last Explanation," the original intention was that this gesture was to mark the end of Kierkegaard's authorship. As we know, this did not happen. On the contrary, the *Postscript* marks the beginning of a new era in Kierkegaard's authorship. His well-known dispute with *The Corsair* is used as an argument to recommence writing, and his authorship is now interpreted as his actual calling in life. Writing, then, cannot be halted. It appears to be reborn again and again in Kierkegaard's life.

Finally, I would like to emphasize Kierkegaard's attempt some years later to explain his authorship in *The Point of View for My Work as an Author* and *On My Work as an Author*, of which the former was only published posthumously in 1859. Having finished *The Point of View for My Work as an Author*, Kierkegaard was seized by qualms since he was worried that the explanation would create confusion with regard to his position on the written word and in that sense would actually work counter to the intention of the text. After this he wrote a shorter version of his account of his authorship, namely, *On My Work as an Author*, which consists of a main text and an accompanying letter. The latter was added at the end of 1850, while the main text was written at the beginning of 1849. The accompanying letter was added with the intention of creating congruence between the first account and the authorship, since in the meantime he had published *The Sickness unto Death* and *Practice in Christianity*. He felt compelled to adjust the first explanation. Similarly, *The Point of View for My Work as an Author* is characterized by a number of postscripts and addendums at the end of the text, the purpose of which was to adjust and clarify the previous accounts. In general, the two texts are characterized by a lack of internal harmony, and it is as if the more the text attempts to describe the authorship, the more the text becomes a reason to generate more text.

These are merely a few examples of general characteristics in Kierkegaard's authorship, the purpose of which is to elucidate similar characteristics in Dalgas' *The Path of Suffering*. This novel, in a similar fashion, contains a postscript, which, so to speak, negates the previous content. This is expressed at a compositional level in the text. The postscript is a compositional break in what one until then could have termed a positivist educational novel, where life is separated into three developmental phases: (1) childhood, which is designated the "theological level" and is characterized by fantasy, (2) youth, which is designated the "metaphysical level" and is characterized by disputes between the levels, and finally (3) manhood, which is designated the "positive level" and is characterized by pure realization, void of illusion, and which has conquered childish fantasy.[33] In the postscript, the protagonist encounters a developmental stage or life-view, which lies completely outside the positivist template. Specifically, he assumes an ascetic position. One could say that Dalgas withdraws the life-view, which until then had been in place as a controlling

---

[33]   This model is inspired by August Comte's positivist three-stage law; cf. Schovsbo "Efterskrift," in *Lidelsens Vej*, p. 288.

structure in the novel. This happens in a way that is not dissimilar to the unfolding of things in *Repetition*. Just as one thinks that one has reached a conclusion to the problem in the novel, a postscript is added which reassesses the entire preceding text. As in the other textual examples by Kierkegaard, one is left with the impression that one has a text which does not quite know itself where it stands.

At one point in time in *The Path of Suffering*, Dalgas has his protagonist Salomon say the following: "These scribbles had one advantage, there were not in verse; but otherwise they were very much influenced by romantic devilry. Salomon had a growing feeling that this illness was like a stake through his heart, of which he would never be free."[34] The scribbles referred to are Salomon's writings in his journal, which forms the basis of the entire novel. We learn that writing is Salomon's secret drive. And we learn that romantic devilry corresponds to a basic loathing of life, a Mephistopheles, who incessantly follows Salomon and is disgusted by everything in the world. To this Mephistopheles, nothing is holy, everything is scorned and mocked. It is this devilish, annihilating spirit that Salomon escapes from through his writings: "a stake through his heart, of which he will never be free."[35] Having filled this first notebook, he continues: "One small notebook was not the end. When you give the Devil your little finger, etc."[36] Here Dalgas appears to be commenting on the text's relationship to itself, namely, that it continually attempts to exhaust itself, but each attempt becomes a reason to fill yet another notebook. And since the journal that is commented on forms the actual basis of the story about Salomon, what we have is the running text commenting on its own problem, which is that it will never bring clarity to itself, and it will never be free from romantic devilry.

If we juxtapose these observations with the other similarities between Dalgas and Kierkegaard, it would make sense to conclude that Dalgas was aware of this textual incongruity in both his own and Kierkegaard's authorship. It appears that it would not be misplaced to conclude that Dalgas appears to be even more conscious of the issue than Kierkegaard himself and that Dalgas, in a quite forward-looking manner, albeit indirectly, elucidates some textual relations, not only in his own, but also in Kierkegaard's authorship.

III. The Course of Events in The Path of Suffering

The plot in the novel unfolds as the old City Treasurer Salomon Simonsen is sitting in an unknown town, attempting to reconstruct his life. The narrative conditions are accounted for in Salomon's introduction to the book. As a subsequent introduction, it is described how Salomon grew up in the town, and we learn that he had a stepfather, who was also City Treasurer in the same town. His stepfather was a real father figure and Salomon's role model during his younger years, but he breaks with him as he grows older and moves to Copenhagen.

In Copenhagen, Salomon meets his new role model, a certain Councilor, who in his outlook on life clearly has characteristics in common with Johannes the Seducer.

---

[34]   Dalgas, *Lidelsens Vej*, p. 84.
[35]   Ibid.
[36]   Ibid., p. 85.

It turns out that the Councilor is Salomon's biological father. They, however, are never able to resolve this issue. The Councilor becomes Salomon's ironic teacher, and Salomon quickly learns the masquerade of irony. A Kierkegaardian period begins to take shape. During this period, however, a painful duality develops in Salomon's life. Due to a loathing of the masquerade of irony, he joins Kierkegaard's movement toward more religious texts and begins reading the New Testament. This Kierkegaardian period is marked by a duality, where during the day with the Councilor he lives with ironic figures, while at home, and in his journal entries, he delves into more intense religious studies. During this period, Salomon meets the girl Prosa, the Councilor's foster daughter, who becomes his fiancée, but whom he—in the true spirit of Kierkegaard—leaves, apparently due to a feeling of remorse of not being able to lead a life of normalcy; it is merely an idea with which he is in love, not with devoted Prosa herself, who, in fact, offers herself as Salomon's great life opportunity. Just as Kierkegaard, "the young man" in *Repetition*, and Dalgas himself, Salomon must also end his betrothal to the woman he loves because of religious scruples.

This break will come to mark the transition to Salomon's years of manhood, where he returns to his own childhood town and takes over his stepfather's position as City Treasurer. He lives as a dry and pedantic civil servant during the day but is still deeply spiritually involved with religious and existential thought. In particular, he seems very concerned with breaking with Lutheranism and interposes a detailed dissertation on his viewpoints titled: "The Reformation's Moral Progress and its Fruits."[37] Here we see a commonality with Kierkegaard's attack on the existing church in his famous leaflets.

One day Prosa turns up in the town. This time as a happily married mother and, moreover, a famous pianist. On this occasion, Salomon meets her, which subsequently makes him revise his attitude to life. He interprets her significance in his life as a step toward a more authentic life, namely, an ascetic life, and hence a final withdrawal from life, a dying from oneself—not unlike "the young man" in *Repetition*, Kierkegaard, and Dalgas himself.

IV. Kierkegaardian Themes in The Path of Suffering

Dalgas' *The Path of Suffering* seems to be inspired by Kierkegaard not just in its form, but also in terms of content. This appears as both direct and indirect references to Kierkegaard in the novel. In the following section, I will elucidate some examples where Dalgas, at a thematic level, draws on Kierkegaardian thought.

A. Criticism of "Christendom"

The first example is Dalgas' criticism of what he calls "high-church,"[38] which is personified by the local pastor in Salomon's childhood town, Reverend Pedersen. This is the version of Christianity in which his stepfather believes, and for this

---

[37]   Ibid., p. 174.
[38]   Ibid., p. 39.

reason Salomon uncritically assumes the same faith. However, at the exact time of his confirmation, Salomon recognizes what he finds to be phony in Reverend Pedersen's message, and starting then, he develops a strong antipathy towards Reverend Pedersen and the type of Christianity for which he stands. In the novel this is expressed as a number of sharp caricatures of Reverend Pederson. These caricatures have indeed borrowed pictures from Kierkegaard's negative account of what he termed the "official Christianity"[39] or "Christendom."[40]

Just like Kierkegaard, Dalgas takes up the battle against the hypocrisy in "Christendom." As an image of this, Reverend Pedersen is—among other things—characterized as "a small, heavy man with fat red cheeks,"[41] which more than hints that he is not in want of food and drink and is quite well positioned as a civil servant of the state.[42] Furthermore, Dalgas writes that this Reverend Pedersen, in spite of his resemblance to a Cherub "did not blow in the doomsday trombone, but stuck to a more modest direction."[43] He represents a version of Christianity which does not require much from the individual human being. It is set up in such a manner that "all proper folk advance to salvation at the time of their demise."[44] The entrance to heaven is ensured if one sticks to the path of the majority and "does not act contrary to King Christian V's Law of the Land."[45] With regard to his childhood religion's relation to heaven, Salomon realizes that at its core it was only about "walking down the road," and "eventually one would arrive there; for just about all roads lead to heaven."[46]

It is not hard to see that this is completely contrary to both Dalgas' and Kierkegaard's view of Christianity. That Christianity, according to Kierkegaard, represents a massive effort and complication, is often put into perspective by him as he elucidates how contrary this is to the lightness with which his contemporaries treat Christianity. This is a recurrent theme in Kierkegaard's authorship and is clearly seen in, for instance, the *Concluding Unscientific Postscript*, *The Point of View for My Work as an Author*, and *The Moment*.

In his struggle against what he terms "high-church," Dalgas avails himself of Kierkegaardian arguments, supported by direct references to Kierkegaard in *The Path of Suffering*. When during his youth Salomon gets fed up with the Councilor's ironic quips, he, for instance, recounts of himself:

> During this time, Salomon sought refuge in an old book, which, as Kierkegaard mentions, is not known in this country. For in his arrogance, he read into the New Testament what he wished, without the correct Protestant interpretation, and as he was blasphemous to the point of interpreting the words literally, he derived many a strange and heretical thing therefrom.[47]

---

[39]   E.g. *SKS* 13, 173 / *M*, 127.
[40]   E.g. *SKS* 12, 48 / *PC*, 35.
[41]   Dalgas, *Lidelsens Vej*, p. 39.
[42]   E.g. *SKS* 13, 311 / *M*, 255.
[43]   Dalgas, *Lidelsens Vej*, p. 39.
[44]   Ibid.
[45]   Ibid., pp. 30–1.
[46]   Ibid., p. 39.
[47]   Ibid., p. 108.

Here Kierkegaard appears to become Salomon's argument for reading the New Testament and for doing so in such a way that stands contrary to the current "correct Protestant interpretation."[48] Not unlike Kierkegaard, the image has now been turned on its head, so that the heresy becomes identical with what Salomon or Dalgas views as the true interpretation of Christianity, and where the "correct Protestant interpretation" becomes identical with the country that, according to Kierkegaard, does not even know the New Testament and therefore the actual untrue interpretation.

Another example of Dalgas incorporating Kierkegaardian arguments can be seen at the end of the novel, where Salomon after having attained greater wisdom in life comments on his own aversion to Lutheranism. He says:

> Yes, even toward my archenemy, Lutheranism, I feel more conciliatory. Not that I take anything back. I am increasingly fortified in my belief that the inhuman form of Christianity, which Kierkegaard has resurrected from oblivion and which I have attempted to transfigure into a positive language, is the true one and the original, and that the modern, humane, or semi-humane Christianity is a falsity. For Christianity is the religion of suffering. That the religion of the nineteenth century was not Christianity, although it adamantly insisted on being called by that name, will one day be seen as a historical fact, just like it now is viewed as a historical fact that the Aristotle of the Middle Ages was a distorted Aristotle—although the scholars of the time insisted on the contrary with the same rage that Reverend Petersen displayed against Kierkegaard.[49]

Hence, Lutheranism is seen as the reason for the state of the nineteenth century, which, according to Salomon, was not true Christianity.[50] In opposition stands Kierkegaard as a representative of the true interpretation of Christianity—an interpretation which makes Christianity a religion of suffering, as opposed to the far too mild version of Christianity in the nineteenth century, here represented by Reverend Pedersen. Furthermore, we see that Kierkegaard's position is designated the "inhumane Christianity," while the current state is designated "the humane or semi-humane." Here we also see Dalgas give way to a specific interpretation of Kierkegaard, which probably was passed down by Brandes, namely, that Christianity in the world of Kierkegaard is pushed to its limit, and that it thereby follows that Christianity is not humanly possible.[51] To Brandes this meant that Christianity had been pushed into the realm of the absurd; for Dalgas, Christianity cannot be placed in human categories but, rather, requires a superhuman assertive effort.[52]

---

[48]   Ibid.

[49]   Ibid., p. 248.

[50]   Garde, *Dansk Aand*, p. 72.

[51]   Georg Brandes, *Søren Kierkegaard. En kritisk Fremstilling i Grundrids*, Copenhagen: Gyldendal 1877.

[52]   Garde, *Dansk Aand*, p. 64.

B. The Aesthetic

As we already have mentioned, Salomon goes through an aesthetic Kierkegaardian period in his life, and the Councilor who represents this position is Salomon's role model. In the following exchange of words between the two, we see how each of them handles the aesthetic perspective:

> "Søren Kierkegaard," said the Councilor, "is my favorite author, just like I hear that he is yours. Which of his Symparanekromonoi do you appreciate the most?" "I think I would be likely to cast my vote for Victor Eremita," said Salomon. "What a shame!" said the Councilor. "The hermit crab is an ugly animal. No, most power lies with Johannes the Seducer and thereafter the Fashion Merchant. Do you realize, there was a time when I had the greatest of desire to become a fashion merchant."[53]

While Salomon is attracted to the more pensive Victor Eremita, the Councilor is more drawn to the two bon vivants, the Fashion Merchant and Johannes the Seducer. What the three characters mentioned have in common is that they all are highly reflective when it comes to aesthetics. The Councilor is himself an incarnation of Johannes the Seducer or the Fashion Merchant. He is charming, jovial, and well spoken. His goal in life is hedonism, and the means to achieve this is the "illusion." "The great illusionists are the great men."[54] Through illusion or seduction we become masters of our own lives and thereby reach a hedonistic state. Salomon's position, inspired by Victor Eremita, is, as we have already mentioned, colored by bitterness toward life. He is disgusted by the triviality of life. Hereby Dalgas brings life to the characters in his novel by using some already known characters from Kierkegaard's authorship. The Councilor is consciously given traits from Johannes the Seducer and the Fashion Merchant, while Salomon consciously is afforded traits from Victor Eremita. In this way Kierkegaard's text assumes the role of a subtext under *The Path of Suffering*, a frame of reference underlying the novel, which is necessary to understand certain existential elements.

It is clear that "In vino veritas" from *Stages on Life's Way* must be assumed as an interpretative framework for these two characters and life categories in the novel. But *Either/Or* is also included in this context through the reference to "Symparanekromenoi." Since Salomon during this period is fed up with his own spleen-like position and is moving toward a more religious lifestyle, it seems justified to interpret a close relation between the highly reflective aesthetic position represented by Victor Eremita and a religious position. It would seem that Victor Eremita, according to Dalgas, marks the transition from the aesthetic to the religious.

C. The Ascetic

In the journal entry, as we remember, Dalgas explains what impact *Either/Or* had with regard to the development of a certain ascetic frame of his mind. It would appear reasonable to interpret this Kierkegaardian inspiration as defining the ascetic point of view that is depicted in *The Path of Suffering* and which appears to be the

---

53   Dalgas, *Lidelsens Vej*, p. 103.

54   Ibid., p. 104.

most authentic life position for the protagonist Salomon. As we know, this journal entry was written shortly before Dalgas died and at a time when he still was working on *The Path of Suffering*. It would therefore be an obvious choice to interpret *Either/ Or* as a model for the entire developmental structure that we see in *The Path of Suffering*, if it is read as an educational novel.

Apparently what we have is a positivist educational novel, which at the end steers toward an ascetic-religious target, rather than a positive life outlook devoid of religious thoughts. As we have already mentioned, the positivist structure is withdrawn through the unexpected shift toward the ascetic position. As described above, Salomon goes through the three stages—childhood, youth, and adulthood— but once he reaches this final stage of development, something occurs which makes him revise his self-image. Once he has returned to the stage of youth and taken over his stepfather's position as City Treasurer, he would, according to the model, have reached the final years of manhood, and the circle would be complete. He should at this point have attained the highest level of insight into life, that is, pure realization, void of illusion and free from religious categories. During this period he not only takes over his stepfather's civil servant position, but he assumes the latter's entire attitude toward life and existence. He lives his life as a true first-class citizen, gets up every morning, goes to work on time, eats his meals regularly, and gets a good night's rest. He does not have the same grand social life as his stepfather, but he sticks to etiquette and does not go against convention. In that sense he lives in accordance with his surroundings. One could say that during this period, he is much like Judge William and tries to live an ordinary life.

Salomon, so to speak, worships the ordinary and finds value in even the most trivial things in life. For example, he appears to have completely mended his relationship to his old arch-enemy, Reverend Pedersen, with whom he at times speaks "across the fence, when he wears clogs, and, smoking on his long pipe, trims his roses."[55] He refers thus to the Reverend: "He gives me good advice about my grapes. And I have at times lent him apologetic arguments."[56] And finally he underscores: "Of course, I love the inhabitants of the town, and its poultry, and all that belongs to the town."[57] Yet while the City Treasurer lives in apparent harmony with the old town, we learn that he at home, secretly, is still preoccupied with his religious interests. It appears then, that the conflict is not quite over, for yet a leap awaits Salomon—the leap into the ascetic dimension of life.

It is up for debate what actually occurs during this last leap. At the outset, it could be interpreted as a fourth developmental step following the three positivist stages described above, but if one takes a closer look, there may be just two steps in the development, in the sense that the first three come together and become one. Salomon's comment above on his own textual output, namely, that it appears to be haunted by an incurable romantic devilry, may serve as an argument that there actually are only two basic categories in Salomon's life, the romantic and the religious-ascetic. In this sense, *The Path of Suffering* can be seen as going through

---

[55]   Ibid., p. 202.
[56]   Ibid.
[57]   Ibid.

a developmental structure that reminds one of *Either/Or*, rather than, as others have claimed,[58] an August Comte-inspired positivist development process.

The all-engulfing romantic irony appears to be present throughout the novel up until the postscript, where Salomon makes the final leap into the ascetic position. As we saw earlier, Salomon's aesthetic position is identified with Victor Eremita's, and we learn that he already at this point is torn between an ironic masquerade and a more serious religious attitude toward life. During the so-called manhood years, he appears to be at ease in a normal bourgeois lifestyle. During this period, Salomon's rhetoric, which forms the basis of his new outlook of life, has much in common with that of Judge William in *Either/Or*. This is expressed through his glorifying statements on life and the citizens of the old town as described above. But it is already seen in the preface to *The Path of Suffering*.

The author who writes the preface is namely the same man who writes in the period during which Salomon apparently found himself again in his old stepfather's position as City Treasurer. Here the narrative voice meets itself, so to speak. During this period the perspective shifts from a past tense narrative to a present tense narrative, as in the preface. The preface ends like this: "So, I move the chair to the writing desk, light my pipe with a wax taper and commence work. But first, for the sense of order, I legally authorize this protocol as a private protocol for—Salomon Simonsen, tenured treasurer of this town."[59] So the point of departure for the novel is that he sits at his desk and commences writing the novel from a position where he clearly identifies himself with his position as City Treasurer.

From here on, the novel moves forward through a backward-looking perspective, through which Salomon's life is told, starting from his childhood years to his manhood years. A little into the last phase, the narrative shifts to the present, and the story appears to have come full circle with the following comment:

> And now I think that I can say "I," for this Salomon, who lives in the small house, in the small town, is the same as he who has taken on the task of writing Salomon's story for his own and Fidivav's edification. I, the person, who calls himself "I," am not the poet Salomon or the Anarchist Salomon or the Worshipper of Prose. It is the good citizen, City Treasurer Salomon of the town.[60]

Salomon here believes that he has reached his life's final and authentic target, which he clearly correlates to being "The Good Citizen," whose calling is to be "City Treasurer Salomon of the Town." This position corresponds exactly to Judge William's ethical position in *Either/Or*. But as we know, there is more to add to Salomon's life than he had expected at the outset of the novel.

Referring to the previously mentioned indications of an underlying destructive irony in the text, I would claim that it is actually the position of the aesthetic romantic Victor Eremita which remains dominating, also during the ostensibly ethical period, and this means that the ethical position is never truly attained in Salomon's life, nor does it attain status as a true existential category. This is

---

58   Schovsbo, "Efterskrift," in *Lidelsens Vej*, p. 288.

59   Dalgas, *Lidelsens Vej*, p. 9.

60   Ibid., p. 199.

primarily supported by the ethical Salomon pointing out that he possesses an inner romantic irony of which he will never be free. This is, I would claim, the same irony that we see at the transitions to the ascetic position and which annihilates the ethical. When Salomon returns to his childhood town and assumes the position as City Treasurer, he does not propel himself into a higher existential state of being. Rather, he reverts to a previous bourgeois (or petit-bourgeois, at that) state, but he attempts, just like "the young man" from *Repetition* to argue that he has attained a higher level of reflection. To Dalgas, the ethical position, represented through Salomon and Judge William, appears to be an expression of an imagined existential category, a regression to a lower state of being. Instead, he appears to suggest that if the all-destroying romantic irony is to be combated, one must transition to an ascetic-religious way of life.[61]

When Dalgas in his journal entry shortly before his demise writes about *Either/ Or* that it in a decisive way has given ascetic shape to his life, it would necessarily follow that he has observed such asceticism in *Either/Or*. This work does indeed seem to promote such an ascetic position, just as Dalgas argues, and this again could serve as support for my assertion that *The Path of Suffering* at bottom uses *Either/Or* as its built-in frame of reference, that it should be read as a novel that is constructed using the same structure as *Either/Or*, and that it, in terms of content, deals with the life cycle using the same categories as we see in *Either/Or*.

At the end of *Either/Or*, Judge William reflects, at a hypothetical level, to what extent it is possible to realize an ascetic way of life. In this connection he philosophizes that such a way of life, under certain given circumstances, can be acknowledged as a real way of life, but in the end concludes: "This whole struggle, however, is a purgatory, the dreadfulness of which I can at least form an idea. People should not aspire to be extraordinary, because to be that means something different from a capricious satisfaction of one's arbitrary desire."[62] Living ascetically, then, is portrayed as both a possible and acceptable way of life. William has not realized this himself, but he imagines what it would be like, should it be realized in the right manner. We learn that, according to William, this is definitely not a desirable position to place oneself in, but if one is willing to undergo the suffering it entails to live secluded from other human beings, then it is actually possible to live as an exception in this world, and not necessarily have to realize normalcy at every moment in life, which has been his standpoint until now. A person who, in a positive sense, lives an ascetic life, would, according to William,

> feel that he has placed an enormous responsibility upon himself. At this point, he says, I have placed myself outside the universal; I have deprived myself of all the guidance, the security, and the reassurance that the universal gives; I stand alone, without fellow-feeling, for I am an exception. But he will not become craven and disconsolate; he will confidently go his solitary way; indeed, he has demonstrated the correctness of what he did—he has his pain.[63]

---

[61]   Garde, *Dansk Aand*, p. 65.
[62]   *SKS* 3, 312 / *EO2*, 331.
[63]   *SKS* 3, 312 / *EO2*, 330.

But we also learn that William has no personal desire to transition into such a way of life. It is, so to speak, a life form, which lies outside the ethical category to which he belongs. Rounding off Chapter 2 thus, he points us in the direction of the third and final chapter in *Either/Or*. Here William, as mentioned earlier, relinquishes his voice and passes the narrative on to his old friend, who is now a pastor in Jutland. This chapter is titled "Ultimatum," and in it we will be introduced to a sermon titled: "The Upbuilding That Lies in the Thought That in Relation to God We Are Always in the Wrong." This opens up the possibility of interpreting the previous ascetic ruminations in a religious direction. In a painful ascetic life, one might be able to find edification in the thought that against God, we are always in the wrong. Through the title "Ultimatum" it is suggested that this is where the actual choice is to be made, not between the aesthetic and ethical, but between the aesthetic and religious.

This appears to be Dalgas' interpretation of *Either/Or* and is probably the reason that he writes that this book influenced him in an ascetic direction. Salomon only defeats the romantic irony that haunts him throughout the novel at the time when he transitions to the ascetic position to which he attaches a religious meaning. It is only in this situation that he can unite with the world, only here that he can get over the loss of Prosa and incorporate her as a higher meaning in his life, precisely by not claiming her as his, but rather realizing that against God he is always in the wrong. It is not possible to defeat irony through an understanding of the abnormal in a normal bourgeois life, which is what Salomon attempts upon his return to the town as City Treasurer. For this reason, the ethical position is for Dalgas not an actual existential possibility, and therefore his educational novel ends up consisting of just two developmental steps: the romantic and the ascetic-religious.

Because of Salomon's identification with Victor Eremita, it appears that this aesthetic hermit position constitutes the closest developmental state at the transition to the, according to Dalgas, pure religious-ascetic state. Thus, Dalgas, in *The Path of Suffering*, sets forth a particular interpretation of *Either/Or*. This is an interpretative possibility that primarily rests on Dalgas' own statement that *Either/Or* has pushed his life in a particular ascetic direction and on the clear-cut references to known characters and categories from *Either/Or*. Also in this example we see Dalgas working with foresight, anticipating a trend in modern Kierkegaard research, which precisely has problematized the status of the ethical category in Kierkegaard's existentialist philosophy.[64]

D. Anxiety

A final example that supports the just proffered interpretation of the relation between the aesthetic, ethical, and religious in the world of Dalgas is taken from Salomon's preface to *The Path of Suffering*. There he writes:

---

[64]   E.g. Garff, *"Den Søvnløse". Kierkegaard læst æstetisk/biografisk*, p. 148. Bøggild, *Ironiens tænker. Tænkningens ironi. Kierkegaard læst retorisk*, p. 93. Winkel Holm, *Tanken i billedet. Søren Kierkegaards poetik*, p. 182. Dehs, *Kunst og æstetik*, p. 247.

Often I compare myself to the pupil of possibility, as mentioned by Vigilius Haufniensis, who lives in the Jutland heath, where the most obscure of events is when a black grouse noisily flaps his wings and takes off, but who is educated in the world of possibilities, and learns more there than many an actor at the theater of world history.[65]

Here Salomon refers to the following passage taken from the last chapter of *The Concept of Anxiety*:

Take the pupil of possibility, place him in the middle of the Jutland heath, where no event takes place or where the greatest event is a grouse flying up noisily, and he will experience everything more perfectly, more accurately, more thoroughly than the man who received the applause on the stage of world-history if that man was not educated by possibility.[66]

As we know, this last chapter is titled, "Anxiety as Saving through Faith," and Vigilius Haufniensis describes a person wrought from anxiety as "the pupil of possibility." Through anxiety, events in the world are experienced more vividly and clearly than if one were not in a state of anxiety, even those events that at face value appear to be insignificant. In accordance with this, Salomon writes about himself that he—at a superficial level—has not experienced a lot, but that he in another sense has experienced quite a lot: "For what to anyone else would have been mere triviality, assumed enormous proportions for me."[67] In Kierkegaard we read: "So when the individual through anxiety is educated unto faith, anxiety will eradicate precisely what it brings forth itself."[68] Anxiety then has a negating effect with regard to the thoughts generated by itself. It is always possible for anxiety to invent new elements of thought that annihilate the old. In this sense, anxiety perpetuates endless motion. It can at all times see new possibilities and can therefore transform even the most trivial of events into momentous ones.

Salomon appears to be in the throes of such anxiety, which constantly destroys its own creations. The entire educational novel is predominantly driven forward by this anxiety. In Salomon's life it manifests itself at its highest level in the romantic irony we see in the identification with Victor Eremita. He does not manage to stop his anxiety, this endlessly negating irony, until he reaches asceticism, where he acknowledges his mental disorder, and thereby learns to control it. With regard to the condition in which he find himself, he writes: "Never was I more distant from Romanticism and mysticism than now, never more sober than now, and delirium can no longer enter my mind, but it has the power to shut eyes and ears, and lay a dark veil on remembrance, and let thoughts die."[69] Physically, Salomon's illness is characterized by epileptic seizures. In this sense his eyes and ears are closed, and the thoughts die. But he has learned to control his seizures by rendering the thoughts harmless. This corresponds to the faith that we read about in Kierkegaard, where

---

[65]   Dalgas, *Lidelsens Vej*, p. 9.
[66]   *SKS* 4, 458 / *CA*, 159.
[67]   Dalgas, *Lidelsens Vej*, p. 9.
[68]   *SKS* 4, 458 / *CA*, 159.
[69]   Dalgas, *Lidelsens Vej*, p. 243.

faith stops the runaway thoughts, and learns to move in the direction he desires, so that anxiety becomes an important force in life. In spite of the illness raging in his mind and body, Salomon maintains "solid self-consciousness,"[70] and nothing can distract his "peace of mind."[71]

V. Conclusion

In this article my point of departure has been Ernesto Dalgas' novel *The Path of Suffering*. I have attempted to show how Dalgas was influenced by and availed himself of Kierkegaard in his authorship. *The Path of Suffering* is the piece of work by Dalgas where Kierkegaard's influence is seen most clearly. But Kierkegaard's influence can also be sensed at other levels in Dalgas' life and authorship. The clear Kierkegaardian influence in *The Path of Suffering* can be transferred to Dalgas' life and authorship in general.

At a thematic level, *Either/Or* appears to be a central source of inspiration for the existential development that the protagonist, Salomon, experiences in *The Path of Suffering*. Here Dalgas, in a visionary manner, seems to suggest the interpretative possibility that the choice with which we are confronted in *Either/Or* is not actually the choice between an aesthetic and ethical life view, but rather between an aesthetic and religious life view. We see a similar usage of Kierkegaard's existential categories in Dalgas' other main work *The Book of Doom*, in which Dalgas seems to suggest that there basically are two paths that may be followed in life, the aesthetic and the ascetically religious, but that both paths in the end, as the ultimate goal, will lead to the final stage of Buddhist nirvana. In *The Path of Suffering*, as well as in *The Book of Doom*, we furthermore see a clear usage of Kierkegaard's sarcastic imagery in the struggle against "official Christianity," and in both novels we furthermore see a conscious usage of Kierkegaardian angst motifs.

Not just in terms of content, but also with regard to form, Dalgas appears to be influenced by Kierkegaard. *The Path of Suffering* is thus encompassed by an enigmatic atmosphere that corresponds to Kierkegaard's *mise-en-scène* of his pseudonymous works. The novel consists of several narrative layers that—like Kierkegaard's pseudonyms—enter into mutual dialogue and contradict each other, and, furthermore, Dalgas avails himself of a strategy of recollection, which seems to consciously be imitating Kierkegaard. Such stylistic characteristics are also found in *The Book of Doom*, where Kierkegaard's pseudonym Johannes de silentio makes an appearance as the protagonist's loyal companion on his travels through the realm of the dead. Through this character, Kierkegaard is included as a pervasive reference throughout the novel. A thought-provoking usage of Kierkegaard's characters is seen as Dalgas chooses to let Johannes de silentio convert to Islam. It is also the case that we find a Kierkegaard reference on the title pages of both *The Path of Suffering* and *The Path of Doom*. The title page for *The Path of Suffering* contains a reference to the symparakromenoi of *Either/Or*, and the title page for *The Book of Doom* contains the

---

[70]   Ibid., p. 244.
[71]   Ibid.

quotation "Subjectivity is truth," referring to the *Concluding Unscientific Postscript*. In both cases, elements from Kierkegaard's thought are included as an interpretative framework for the book.

Finally, one may draw clear parallels between the two authors' lives. Dalgas clearly sees Kierkegaard as a figure with which he identifies. Just like Kierkegaard, Dalgas grew up in a family with a dominating and extroverted father. Both fathers were reputed businessmen. Both Søren and Ernesto reacted in opposition to their fathers, and, for both, this reaction turned out to have a great impact on their lives and authorships. Just like Kierkegaard, Dalgas breaks his engagement to the woman in his life. Both Kierkegaard and Dalgas appear to bury themselves in writing and thus process the conflicts that they encounter in life. Both are afflicted by mental disorders with which they fight to the end of their lives. To Dalgas, the suffering appeared insurmountable, and he saw no other way out than to end his own life at just 28 years of age. Kierkegaard died at the age of 42. His body succumbed, probably worn out by the exhausting internal struggles. In spite of their untimely deaths, the authorships of both men bear witness to great insight. Dalgas' remembrance of the inscription on Kierkegaard's tombstone, therefore, seems fitting for both Dalgas and Kierkegaard: "the old verse, in which Kierkegaard found comfort at the end, comes to mind: 'Just a short while, then I have won. Then the whole struggle entirely disappears.' "[72]

---

[72]   Dalgas, *Lidelsens Vej*, p. 256.

Bibliography

I. References or Uses of Kierkegaard in Dalgas' Corpus

Dommedags Bog, ed. by Henrik Schovsbo, Copenhagen: Det Danske Sprog- og Litteraturselskab/Borgen 1996 (*Danske Klassikere*), pp. 14–15; pp. 30–1; p. 40; p. 75; p. 91; pp. 158–9; p. 160; p. 191; p. 310.
Lidelsens Vej, ed. by Henrik Schovsbo, Copenhagen: Det Danske Sprog- og Litteraturselskab/Borgen 1996 (*Danske Klassikere*), p. 8; p. 9; pp. 30–1; p. 39; p. 75; p. 79; p. 84; p. 85; p. 94; pp. 103–4; p. 105; p. 108; p. 113; p. 199; p. 202; p. 228; p. 229; p. 237; p. 239; p. 243; p. 244; p. 248; p. 249; p. 254; pp. 256–7.

II. Sources of Dalgas' Knowledge of Kierkegaard

Brandes, Georg, *Søren Kierkegaard. En kritisk Fremstilling i Grundrids*, Copenhagen: Gyldendal 1877.
Høffding, Harald, *Søren Kierkegaard som Filosof*, Copenhagen: Det Danske Forlag 1892.
Nielsen, Rasmus, *Magister S. Kierkegaards Johannes Climacus og Dr. H. Martensens Christelige Dogmatik. En undersøgende Anmeldelse*, Copenhagen: C.A. Reitzel 1849.
— "Om S. Kierkegaards mentale Tilstand," *Nordisk Universitets-Tidsskrift*, vol. 4, no. 1, 1858, pp. 1–29.
— *Paa Kierkegaardske Stadier*, Copenhagen: Gyldendal 1860.

III. Secondary Literature on Dalgas' Relation to Kierkegaard

Boisen, Henry, "En glemt filosof," in *Kristendom og Humanisme*, Copenhagen: Levin og Munksgaards Forlag 1922, pp. 51–61; p. 59; p. 60.
Bukdahl, Jørgen, *Det moderne Danmark*, Copenhagen: Aschehoug 1931, pp. 25–6.
Garde, Axel, *Dansk Aand*, Copenhagen: Gjellerups Forlag 1908, p. 59; p. 72; p. 79.
Gelsted, Otto, "Ernesto Dalgas," in *Sirius. Dansk Litteraturtidende*, no. 3, Copenhagen: P. Haase og Søn 1924, pp. 139–40; p. 139.
Henriksen, Aage, "Forord," in Dalgas' *Noveller og Fragmenter*, ed. by Aage Henriksen, Copenhagen: Steen Hasselbalchs Forlag 1942, pp. 5–12; pp. 6–8.
— "Ernesto Dalgas: Lidelsens Vej. En studie i romanens tilblivelseshistore," *Orbis Litterarum*, no. 6, Copenhagen: Gyldendal 1948, pp. 133–50.
— "Kompositionens sprog," in his *Gotisk tid*, Copenhagen: Gyldendal 1971, pp. 175–237; p. 182.

— "Det borgerlige oprør," in his *Svanereden*, Copenhagen: Amadeus 1990, pp. 7–23; p. 17.

Jaurnow, Leon, "Indledning," in Dalgas' *Kundskabens Bog*, ed. by Leon Jaurnow, Copenhagen: Hans Reitzels Forlag 1995, pp. 7–15; p. 12; p. 13.

Paludan, Jacob, *Litterært Selskab*, Copenhagen: Hasselbalch 1956, p. 10; p. 12.

Plesner, K.F., "Dansk Dommedag," in *Kulturbærere*, Copenhagen: Aschehoug 1938, pp. 19–26; pp. 22–4.

Poulsen, Mogens, "I Kierkegaards skygge—Ernesto Dalgas," in *Kierkegaardske skæbner, fire radioforedrag*, Copenhagen: Petit Forlaget 1955, pp. 33–42.

Schovsbo, Henrik, "Mulighedens discipel," in *Den blå port*, no. 17, Copenhagen: Rhodos 1991, pp. 7–13; p. 7; p. 11.

— "Efterskrift," in Dalgas' *Dommedags Bog*, ed. by Henrik Schovsbo, Copenhagen: Det Danske Sprog- og Litteraturselskab/Borgen 1996 (*Danske Klassikere*), pp. 341–66; p. 341; p. 342; p. 344; p. 348; p. 354; p. 361; p. 362.

— "Efterskrift," in Dalgas' *Lidelsens Vej*, ed. by Henrik Schovsbo, Copenhagen: Det Danske Sprog- og Litteraturselskab/Borgen 1996 (*Danske Klassikere*), pp. 281–300; p. 283; p. 288; p. 290; p. 292; p. 294; p. 295.

Stjernfelt, Frederik, "Buddhas København," in *Københavnerromaner*, ed. by Marianne Barlyng et al., Copenhagen: Borgen 1996, pp. 137–53; p. 143; p. 146; pp. 148–50.

Woel, Cai M., "Ernesto Dalgas," in his *Troubadourer, literære Tidsbilleder*, vols. 1–2, Copenhagen: Woels Forlag 1930–34, vol. 1, pp. 35–46; p. 42; p. 43.

Martin A. Hansen:

Kierkegaard in Hansen's Thinking and Poetical Work

Esben Lindemann

On June 4, 1954, approximately one year before his death, Martin A. Hansen (1909–55) gave an interview to the Danish newspaper *Aarhuus Stiftstidende* under the title "A Conversation with Martin A. Hansen." In it, the interviewer poses the question: "Do you dare call yourself a Christian poet?," to which Hansen responds: "Well, what, in fact, is a Christian poet? I shun ideological religiousness like the plague. But what would I have gained in life without Søren Kierkegaard as one of the recurring pillars on my path!"[1]

In this response, Hansen acknowledges the immense significance that Kierkegaard had on his life and poetry. Upon a closer examination of Hansen's collected body of work, one will indeed find a large number of references to titles and themes from Kierkegaard's authorship. This means that when we examine the relation between these two Danish authors and thinkers, the question will concern not so much *whether* Hansen was affected by Kierkegaard, but rather *how* Hansen applied Kierkegaard's philosophy in his own thinking and poetry. Kierkegaard is incontestably a central source of inspiration in Hansen's authorship. Both direct and indirect statements from Hansen pay testimony to this.

The reason that Hansen in the interview is asked the question whether he dares call himself a Christian poet, is because Christianity is a recurring theme in his texts. Just like Kierkegaard, he despises "ideological Christianity," and not unlike Kierkegaard, he refuses to refer unambiguously to himself as a Christian. Already this suggests a significant similarity between Hansen and Kierkegaard, but it is precisely because of the recurring Christian motifs in Hansen's work that his status as a poet in the history of Danish literature has been debated. In this connection he has been accused of being a romantic proponent of the past and peasant life.[2]

In this article, by contrast, I intend to follow a path laid out in the latest Hansen research, as represented by Anders Thyrring Andersen, who has shown that Hansen

---

[1]   Sverre Riisøen, "En samtale med Martin A. Hansen," in *Aarhuus Stiftstidende*, June 4, 1954, p. 12. I would like to thank Olav Balslev for his translations of Hansen's works that appear in this article.

[2]   For example, Thomas Bredsdorff, *Dansk litteratur set fra månen*, Copenhagen: Gyldendal 2006, pp. 222–3.

holds a position as a ground-breaking modernist in Denmark.[3] Andersen has in several articles demonstrated that Hansen was markedly inspired by Kierkegaard and has suggested that one designate Hansen as a "Christian Modernist."[4] In extension of this, the thesis of this article will be that that it is precisely under the influence of Kierkegaard that Hansen develops his distinct, modernistic characteristics.

Since Kierkegaard, so to speak, is present everywhere in Hansen's work, I have chosen to concentrate on passages where Hansen explicitly comments on his relation to Kierkegaard or expounds on his interpretation of Kierkegaardian ideas. This article, then, will predominantly be an exposition of how Kierkegaard's effect on Hansen's thinking manifests itself in diary entries, letters, and essays. This is done, however, with the aim of throwing light on the importance of Kierkegaard in Hansen's poetry, and on how Hansen in this connection becomes a main figure in Danish modernistic literature.

I. Hansen's Life with Kierkegaard

> When I, as a seventeen-year old, entered teachers' college, I was well-versed in our Golden Age literature, and in addition to that Holberg and Johs. Ewald. I had read Poul Møller, Goldschmidt, Drachmann, Aakjær, Skjoldborg, and some Pontoppidan. I had read *Either/Or*, but did not know Johs. V. Jensen and J.P. Jacobsen, or anyone more contemporary—not even by name.[5]

This was the wording of a diary entry from 1940, where Hansen thinks back on a crossroads in his life. As it appears, Hansen at the age of 17 read *Either/Or*. The story does not recount what had incited the peasant boy, whose name originally was Alfred Martin Jens Hansen, to read Kierkegaard. It had most probably played some role that Hansen's parents were active representatives for both The Church Association for the Inner Mission, and the Grundtvigians. This means that he had been accustomed to theological debates at home and had been in close contact with the inherent tension between Pietism and Grundtvigianism. After some years of financial instability, the family bought a small farm in 1918 in their native area of Stevns, and in this connection, Hansen shifts to a small school in the village of Strøby Egede. Here, the couple Marie and Erik Heding became his teachers. This encounter also probably influenced the development of Hansen's early interest in Kierkegaard. The two teachers definitely had an inspirational effect on Hansen, and during these years he was very preoccupied with historical and religious literature. After finishing school in 1923, Hansen found work on different farms in the surrounding area of

---

[3]   Anders Thyrring Andersen, "Midt i en refleksionstid. Martin A. Hansens dagbøger—kristendom og modernisme," in *Kritik*, vol. 118, 1995, pp. 13–23. Anders Thyrring Andersen has been responsible for publishing Martin A. Hansen's *Dagbøger 1931–1955*, vols. 1–3, in 1999 and *Kætterbreve. Martin A. Hansens korrespondance med kredsen omkring Heretica*, vols. 1–3, in 2004. In this connection, he has written a number of articles on Martin A. Hansen and the legacy from Kierkegaard (cf. the bibliography at the end of this article).

[4]   Ibid.

[5]   Martin A. Hansen, *Dagbøger 1931–1955*, vols. 1–3, ed. by Anders Thyrring Andersen and Jørgen Jørgensen, Copenhagen: Gyldendal 1999, vol. 1, p. 84 ("March 7, 1940 b").

Stevns. And in 1925, at one of his places of work, he met the well-read farm foreman Hans Jørgensen, who introduced him to a broader selection of literature. It is during this period that Hansen read *Either/Or*.[6]

Ready for the task, Hansen was admitted to Haslev Teachers' College at the age of 17. Here Kierkegaard was on the syllabus, together with the younger Danish authors Johannes V. Jensen (1873–1950) and J.P. Jacobsen (1847–85), the names of whom Hansen did not even know when he started the program of study. This source of inspiration, coupled with the fact that Hansen wrote a number of articles for the Teachers' College magazine, were probably contributing factors to Hansen deciding in 1929 that he wanted to be a fiction writer. Additionally, during this period Hansen began to distance himself from the Pietistic legacy from home.[7]

In 1935, Hansen's social-realistic debut novel *Now He Gives Up* was published.[8] After the novel *Jonathan's Journey* from 1941,[9] there followed a number of short-story collections and novels, which all maintained a more narrative, and occasionally experimenting style. The big breakthrough with the critics came in 1946 with the short-story collection *The Thorn Bush*,[10] while his main work, the novel *The Liar*, was published in 1950.[11]

Hansen's authorship also includes a number of articles and essays. He, for instance, wrote illegal articles for the resistance movement during World War II, and wound up being one of the pivotal forces behind the illegal magazine *People and Freedom*. In this connection, he also wrote a series of articles titled *The Moment* with a direct reference to Kierkegaard's rebellious flyers during the well-known church feud. In addition, Hansen in 1947 became co-founder and editor of the recognized Danish literary journal *Heretica*.

After the publishing of *The Liar*, Hansen's fictional writing subsided. Instead, he delved into extensive studies on the history of the church, which, among other things, resulted in the book *Worm and Bull* from 1952,[12] as well as a large-scale series of lectures. As we will see later, there is a connection to be made between Hansen's interpretation of some aspects of Kierkegaard's philosophy and Hansen's sudden stop in creating fictional literature.

As said, Kierkegaard's influence is tangible in practically everything that Hansen wrote. Diaries and letters from the period testify to an in-depth knowledge of Kierkegaard's work. Hansen, just having arrived for a study visit at the Lysebu Institution in Norway, recounts the following on January 18, 1948 in a letter to his friend, the Danish poet and author Thorkild Bjørnvig (1918–2004):

> I have now laid in front of me on the table the pictures of Vera and the children, the stone axe, Zealand on the map, Johs. Ewald, my pipes (my blank tax return), *The Star*

---

6   Anders Thyrring Andersen and Jørgen Jørgensen, *Martin A. Hansen—Dagbøger—Noter og registre*, vols. 1–3, Copenhagen: Gyldendal 1999, vol. 3, p. 964.

7   Ibid.

8   Martin A. Hansen, *Nu opgiver han*, Copenhagen: Gyldendal 1935.

9   Martin A. Hansen, *Jonatans Rejse*, Copenhagen: Gyldendal 1941.

10   Martin A. Hansen, *Tornebusken*, Copenhagen: Gyldendal 1946.

11   Martin A. Hansen, *Løgneren*, Copenhagen: Gyldendal 1950.

12   Martin A. Hansen, *Orm og Tyr*, Copenhagen: Gyldendal 1952.

behind the Gable (the signed copy, however, stayed with Vera, as it should), 3 volumes of Kierkegaard. —These are the requisites that comfort me in my expatriation....[13]

Kierkegaard, thereby, is a fix-point in Hansen's expatriation, side by side with the pictures of his wife Vera Hansen (1910–58) and the children, his favorite pipes, and other artifacts from home. Out of the three volumes he carried with him, one or two of them is probably the *Concluding Unscientific Postscript*. Hansen's diary entry from January 17, 1948 reveals: "Read substantially from 'Concluding Unscientific Postscript'—just like last year."[14] As one can see, Hansen did not treat this work by Kierkegaard as mere diversion during his trip to Norway. It is a work that he kept returning to, and there is much that indicates that precisely this work had a special significance for him.[15] Two other works that seem to have been important to Hansen are *The Concept of Anxiety*[16] and *The Point of View for My Work as an Author*.[17] In addition, there is testimony to the fact that Hansen was in possession of "Kierkegaard's Collected Works (Drackm.-Heiberg Edition)"[18] and "Kierkegaard's 'Papers.' "[19] He studied closely, among other works, "In vino veritas,"[20] *A Literary Review*,[21] *Philosophical Fragments*,[22] and *Works of Love*.[23]

If we examine the literary sources that Hansen relates to in his understanding of Kierkegaard, it appears that he has been oriented toward authors that—for his time—represented current, and at times innovative, or even critical interpretations of Kierkegaard's philosophy. These authors concurrently challenged and inspired Hansen's own understanding and application of Kierkegaard. Hansen, for instance, read the work *Philosophy of Religion* by the Danish philosopher Harald Høffding (1843–1931),[24] who in his humanistic naturalism challenges the Kierkegaardian idea of a personal relation to God. Hansen challenges Høffding, who, he claims, commits the mistake of wanting to fathom the existence of God through knowledge.[25] Hansen would here be able to find support for his arguments in the author Johannes Hohlenberg's (1881–1960) work, *Søren Kierkegaard* from 1940,[26] which precisely

[13]   Martin A. Hansen, *Kætterbreve. Martin A. Hansens korrespondance med kredsen omkring Heretica*, vols. 1–3, ed. by. Anders Thyrring Andersen, Copenhagen: Gyldendal 2004, vol. 1, p. 180 (Letter to Thorkild Bjørnvig, January 18, 1948).
[14]   Hansen, *Dagbøger 1931–1955*, vol. 2, p. 600 ("January 17, 1948").
[15]   Hansen, *Kætterbreve*, vol. 1, p. 194 (Letter to Aksel Heltoft, April 4, 1948).
[16]   Hansen, *Dagbøger 1931–1955*, vol. 1, p. 466 ("August 28, not, 1946").
[17]   Hansen, *Dagbøger 1931–1955*, vol. 2, p. 648 ("June 30, 1948"); p. 677 ("October 16, 1948"). Hansen, *Kætterbreve*, vol. 1, p. 249 (Letter to Ole Wivel, March 2, 1949).
[18]   Hansen, *Dagbøger 1931–1955*, vol. 1, p. 202 ("January Friday 16, 1942").
[19]   Hansen, *Dagbøger 1931–1955*, vol. 2, p. 679 ("November 5, 1948").
[20]   Hansen, *Dagbøger 1931–1955*, vol. 1, p. 246 ("June 19, 1942").
[21]   Hansen, *Dagbøger 1931–1955*, vol. 1, p. 421 ("January 30, 1946").
[22]   Hansen, *Dagbøger 1931–1955*, vol. 1, p. 421 ("February 3, 1946").
[23]   Hansen, *Dagbøger 1931–1955*, vol. 2, p. 486 ("February 28, 1947").
[24]   Harald Høffding, *Religionsfilosofi*, Copenhagen: Gyldendal 1901.
[25]   Hansen, *Dagbøger 1931–1955*, vol. 1, p. 134 ("February 8, 1941 a").
[26]   Johannes Hohlenberg, *Søren Kierkegaard*, Copenhagen: Aschehoug 1940.

emphasizes Kierkegaard's personal and passionate aspects.[27] Hohlenberg represented a trend at the time to break with positivism and to make Kierkegaard topical again, and to make him a source of inspiration for more new trends at the time. Hansen seems to be following these new trends, and in the physician Olaf Pedersen's (1920–97) *From Kierkegaard to Sartre*,[28] Hansen could read about the relation between Kierkegaard and the fashionable philosophy of the time: French existentialism.[29] Finally, Hansen enthusiastically reads the Danish literature researcher Aage Henriksen's (1921) dissertation *Kierkegaard's Novels* from 1954,[30] in which he sees an interpretation of Kierkegaard that offers a "refreshing" break with "the usual set-in-stone view of prose-ification."[31]

Moreover, letters and diary entries bear witness to the fact that Hansen regularly attended lectures or participated in debates on Kierkegaard.[32] For example, he attended lectures with Vilhelm Grønbech (1873–1948),[33] a Danish historian of religion, who evidently was inspired by Kierkegaard, but who in his critical approach developed his own independent program, and Knud Hansen (1898–1996), a Danish theologian, who accuses Kierkegaard of merely benefiting from the church, which he thinks that he is breaking with.[34] Martin A. Hansen was also present at the inauguration of the Kierkegaard Society in Denmark, May 4, 1948.[35] Here he met a number of the association's prominent representatives and from then on participated in its meetings. Finally, Hansen undoubtedly also gained insight into Kierkegaard's works through his position as editor for *Heretica*. The journal published a series of articles relating to Kierkegaard.[36]

All this shows that Hansen was open to new ways of applying Kierkegaard, and that he took critical approaches to Kierkegaard seriously. Furthermore, in Hansen's interest in Kierkegaard, there appears to be a tendency that serves as an extension of his general break with pietism.

---

[27]   Hansen, *Dagbøger 1931–1955*, vol. 1, p. 154 ("April 2, 1941"). Ibid., vol. 1, p. 168 ("August 5, 1941").
[28]   Olaf Pedersen, *Fra Kierkegaard til Sartre*, Copenhagen: Arne Frost-Hansens Forlag 1947.
[29]   Hansen, *Kætterbreve*, vol. 1, p. 160 (Letter to Bjørn Poulsen, November 29, 1947).
[30]   Aage Henriksen, *Kierkegaards Romaner*, Copenhagen: Gyldendal 1954.
[31]   Hansen, *Kætterbreve*, vol. 2, p. 1239 (Letter to Tage Skou-Hansen, November 10, 1954).
[32]   Hansen, *Dagbøger 1931–1955*, vol. 1, p. 479 ("November 14–15, 1946"); vol. 2, p. 678 ("October 26, 1948").
[33]   Hansen, *Dagbøger 1931–1955*, vol. 1, p. 433 ("April 2, 1946").
[34]   Hansen, *Kætterbreve*, vol. 1, p. 606 (Letter to Ole Wivel, September 27, 1950). Ole Wivel, in Hansen, *Kætterbreve*, vol. 1, p. 565 (Letter to Martin A. Hansen, June 13, 1950).
[35]   Hansen, *Dagbøger 1931–1955*, vol. 2, p. 618 ("May 4, 1948").
[36]   Ole Wivel, in Hansen, *Kætterbreve*, vol. 1, p. 515 (Letter to Martin A. Hansen, June 13, 1950); vol. 1, p. 565 (Letter to Martin A. Hansen, August 18, 1950). Hansen, *Kætterbreve*, vol. 1, p. 594 (Letter to Ole Wivel, September 14, 1950); vol. 1, p. 606 (Letter to Ole Wivel, September 27, 1950); vol. 2, p. 1239 (Letter to Tage Skou-Hansen, November 10, 1954).

II. Hansen's Conscious Use of Kierkegaardian Motifs in Fiction

It may rightly be said that Kierkegaard's philosophy is a main pillar in Hansen's thinking and poetry.[37] Many of Hansen's fictive texts actually seem to have been constructed by way of Kierkegaardian thought diagrams. An example of this is "The September Fog" from the short-story collection *The Thorn Bush*. In his dissertation on Hansen's poetry and thinking, Thorkild Bjørnvig writes the following about the construction of this short story a few years after Hansen's death: "'The September Fog' disintegrates."[38] And Bjørnvig gives as one of the main reasons for this that

> The philosophy is not artistically assimilated into the story. The philosophy stems from, among others, Søren Kierkegaard's *The Concept of Anxiety*, which the author himself highlights as an explanatory book for the hardship of the times and the nature of demonism: The fear of the good, the true—the *real*! "The Midsummer Party" is also based on *The Concept of Anxiety*, but has there been assimilated with success.[39]

According to Bjørnvig, "The September Fog" has turned out be more of a philosophical than an artistic text, and "The reader is left with a feeling, as if a core had fallen out, a glowing core, whose rays still may be felt in the material."[40] On the other hand, Hansen has, according to Bjørnvig, managed to incorporate the Kierkegaardian concept of anxiety in an artistically viable way in "The Midsummer Party" from the same collection of short stories. It is, in other words, clear that *The Concept of Anxiety* has had a certain importance for the construct of *The Thorn Bush*.

Bjørnvig, furthermore, is not the only one to have noticed this. Hansen, then, on October 10, 1946, comments on the critic Preben Ramløv's (1918–88) draft for a review of *The Thorn Bush*, which was to be published in the Danish newspaper *Information*: "Far exceeds the scope of a short story. Drowned in Kierkegaard. I am being forced to accept opinions that I do not have."[41] And a few months after the review was published, Hansen writes to Ramløv: "I should say that there I do have a point of criticism or two against the assessment of the Kierkegaardian, but a review should surely not be in accordance with what the person critiqued thinks himself (a review is a work, personal, independent, like other literary genres)."[42]

Hansen feels that he is being force-fed opinions not his own, and, staying in close proximity to Kierkegaard, he transfers the understanding of the work to the reader and distances himself further from the review by proclaiming its autonomy as a genre. The question now is whether it is pure coincidence that Bjørnvig thinks that "The September Fog" collapses under the Kierkegaardian philosophy, and that

---

[37]   Thorkild Bjørnvig, *Kains Alter. Martin A. Hansens Digtning og Tænkning*, Copenhagen: Gyldendal 1964, p. 532.

[38]   Bjørnvig, *Kains Alter. Martin A. Hansens Digtning og Tænkning*, p. 121. Translated by Olav Balslev.

[39]   Ibid.

[40]   Ibid.

[41]   Hansen, *Dagbøger 1931–1955*, vol. 1, p. 475 ("October 10, 1946").

[42]   Hansen, *Kætterbreve*, vol. 1, p. 99 (Letter to Anne-Marie and Preben Ramløv, December 31, 1946).

Ramløv in his interpretations drowns in Kierkegaard. Hansen, most definitely, has, through his clear references to Kierkegaard and an evident Kierkegaardian structure, set up a clear interpretative frame for the text.

The reader is left with the impression that Hansen has attempted to incorporate Kierkegaardian motifs in *The Thorn Bush* by casting a glance at a few diary entries and a letter, in which Hansen comments on the creation of *The Thorn Bush*. Firstly, the diary entry from September 17, 1945:

> Continued this spring on the short stories that I had commenced already in December, in particular the more extensive one, "Grandfather Is Ill"—and the other on "The Easter Bell." Some of these had been sent to Gyldendal, the publishing house, which wanted to publish them by autumn, but this was rendered impossible due to illness and fatigue. I am now considering removing the shorter stories, and publishing the two long ones with a third long one under the title "Three Stages" (this is perhaps pretentious).[43]

In the end, *The Thorn Bush* ends up comprising the three stories, as Hansen has planned. "Grandfather Is Ill," which becomes "The Midsummer Party," is one of them. "The Easter Bell" and "The September Fog" are the two others. Note that *The Thorn Bush* originally was to be named *Three Stages*, which is a direct allusion to Kierkegaard's *Stages on Life's Way*. This is the first piece of evidence that Hansen consciously sought to incorporate Kierkegaardian motifs in *The Thorn Bush*, that is, the three most basic stages in Kierkegaard's portrayal of human existence: the aesthetic, the ethical, and the religious. Each of the stories in *The Thorn Bush* represents a stage. In a letter to his friend Bente Hammerich (1921–2002), shortly before *The Thorn Bush* was published, Hansen explains: "Each of the three stories is about a different stage, in different shapes based on the choice. From here, then, the book has its title, which also, as in Nis Petersen's poem, and in the symbolic usage of the thorn bush in the last story, evokes the notion of suffering."[44]

The other piece of evidence that Hansen consciously works with Kierkegaardian motifs in the text lies in his use of the concept *choice*. This corresponds to a dialectical pattern in Kierkegaard, and Hansen, like Kierkegaard, understands *choice* as a deciding existential choice that implies suffering. To Hansen, this is more than a mere psychological choice, which only can be described in psychological terms. In his letter to Hammerich, he writes about the choice: "it is more; it can be an event that both fetters and releases powers outside man."[45] Just like Kierkegaard, Hansen operates with *choice* in such a way "that it gains a metaphysical perspective."[46]

The third piece of evidence that Hansen consciously works with Kierkegaardian motifs in *The Thorn Bush* is to be found in another diary entry, which was written during the creation of "The September Fog," in which Hansen points out the following about one of the characters in the short story: "In the following, Fyrre's confession must be renewed, so that it organically connects to the story's 'anxiety'

---

[43]   Hansen, *Dagbøger 1931–1955*, vol. 1, p. 396 ("September 17, 1945 b").

[44]   Hansen, *Kætterbreve*, vol. 1, p. 106 (Letter to Bente Hammerich, February 3, 1947).

[45]   Ibid., p. 107.

[46]   Ibid.

motif; for this purpose it is evident."[47] During the period while Hansen was writing "The September Fog," he was deeply involved in reading *The Concept of Anxiety*.[48] It therefore seems evident that the anxiety motif to which he here refers has been taken from Kierkegaard.

In spite of the evidence indicating that he worked with Kierkegaardian motifs in *The Thorn Bush*, Hansen maintains the following in his letter to Hammerich: "The short story is not an intellectual conundrum, a disguised dialectical assignment to which a key can be handed over, a philosophical formula that, like these keys, with which you open the tin lid of a can, can open everything so that each detail lies like a piece of mosaic in a properly ordered thought pattern."[49] Hansen here seems to oppose the criticism hinted at by Bjørnvig and Ramløv, namely, that the artistic aspect is suffocated by the pretentiously constructed Kierkegaardian thought structures. We will here leave it open whether Hansen manages to refute the criticism, and let it suffice to observe that Kierkegaard's philosophy is very much present in Hansen's poetry. Hansen would probably be willing to accept this. Briefly summarizing a letter from his friend, the Danish author Ole Wivel (1921–2004), Hansen writes in his diary entry of June 9, 1948: "Letter from Ole—about the prose— Emphasis on my prose in the story and the critique thereof in the articles—points to a tradition [from] Kierkegaard to Johs. V. J. to which I belong…and this is perhaps true."[50] Some other works of fiction that, like *The Thorn Bush*, are fundamentally inspired by Kierkegaard, are *Lucky Kristoffer*, "The Waiting Room," and *The Liar*.[51]

III. Indirect Communication

In the letter to Bente Hammerich, it is interesting to note that Hansen, completely in the spirit of Kierkegaard, refrains from explaining the meaning behind his works of fiction. He, in fact, sees it as a fulfillment of his highest goal as an author to be asked by his readers for such an explanation, because "You should be able to surmise that such a question, that directly or concretely concerns the story, in fact is symbolic in itself, since another question underlies the concrete question that is relevant to he who asks the questions, and which concerns something that is above and beyond the story."[52] Hansen's own intention with the fictional texts, then, is the diametrical opposite of what they are criticized for. According to Hansen, they in fact differ from the philosophical texts by intrinsically being mysterious—unsolvable riddles, that is, to which no "key can be handed over." Rather, the texts must be able to speak *to* and *in* the individual reader, and thereby obtain a life that lies beyond the story. These thoughts completely resonate with Kierkegaard's thoughts about indirect communication. Kierkegaard, in fact, maintained that the foundation of his authorship

---

[47]   Hansen, *Dagbøger 1931–1955*, vol. 1, p. 468 ("September 2, 1946").
[48]   Hansen, *Dagbøger 1931–1955*, vol. 1, p. 466 ("August 27, 1946"). Andersen and Jørgensen, *Martin A. Hansen—Dagbøger—Noter og registre*, vol. 3, p. 1124.
[49]   Hansen, *Kætterbreve*, vol. 1, p. 106 (Letter to Bente Hammerich, February 3, 1947).
[50]   Hansen, *Dagbøger 1931–1955*, vol. 2, p. 637 ("June 9, 1948").
[51]   Andersen, in Hansen, *Kætterbreve*, vol. 3, p. 1310.
[52]   Hansen, *Kætterbreve*, vol. 1, p. 106 (Letter to Bente Hammerich, February 3, 1947).

was based on a particular indirect communication strategy that did not address the masses but rather the individual reader, whom Kierkegaard wished to propel, of their own volition, to learn existential truth. As an example, Kierkegaard describes in the *Concluding Unscientific Postscript* the indirect message form as a *mise-en-scène* of a conflict that does not offer a concrete result, but which precisely leaves it up to the reader to find the solution.[53]

In his capacity as editor of the periodical *Heretica*, Hansen does indeed use the concept of indirect method. In a letter to his co-editor Ole Wivel on October 8, 1950, we learn that the goal of the periodical is to "apply the 'indirect method' in essay writing."[54] Hansen saw a possibility of rechristening modernity through the young, contemporary generation of poets.[55] The indirect method meant allowing these young poets to speak their mind, and thereby orchestrate dialectical contradictions which, in Kierkegaardian terms, would give the generation incentive to act of their own volition. In other words, Hansen, through this orchestration, wanted to seduce the youth into Christianity.

Two letters and a diary entry from mid-September 1946 bear witness to the fact that a similar communication strategy also constitutes the basis of Hansen's works of fiction. One of these letters is to Thorkild Bjørnvig. Hansen here presents a controversial and forward-looking interpretation of precisely Kierkegaard's form of communication:

> Recently, a friend did point out that I—in all modesty—at times enjoy applying similar "disguises" as Kierkegaard, to manufacture a fake "I," which then becomes responsible for the meaning. I do view the psychological consistency, not to mention the moral consistency, in a slightly different manner. I have been educated to the fact that Kierkegaard used these pseudonyms in order to express the different stages' messages subjectively, whereas he in his edifying works published under his true name, because he here speaks in his own name. I do not hold this to be completely true. The edifying works contain the least of Kierkegaard; here he, in faith and good belief, subjects himself almost slavishly to the idea, the message, the gospel. Whenever he says "I" in his own name, it is not he who speaks first, but the message. But the pseudonyms are confessions, the disguise is unveiling, probably the most merciless ever seen. Here he merely speaks on behalf of his own person. He was refined; it is certain that it has drawn enjoyment, that temptation has been involved; but as refined as he may be, he has never been tempted, like Gide, to embrace shrewd, yet barren refinement: to turn his own "I" into a mask. This temptation of which he naturally has been aware, he did not fall for. One of course may claim that the historical source for "Johannes the Seducer" was the aesthetician P.L. Møller, and Realia does show good reasons for this, but it is not decisive, either psychologically or ethically, for the truth about "The Seducer's Diary." The truth is, of course, that Kierkegaard himself was the seducer, whether he seduced a damsel or not. The sting is pointed toward himself, the confession is his own, and it becomes so much the more true and relentless since it is not conveyed by an "I" that carries his own name;

---

[53]   *SKS* 7, 228–73 / *CUP1*, 251–300.

[54]   Hansen, *Kætterbreve*, vol. 1, p. 622 (Letter to Ole Wivel, October 8, 1950).

[55]   Anders Thyrring Andersen, "'Jeg tænker ved at skrive.' Den forførende dialog i Martin A. Hansens *Heretica*-korrespondance," in *PS. Om Martin A. Hansens korrespondance med kredsen omkring Heretica*, ed. by Anders Thyrring Andersen, Copenhagen: Gyldendal 2005, pp. 117–47; p. 131.

if it were, regardless of how wonderful and adamant it is, it would become poetry and universally valid and thereby transformed into something impersonal, regardless of the inherent personal pain. Using a pseudonym, he retains it in the sphere of the personal; it is not a poetical but a moral document; it is an appendix to the characterization of the person and its defects…and it can be said something similar is true of my use of fake "I's"…[56]

Hansen here, in an undetailed manner, assaults an interpretation of Kierkegaard's communication strategy, which only truly finds resonance several years after Hansen's death.[57] As one may note, Hansen opposes both the common and Kierkegaard's own interpretation of the communication relationship. The reality is then decidedly not the way one would want it to appear: that Kierkegaard uses pseudonyms in order to distance himself from the content. In a similar vein, it is not completely true that it is Kierkegaard's own voice that resonates in the texts published under his own name, for example, the edifying discourses. According to Hansen, it is the exact opposite. It is in the pseudonymous works that one senses Kierkegaard most clearly, "the disguise is unveiling." When Kierkegaard writes under his own name he is rather less honest, since he here subordinates himself to the message, the gospel.

The interesting thing in this connection is to notice that Hansen uses this controversial interpretation of Kierkegaard's communication form to say something about his own. When Hansen then uses his fake "I's," it is not to make these responsible for the meaning, but rather because he in the fictive "I's" sees some possibilities to express himself personally. These are possibilities that do not exist in the same way if one orchestrates one's "I" within the frame of fiction. The friend, to whom Hansen refers above, and who recently has compared Hansen to Kierkegaard is Preben Ramløv in the review from *Information*. A few days before Hansen writes to Bjørnvig, he wrote a letter to precisely Ramløv, in which he comments on the latter's interpretation of *The Thorn Bush*. In this connection, Hansen touches upon the comparison with Kierkegaard's form of communication:

It amused me tremendously to read how you have noticed that I here and there have appeared in disguise in the works, and then you thought of the Kierkegaardian illusion tricks. I have often thought that this extremely refined writer, when it comes to form, strangely enough never used the most shrewd disguise of them all, namely to project his own "I" directly within the frames of fiction. Naturally, he played with the thought, but it must be the case that he wanted to be included *himself*, and therefore used fictional characters, because in those you *are*.[58]

If Kierkegaard, like the French writer André Gide (1869–1951), had portrayed his "I" directly within the frames of fiction, he would not have been able to include himself in the same way as when using the fictive pseudonyms, "because in those you *are*."

[56]   Hansen, *Kætterbreve*, vol. 1, pp. 82–83 (Letter to Thorkild Bjørnvig, September 17, 1946).
[57]   Joakim Garff, " '…da er der en, der nikker i Smug nær dig.' Om at fornemme det fremmedes medvirken i teksten—kierkegaardsk kætterbrev," in *PS. Om Martin A. Hansens korrespondance med kredsen omkring Heretica*, ed. by Andersen, pp. 148–64.
[58]   Hansen, *Kætterbreve*, vol. 1, p. 75 (Letter to Preben Ramløv, September 14, 1946).

The problem, as indicated in the letter to Bjørnvig, is that a disguise, à la Gide, would have turned Kierkegaard's texts into poetry and thereby become universally valid, which would have heightened them to something impersonal. According to Hansen, Kierkegaard refrains from doing so because he wants to include himself in the texts. And for this reason, Hansen writes that Kierkegaard's texts are not works of poetry, but rather moral documents. They are an expression of Kierkegaard's personal confessions. What is interesting is that Hansen presupposes that this is a conscious choice made by Kierkegaard, that is, that Kierkegaard consciously, in spite of his own assurances and the commonly accepted interpretations, wanted to express his personal confessions through the pseudonyms.

IV. The Communication of Existence is Fiction

It could here be argued or added that it is precisely in the edifying discourses that Kierkegaard appears within the frames of fiction, disguised as his own "I." In this way, the relationship would be turned upside down. The edifying discourses would be poetry, and the pseudonymous texts that honest and confessing. This, however, would presuppose that one could show that the edifying discourses were to be seen as fictional frames, a path down which neither Hansen nor Kierkegaard goes. However, if one allows oneself to think the two authors' thoughts through, it could very well end up having this consequence.

According to Hansen, his own way of writing reminds him of Kierkegaard's usage of pseudonyms. Just like Kierkegaard, Hansen aspires to write personally, and like Kierkegaard, he is of the opinion that one through imagined "I's" comes closer to the author than if one in a straight manner and under one's own name confesses the truth about oneself. This is ascertained in the diary entry of September 15, 1946:

> More about "The Reader"—and my true reader, the two of which are not actually identical—and "The Author," who as a character is dislocated—so it must be—vis-à-vis his own self.—About how the construct of "I" directly is a particularly refined disguise (not the format here)—but Kierkegaard used disguises, precisely not to hide, but to be able to confess.[59]

This record further suggests why Hansen views the fictive "I's" as more realistic than a straightforwardly expressed "I." Hansen here marks a distinction between "The Reader" and the "True Reader," and between "The Author" and "One's own I." There is a difference between the orchestrated reader and the true reader, just as there is a difference between the orchestrated author and the author's true "I." It is evident that there must be a difference between the character "The Reader" as portrayed in "The Midsummer Party" and the reader who in reality receives the short story. It is also clear that since the author expresses himself within the framework of fiction, one cannot just offhandedly identify the author's text with the author's actual "I." But the distinction that Hansen makes seems to delve deeper than such basic fictional sender–recipient relationship. To Hansen, it appears to be a basic tenet for

---

[59] Hansen, *Dagbøger 1931–1955*, vol. 1, p. 472 ("September 15, 1946").

all existential communication. By expressing ourselves about existence, the actual message is displaced from the message it is conveying. By attempting to convey our understanding of ourselves, the message is displaced from the self it seeks to express. This basic asymmetric relationship between messenger and message makes a straightforward confession impossible.

The essential argument for this interpretation of Hansen's thoughts regarding the possibilities inherent in the existential communication lies in his experiences with the diary genre. Hansen touches upon this in his letter to Bjørnvig: "Or have you experienced the converse, namely, that one writes more personally, more truly, spirited, sincerely, honestly toward oneself, in secret correspondence with oneself in, for example, diaries? This is not my experience. This could be attributed to a flaw in my personality, but it is my experience that a diary is the most shallow one can write."[60] And as an argument for this distrust of the diary, he, later in the letter, writes

> because self-confession is like a race with no finish, it is without goal, without grounds for assessment, it is endless, no matter where you halt, no matter how long you keep on going; confession is unreliable, no matter how "sincere" you are; it continues to be not credible, because it has not ended; it is endless, and at every instant it triggers new psychological mirror images that can be fixated in the infinite. For this reason, confession might as well be called an endless series of disguises that deceive you; confession is but a new mask.[61]

The confession always shirks the actual confessor. It is like the sky that, the moment you embrace it, escapes from your embrace. Confession is an infinite regress. It is meaningless, since you can never capture the actual meaning. It will always be possible to view it from another perspective; it will always already have other possible meanings. Hansen, therefore, ends up concluding that confession, *per se*, is a disguise, a mask. Diary writing, where one otherwise should hope to find an "I," that in the most sincere way confesses to itself, is then, according to Hansen, fiction. It is an orchestration of an "I" that confesses to a fabricated "You."

One does consider why Hansen, in the same letter to Bjørnvig, stresses the letter genre as a more sincere form of expression than the diary.[62] The difference between diary and letter appears to be that one in the letter does not address a fabricated "You," but an actually existing "You," which therefore does not lead to the same infinite regress. It is difficult to fathom why the ideal relation of communication between the letter writer and the recipient, of which Hansen speaks, does not "at every instant" trigger "new psychological mirror images." The letter-writing scenario is not that isolated a phenomenon that it excludes other possible perspectives. It is difficult here to see that it should make a big difference whether the "you" to whom one is writing is fictive or actually existing. Rather, the problem seems to be that the phenomenon about which one wishes to communicate, namely a self, in itself is an infinite relation. It cannot be contained in communication, because once communicated, it has already passed. To use a Kierkegaardian term,

---

[60]   Hansen, *Kætterbreve*, vol. 1, p. 81 (Letter to Thorkild Bjørnvig, September 17, 1946).
[61]   Ibid., p. 84.
[62]   Ibid., p. 81.

it is constantly incipient.[63] If, as Hansen appears to assume, this is the case, any existential communication must be fiction.

For this reason, a confession also becomes more credible if it presents itself as fiction than if it pretends to be able to present itself in a direct "I" form. Using pseudonyms, Kierkegaard, according to Hansen, reflects on the basic problem of existential communication. The reason is that pseudonyms reflect the relation that the "I" does not allow itself to be expressed unequivocally. They speak on behalf of Kierkegaard himself. According to Hansen, Kierkegaard is, through the pseudonyms, viewed from different perspectives, and hereby Kierkegaard approximates an understanding of a relation that cannot be captured, because it is always incipient. But it is precisely because Kierkegaard through the pseudonyms expresses his consciousness regarding his own problem of communication that the confession becomes so much the more honest. One could label this Hansen's interpretation of Kierkegaard's reflections on the double-reflective communication[64] applied to Kierkegaard himself.

If it is in fact the case that the communication which orchestrates "I persons" that speak on behalf of one's own "I" is the most honest, it should necessarily follow, within the framework of Hansen's interpretative horizon, that the message in which one speaks on behalf of oneself in "I" form is less honest. This is why Hansen writes that it is precisely Kierkegaard's edifying writing that contains the least of Kierkegaard. At the same time, Hansen contemplates why Kierkegaard never presented his own "I" within the framework of fiction, and concludes that Kierkegaard refrained from doing so because he wanted to include himself in the text. Had he presented his "I" directly within the framework of fiction, his texts would transform into poetry, and thereby become universally accepted and elevated to the level of the impersonal.

If we try to follow Hansen's train of thought, Kierkegaard's edifying texts, according to Hansen's definitions, must still be defined as poetry. In these texts, Kierkegaard could be said to be in agreement with Hansen's interpretation of setting his "I" within the framework of fiction, in spite of the fact that Hansen wonders why Kierkegaard never uses this means of disguise. It was precisely a consequence of Hansen's diary writing experiences that any existential message would have to be fiction. In line with this, the edifying discourses that attempt to throw light on human existence must be fiction, and Kierkegaard could here be said to present his own "I" within a framework of fiction. The difference between the pseudonymous and edifying texts, then, is not that one is more fictional than the other. Both are fiction, but the pseudonyms merely express a more personal type of fiction and can thereby be seen as a type of confessional literature, while the edifying discourses are an expression of a universally acknowledged, impersonal type of fiction, and therefore constitute poetry.

Hansen's interpretative frame is original, since it on the one hand allows itself to oppose Kierkegaard's own assurances regarding his authorship, and his relation to his pseudonyms. On the other hand, Hansen offers a reading of Kierkegaard, which makes sense with regard to Kierkegaard's statement about both the pseudonymous and the edifying texts. Kierkegaard relinquishes any personal connection to

---

[63]   *SKS* 4, 321 / *CA*, 12–13.
[64]   *SKS* 7, 73–80 / *CUP1*, 72–80.

his pseudonyms,[65] but identifying with the pseudonyms would in fact nullify their sincerity, according to Hansen's interpretation. When Kierkegaard then refrains from identifying with the pseudonyms, it should be seen as a consistent adherence to an extremely personal style of communication. For this, according to Hansen, Kierkegaard must with the same level of consistency maintain his "tricks of illusion."

Furthermore, Kierkegaard acknowledges that in the edifying texts he writes under his own name, since he deals here with universally valid subjects.[66] Within Hansen's framework of interpretation, this could precisely make sense if one viewed the edifying texts as poetry. The edifying texts thereby become part of the illusionary tricks. They are no less fictional than the pseudonymous texts. They are merely an expression of a particular form of fictional message that approximates the lyrical, and therefore is within the realm of universally valid conditions. According to Hansen, the edifying texts hereby are elevated to something impersonal, which is the reason for which Kierkegaard here, without problems, can write under his own "I."

It should be underscored that elements of this interpretation of Kierkegaard's communication strategy are an expression of how Hansen's frame of interpretation could have been taken one step further. The purpose has merely been to elucidate the perspectives in the very original and forward-looking interpretations that undeniably are inherent in the manner in which Hansen applies Kierkegaard within this area. Hansen pre-empts a very current trend in Kierkegaard research that focuses on the rhetorical aspects of Kierkegaard's authorship, as opposed to the epistemological or categorical.[67]

V. Reflection—Simplicity

There is one theme in particular which seems to be instrumental to Hansen's collective application of Kierkegaard.[68] The theme in question concerns Kierkegaard's diagnosis of his time and modern man. Hansen transfers this critique to his time, and indicates—akin to Kierkegaard—that time and modern man suffer from an all-pervasive ailment of reflection. In this section I outline how the critique is expressed in Hansen's thinking and use this analysis as an offset for the remainder of the article.

One day at the beginning of December 1940, Hansen was sitting and reflecting on three new notebooks he had acquired. He was exalted. He loved taking meticulous notes and had to restrain himself from transcribing entire books verbatim. Suddenly, in extension of these reflections, he writes: "Good allusion: I do not lament that

---

[65]   *SKS* 7, 569–73 / *CUP1*, 625–30.

[66]   *SKS* 16, 95 / *PV*, 115.

[67]   See, for instance, Joakim Garff, *"Den Søvnløse": Kierkegaard læst æstetisk/ biografisk*, Copenhagen: C.A. Reitzel 1995.

[68]   Andersen, "Midt i en refleksionstid. Martin A. Hansens dagbøger—kristendom og modernisme," p. 16. Anders Kingo, "Åndsfrændskab. Om ligheder og forskelle i Martin A. Hansens og Søren Kierkegaards tænkning," in *PS. Om Martin A. Hansens korrespondance med kredsen omkring Heretica*, ed. by Andersen, pp. 165–77; p. 169.

the heart is evil, but that it is wretched."[69] The allusion made is to "Diapsalmata"
in *Either/Or* and goes: "Let others complain that the times are evil. I complain that
they are wretched, for they are without passion."[70] There is a direct connection
between Hansen's reflections on his meticulous notes in the notebook and the
allusion to Kierkegaard. Hansen, as one sees, is inflicted with the ailment about
which the aesthete in "Diapsalmata" complains. First, Hansen is guilty of being
hyperconscious about his own self, and secondly of an exaggerated proclivity toward
barren thoughts and ideas. This is precisely what the aesthete complains about as
regards his times. His age is void of passion and overpopulated with "mercenary
souls," who unequivocally live their lives according to reason, perform their duties,
or use argumentation to obtain a placid world-view. According to the aesthete, man
loses himself in thought, just like Hansen loses himself in his reading notes. The
allusion to "Diapsalmata" is later used as a motto for the previously mentioned series
of articles "The Moment" in *People and Freedom*.[71] Hansen, thereby, seems to direct
the aesthete's critique of the times toward his own times, hence implying that the
problem of his contemporaries is that they through reflection reason themselves
away from the actual core of existence. Time and modern man become alien to
themselves through reflection.

Seven years later, we find the following reflection on the liberated modern man:
"Absolute liberation drew all its passion from what was binding. Once it disappears,
passion and meaning disappear. One lingers in dark melancholy but longs for
attachment. Or in one's liberation, one becomes the uttermost boring philistine,
desiccated by the prejudice of open-mindedness."[72] Once again, Hansen uses a
Kierkegaardian category, "the philistine," to characterize his own times. This is a
characteristic, which appears to predate more current theoreticians' analysis of the
spirit of the times,[73] and Hansen points out that modern man's all-pervasive liberation
frees him from having to find an absolute meaning with existence. It is a leveling
of all values that leads to "dark melancholy," despair, or "the prejudice of open-
mindedness." Modern man is left to his own liberated reflection, but in reflection
one distances oneself from oneself. One indulges in senseless melancholy or turns
into a desiccated, matter-of-fact, limited philistine. Freedom, then, concurrently
implies a limitation: prejudice. In a modern age characterized by an all-pervasive
reflection, open-mindedness, any perspective—in a more current wording[74]—must
be an expression of a reduction of the complexity that freedom implies. Hansen,
then, seems to share Kierkegaard's critique of rationalism. A zeitgeist dominated
by reflection, where passion has been put on the backburner in favor of reason, will
additionally be marked by thought's inherent need to reduce complexity. In other

[69]   Hansen, *Dagbøger 1931–1955*, vol. 1, p. 116 ("December 5, 1940").
[70]   *SKS* 2, 36 / *EO1*, 27.
[71]   Andersen and Jørgensen, *Martin A. Hansen—Dagbøger—Noter og registre*, vol. 3,
p. 1016.
[72]   Hansen, *Dagbøger 1931–1955*, vol. 2, p. 528 ("March 22, 1947").
[73]   See, for instance, Thomas Ziehe, *Plädoyer für ungewöhnliches Lernen*, Hamburg:
Rowohlt Taschenbuch Verlag GmbH 1982, pp. 17–105.
[74]   See, for instance, Niklas Luhmann, *Soziale Systeme*, Frankfurt am Main: Suhrkamp
Verlag 1984, p. 94.

words, the time of reflection, modernity, is, according to Hansen, paradoxically a time of narrow-mindedness.

This Kierkegaardian idea may be supported by another Kierkegaard quotation from Hansen's diaries. Here Hansen quotes *Stages on Life's Way*, "Nebuchadnezzar": "For this reason, bigoted earnestness always fears the comic, and rightly so; true earnestness itself invents the comic."[75] It is precisely in this passage from *Stages on Life's Way* that reflection has a tendency to turn into bigotry. The idea can become too earnest for itself, and thereby an object of the comic. As opposed to "bigoted earnestness," the comic contains a duality. What it contains is the notion that a thought is concurrently finite and infinite—free, but actually not free—that the thought, at the instant it is expressed, loses its freedom. Bigoted earnestness, on the other hand, cannot fathom its own limitation. It cannot—again with a more current expression[76]—see the blind spot that accompanies any thought.

This is a recurring figure in Kierkegaard's authorship, which in the essay "Hos 'hine Enkelte' " propels Hansen—at Kierkegaard's gravesite—to say about *The Concept of Anxiety*: "a landmark work, which can explain a current phenomenon such as the insanity of Nazism in more depth than the many books of the day; a handbook for our times' 'existential' philosophers."[77] Nazism is a symptom of the time of reflection, which Hansen feels that he is living in. It is an idea which has taken itself too seriously, and in its need to reduce complexities, has become blind to the conflict which every idea is subject to.

Hansen's approach is just as Kierkegaardian in the science-critical essay "The Belief in Knowledge": "The more difficult access to scientific knowledge is, and the more determined its conflict with the nature of language appears, the more ill-fated becomes the question of general education."[78] The increasing complexity of science does not merely conflict with the nature of language; it concurrently causes a divide between the intelligentsia and the masses, which actually is "an artificial separation, because the irony of the situation is that we in one sense all belong to the intelligentsia, in our capacity as a specialist within a narrow field, and at the same time all belong to the masses, because of our failing insight within almost all other fields."[79] Hansen here paints a picture of a fragmented and complex societal structure, where everyone is a specialist within a narrow field, and an ignoramus within almost all other fields. It is precisely for this reason that there is—according to Hansen—a particular need for general education, in order to qualify the choices that the ultra-specialized modern society consistently demands that individuals make based on an infinite number of possibilities and on relatively limited scientific knowledge.

---

[75]   Hansen, *Dagbøger 1931–1955*, vols. 1–3, vol. 1, p. 436 ("April 8, 1946"). *SKS* 6, 340 / *SLW*, 366.

[76]   See, for example, Luhmann, *Soziale Systeme*, p. 63.

[77]   Martin A. Hansen, "Hos 'Hine Enkelte,' " in *Tanker i en Skorsten*, Copenhagen: Gyldendal 1948, p. 146.

[78]   Martin A. Hansen, "Kundskabstroen," in *Leviathan*, Copenhagen: Gyldendal 1950, p. 83.

[79]   Ibid., p. 89.

Hansen is here ahead of his time in describing late modern society,[80] and since this forward-looking societal analysis has Kierkegaard as its source of inspiration, it is only fair and correct to view Hansen as an important transitional figure with regards to how Kierkegaard will be viewed later on.

The condition in which modern man finds himself, Hansen—with direct reference to Kierkegaard—terms "demonism." In, for example, the short story "September Fog" (1946), Hansen writes about Kierkegaard's *The Concept of Anxiety*:

> The work is not aimed at the masses, but rather to the individual, who by eating of the Tree of Knowledge—for better and worse—has become guilty, and thereby guilty of everything. As we sit here, there are probably but a few elements that we remember clearly from Kierkegaard's writings. But why is it that what we remember the most clearly in the analysis of the demonic is the fear of what is good? Demonism has made its entrance into history—openly and organized.[81]

Demonism describes a condition in which reality to a degree loses its clout and the individual misses out on his actual self, so to speak. Hansen describes demonism as the fear of good, or the fear of what is real, the anxiousness of being who you actually are, to be what you were destined to be. Demonism is the absence of acquisition. According to Hansen, the exaggerated reflection that "has made its entrance into history—openly and organized"[82] is an expression of a fear of truly living; time thereby lacks acquisition, that is, it lacks wanting to do what it is actually destined to do: "We detest the historical figures of demonism, its way of thinking, its morality; but we live in a nesting box, where the demonic may thrive, the fear of the good, the fear of the true, the fear of the real. When the naive dairyman says, what we ourselves are thinking, we turn against him."[83] The exasperating in the demonic is that we acknowledge what the true and good is; perhaps we even detest the demonic, but yet we turn against truth.

It is no coincidence that Hansen uses the image of the naive dairyman, because—fully in the spirit of Kierkegaard—the realization of the true and good is not a scientific task. Rather, it is something that even the most naive dairyman can understand. Hansen, in concordance with Kierkegaard, finds that truth in itself is naive. On February 8, 1941, we find a fragment of a text in Hansen's diary which can shed some light on this naive truth. Here he discusses Høffding's *Philosophy of Religion* and notes: "Once you have read this, go one step further and read G.K.C., one step further and read P. and K., ascend to the top and read the New Testament. You will then realize that the highest is also the simplest."[84] The actual truth lies, according to Hansen, in the New Testament. The entry shows that Hansen criticizes Høffding for committing the error of wanting to realize this truth through

---

[80]   See, for instance, Anthony Giddens, *Modernity and Self-Identity*, Cambridge: Polity Press 1991, pp. 10–35.

[81]   Martin A. Hansen, "Septembertaagen," in *Tornebusken*, Copenhagen Gyldendal 1946, p. 198.

[82]   Ibid.

[83]   Ibid., p. 210.

[84]   Hansen, *Dagbøger 1931–1955*, vol. 1, p. 137 ("February 8, 1941 c").

reason, and thereby is forced to jettison the concept of a personal God. As the most simple and uncomplicated things in the world, the evangelical truth, according to Hansen, cannot be fathomed by the rational mind, and he refers to the English author G.K. Chesterton (1874–1936), G.K.C., who attempts to show that the New Testament, although it cannot be viewed as a direct reproduction of the life of Jesus Christ, still as fictional material has a shocking and miraculous quality to it, and thereby indirectly approaches the truth.[85] Furthermore, Hansen refers to the French philosopher Blaise Pascal (1623–62), P, who attempts to show that truth lies in the deeds of the heart and the will.[86] Finally, Hansen refers to Kierkegaard, K, who is the last step on the way to the highest truth. Kierkegaard's feat is precisely that he wishes to pave the way to the simple truth. Kierkegaard, unlike Høffding, does not wish to apply more reason in order to understand the truth. Rather, Kierkegaard wants to help individuals rid themselves of the reason that prevents them from realizing the simple and immediate truth. This seems to be Kierkegaard's function as it relates to Hansen's voyage toward the simple evangelic truth. In the spirit of Kierkegaard, Hansen—in this time of reflection—wants to use reflection to free the time from reflection and prepare it for the simple truth, which is only to be found in the New Testament. Kierkegaard, for instance, writes in *On My Work as an Author*: "This, in 'Christendom,' is 'Christianly the movement of reflection; one does not reflect oneself into Christianity but reflects oneself out of something else and becomes more and more simple, a Christian."[87]

This is the basic pattern found in Kierkegaard: through reflection to meet oneself in simplicity, to repeat the simplicity of one's childhood in a new way. Hansen expresses this in a letter to the Norwegian author Per Arneberg (1901–81) as follows: "I am without the aptitude of the critic, but a naive reader. With difficulty, I have returned to this state, that is, to the state of a boy's simplicity in reading, following many years of sagacity, analyses, meaninglessness. A literary work that does not pique naiveté, I put away."[88] What, according to Hansen, holds value is the simple, and a literary work must, like the New Testament, be able to awaken this simplicity. Hansen here seems to suggest that where truth directly circumvents reason, it indirectly can be approached and expressed through aesthetic symbolism. I will elaborate on this later in this article, but here it is important to underscore that since the language of symbols speaks to senses and feelings, Hansen's train of thought is on a par with that of the esthete from *Either/Or*, who laments that his times are void of passion. Hansen wishes to awaken passion, since he—just like Kierkegaard—sees truth to be connected to passion.

Through reflection, then, we must return to a simple, passionate truth as it is found in the New Testament. That this indeed is Hansen's train of thought, and that he has it from Kierkegaard, becomes evident from a diary entry from September 20, 1948. Hansen is in the middle of an artistic and personal crisis, and his wife Vera is

---

[85]   Ibid., p. 136.
[86]   Andersen and Jørgensen, *Martin A. Hansen—Dagbøger—Noter og registre*, vol. 3, p. 1022.
[87]   *SKS* 13, 13 / *PV*, 7.
[88]   Hansen, *Kætterbreve*, vol. 1, p. 37 (Letter to Per Arneberg, New Year, 1945–46).

away traveling after prolonged, serious illness. She is the only person with whom he really needs to talk, although he himself did not manage to be there for her, when she needed his care. He feels loathing for his surroundings, the presence of other people is torturous to him, and suddenly he exclaims: "In truth, in front of God, you are in the wrong. In everything."[89] Like another Job, Hansen feels that everything has been taken from him, and it seems appropriate to assume that he here is alluding to the final section "Ultimatum" in *Either/Or*, where the ethicist recounts his old friend's sermon titled "The Upbuilding that lies in the Thought that in Relation to God we are always in the Wrong." Here we are presented with the friend's interpretation of one of the main themes from the Book of Job, and we are told that the edifying, in spite of reason, is the wish to be in the wrong when it comes to God. Even though all reason points to the individual being in the right, such an individual, out of love of God, does not wish for anything but to be in the wrong. The thought that God, the beloved, should be in the wrong, is too painful to him who truly loves God, and thus he only finds edification in the thought that against God, we are always in the wrong. The friend of the ethicist expresses it thus:

> When thought convinced you that this was correct, that it could not be any other way than that you might always be in the wrong or God might always be in the right, then the acknowledgment followed. And you did not arrive at the certainty that you were in the wrong from the acknowledgment that God was in the right, but from love's sole and supreme wish that you might always be in the wrong, you arrived at the acknowledgment that God is always in the right.[90]

I will not delve further into this thought here but merely acknowledge that it is by suspending the rational that the individual reaches an acknowledgement of the true good; it is through love and an intimate wish. This thought appears to be concordant with Hansen's skepticism with regard to the over-reflected time he finds himself to be a part of.

However, it can be debated whether Hansen really finds the thought of always being in the wrong against God edifying. In this connection, Hansen's allusion to the above-mentioned section from *Either/Or* seems rather to be an expression of profound resignation. Hansen's crisis at this time in his life springs from the fact that he has realized that he himself is subject to reflection, and that it is impossible for him to make the perfect transition to simplicity.[91] He cannot honor the stipulation to accept the thought that against God, we are all in the wrong. He is not capable of jettisoning reflection out of sheer love of God, and one senses a bitter irony when Hansen suddenly remembers Kierkegaard's words.

In spite of this, I will suggest that the allusion to Kierkegaard could be a confirmation of a basic Kierkegaardian dialectic in Hansen's thinking between reflection and simplicity. Hansen's bitterness is not directed toward Kierkegaard

[89]   Hansen, *Dagbøger 1931–1955*, vol. 2, p. 674 ("September 20, 1948").

[90]   *SKS* 3, 328 / *EO2*, 349.

[91]   Anders Thyrring Andersen, "Et jeg i flertal. Fiktion og dialektik i Martin A. Hansens Dagbøger," in *Efterskrifter. Omkring Martin A. Hansens dagbøger*, ed. by Anders Thyrring Andersen and Jørgen Jørgensen, Copenhagen: Gyldendal 2001, pp. 118–38, p. 132.

or the content of the edifying sermon, but is rather an expression of Hansen's astonishment that the Kierkegaardian ideal cannot be applied to his own life. To his own surprise, Hansen is not capable of making the ideal transition from reflection to simplicity in his own life, the reason for which he must resign himself. This, however, does not mean that he dismisses the ideal.

VI. The Cessation of Fiction

Based on the foregoing results, one could rather suggest that Hansen is more Kierkegaardian than Kierkegaard himself. As we know, Kierkegaard was very conscious of his own over-reflection, which he frequently, and in various ways, refers to throughout his authorship, for example, in *The Point of View for My Work as an Author*: "I have had no immediacy, and therefore, understood in a purely and simply human sense, I have not lived. I began at once with reflection, did not accumulate a little reflection in later life, but I actually am reflection from first to last."[92] As opposed to Hansen, Kierkegaard did not bring his literary productivity to a halt, which, as it were, had the same dialectical goal. It is as a result of a specific interpretation of Kierkegaard's dialectic that Hansen must resign himself to no longer write fiction. This will be elucidated in this section.

In his dissertation, Bjørnvig writes the following about the connection between Hansen's crisis as an author and Kierkegaard's philosophy:

> Søren Kierkegaard's dissertation on the difference between a genius and an apostle must have affected him deeply; precisely because he acted ethically and Christianly in practice, and because he did not find that artistic gift entitled anyone to assume a special position, he loathed the modern tendency to place art on a pedestal, as if it could replace religion….This deep and hidden tension is, I believe, and as already mentioned in "Kain's Alter," one of the reasons for the hiatus in Martin A. Hansen's artistic production after "The Partridge" and *The Liar*; both were like a final word before an action, an ill-fated word for the true poet; edifying poetry was no escape; Martin A. Hansen knew exactly what art was, and stipulated the highest requirements on his own.[93]

Bjørnvig, then, ascribes to Kierkegaard's distinction between genius and apostle great significance with regard to Hansen's poetical hiatus. We understand that Hansen should have acquired a certain loathing for art through Kierkegaard. While genius possesses a merely transient, quantitative originality, the apostle, according to Kierkegaard, possesses an absolute and therefore qualitative originality. Genius can, through an exceptional intellect, anticipate a natural historical development. The apostle belongs to transcendence, and he can bear messages about what lies beyond a natural development. According to Kierkegaard, this gives the apostle the authority to speak; the genius, however, does not possess this authority.[94] Bjørnvig supports his claim that Hansen finds himself in a period during which he loathes art by referring

---

[92]   *SKS* 16, 61–2 / *PV*, 83.
[93]   Bjørnvig, *Kains Alter. Martin A. Hansens Digtning og Tænkning*, p. 121. Translated by Olav Balslev.
[94]   *SKS* 11, 98 / *WA*, 94.

to *The Sickness unto Death*, in which Kierkegaard writes: "Christianly understood, every poet-existence (aesthetics notwithstanding) is sin, the sin of poetizing instead of being, of relating to the good and true through the imagination instead of being that."[95] Bjørnvig's point is that Hansen, under the influence of this Kierkegaardian way of thinking, felt guilty about his work as a poet. Because of this ethical and Christian approach to life, Hansen cannot live with this guilt and therefore has to stop writing fiction, since doing so prevents him from living in truth. Hansen is not an apostle and therefore does not have the authority to speak.

There are certain elements in Bjørnvig's analysis of Hansen's ceasing to write fiction that appear unsatisfactory. It is difficult to follow the train of thought that Hansen, under the influence of Kierkegaard's dissertation on the relation between a genius and an apostle, should be spurred to stop writing fiction. As supported by Bjørnvig's interpretation, Hansen was, as it were, particularly conscious about his own status as a poet. Whether he dared call himself a genius is uncertain, but that it never occurred to him to call himself an apostle should be clear to everyone. In this sense, Hansen was influenced by Kierkegaard, but this influence probably incited Hansen more to write fiction than not to. Hansen saw, as has been illustrated, some possibilities—through fiction—to express himself in an indirect manner. Hansen does so in a clear Kierkegaardian realization of the fact that he, unlike an apostle, does not hold the authority to preach. Instead, he can preach in an indirect manner, precisely like Kierkegaard.

As we saw earlier, Hansen's ceasing to write fiction should probably rather be explained by the fact that he, in his own life, cannot seem to bring together the dialectic between reflection and simplicity, which he preaches in fiction. This dialectic had been the actual driving force in his authorship of fiction, which ends after the publishing of *The Liar* in 1950. Three years later, Hansen's belief in dialectics is, however, still intact, and it is even stressed as a poetical advantage. In this vein, he writes the following in a letter to the Danish poet Tage Skou-Hansen (b. 1925) on July 22, 1953:

> As far as ambivalence goes, I believe it to be not…adverse for a writer of prose to have some of it. If he has a certain ethical point of view, it most probably does not involve wavering on the actual field of morality—here he will, through his sense of responsibility, take a stand or have a reaction as far as important actions, opinions, stipulations go, and this is of—great—importance with regard to his character and humanity, and thereby naturally for him as an author. But this would be a rarer central element in his discussion of and obligations to fiction as a *poet*. Here, what is significant will often approximate a discussion of the actual ethical categories and the source of ethics; and if he differentiates, consciously or not, between his position as "apostle" or "dialectician" (the differentiation made by Kierkegaard), and if he, like Kierkegaard must see his calling as the latter…then his "ambivalence" is hostile toward neither life nor poetry. But rather is the true state of discussion, which does not prevent his work from, indirectly, being of a strong preaching quality, but does hinder him in making the preaching both conceptual and moral, and under a compulsion for others' choices; he points to the sources, but the individual must choose whether and how to drink.[96]

---

[95]   *SKS* 11, 191 / *SUD*, 77.

[96]   Hansen, *Kætterbreve*, vol. 2, p. 1131 (Letter to Tage Skou-Hansen, July 22, 1953).

According to Hansen, being conscious about one's own position as a dialectician, as opposed to an apostle, does not result in an attitude hostile to poetry. On the contrary, dialectics or ambivalence are productive elements in poetry. Furthermore, we see that the dialectician—completely in the spirit of Kierkegaard—unlike the apostle has the authority to preach imperatively, but only indirectly by giving the individual incentive to make his own choices.

Bjørnvig's analysis of Hansen's decision to stop writing fiction is furthermore unsatisfactory, since he sees it as the result of an ethical and Christian attitude toward life. As we see in Hansen's letter to Skou-Hansen, Hansen draws a clear distinction between a personal, ethical point of view and the work as an author. There is a difference between the duty one feels in one's personal life, and the duty one feels as a poet with regard to fiction. The author's moral stance is not channeled through fiction and does not affect the assessment of what fiction should communicate. Fiction, rather, relates to the realm of the possible in ethics and allows assessments to remain open. When one takes these thoughts into account, there is not much to indicate that Hansen sees anything ethically wrong with being a poet; and in addition he does not at all stipulate that fiction can be an object of ethical assessment. On the contrary, fiction seems to involve an immanent ethics that is connected to the joy of life, and a belief that one through art can incite the individual recipients to think and act independently. One does not sense the guilty conscience and remorse that Hansen, according to Bjørnvig, should be feeling on his own behalf as a writer of fiction, and on behalf of his work as a poet in general, both of which Hansen supposedly inherited from Kierkegaard.

The reason that Hansen's fictional writing grinds to a halt is not ethical; rather, it should probably be sought in his poetological consideration. He is lacking two of the main prerequisites for being able to produce fiction and these seem to be based on an interpretation of Kierkegaard's poetology. First, for Hansen there must be a dialectical spark that ignited the fiction, and secondly, he must be personally present. Furthermore, the two prerequisites appear to be mutually dependent. The dialectics between reflection and simplicity which—until Hansen stops writing fiction—has been the bearing force, balances out as Hansen realizes that dialectics no longer play a role in his personal life. He thereby no longer has the dialectical spark necessary to write fiction, or he is lacking the personal experience on which he can unfold the dialectics. Ideally, however, dialectics are intact in Hansen's conscience, which means that in, for example, letters and essays, he can comment on it directly. In fiction, it cannot just be realized.

VII. Christian Modernism

A long-lived assertion that has been attributed to Hansen is that his fiction authorship was dominated by formal traditionalism. Through numerous comparisons with Kierkegaard, Anders Thyrring Andersen refutes this and places Hansen in a category which he terms "Christian modernism." Andersen illustrates how this Christian modernism expresses itself in fictional accounts such as *Lucky Kristoffer*, "The

Midsummer Party," and *The Liar.* Here, however, I will show that Hansen's diaries, letters, and essays indicate that Hansen also viewed himself as a modernistic pioneer.

In Hansen's letter to his thirteen-year younger colleague Aksel Heltoft (1922–93), we encounter the following assessment of his own position vis-à-vis the new generation of poets:

> Among the generations, you are now the ones guiding, and my relation to you will primarily be that of the apologist and not that of the leader—perhaps a type of forerunner (I flatter myself that "Jonathan's Journey" is a precursor of a different radical symbolism), but not that of a leader—one reason for this being that I do not intend to take symbolism as far as your contemporaries; for this, I am either too wise or too naive. But I am not lacking in understanding of strict, poetical experiments that take the usual metaphors' atomization process further than I could have done myself (by all means, as a style test, stunt, persiflage, I could scribble down some hyper-symbolism and ultra-allegory, which would be more radical than anything seen so far—which is, I assume, the reason that Kierkegaard never wrote those fairy tales, which he claimed to be able to write in such a manner that it would destroy H.C. Andersen as a storyteller).[97]

Hansen, then, sees himself as a forerunner for the younger generation's more radical symbolism, but he refuses to call himself a leader of the young symbolists. He would rather tend to call himself an apologist. An apologist is typically someone who defends Christianity. Hansen, then, sees himself as a modern symbolist who takes seriously the breaking down of old things—"in the usual metaphors' atomization process," but he is not willing to take this discipline as far as the younger poets, precisely because he occupies the position as apologist. As part of the modernistic symbolism, Hansen sees it as his task to defend Christianity. He participates in a modernistic demolition process, but all the while keeping Christianity in view. In this connection it is interesting to note that Hansen compares himself with Kierkegaard. Just as Kierkegaard refrained from surpassing Hans Christian Andersen (1805–75) in the art of writing fairy tales, although he could have, Hansen refrains from surpassing the young generation in symbolism, even though he could have done so. And, according to Hansen, the reason appears to be the same. Both Kierkegaard and Hansen refrain from cultivating the fashionable since they concurrently have Christianity as the goal of their poetry.

It is common knowledge that Kierkegaard criticizes H.C. Andersen in *From the Papers of One Still Living*, but the passage which Hansen refers to here is more probably from Kierkegaard's papers: "Andersen can tell the fairy tale about the galoshes of good fortune—but I can tell the fairy tale about the shoe that pinches, or, more correctly, I could tell it, but because I do not want to tell it but hide it in deep silence I am able to tell something quite different."[98]

There seems to be a parallel between Hansen's poetry and his considerations on reflection. Just as one, in a time of reflection, must reflect one's way through reflection in order to return to Christian simplicity, one must, in modern times, redefine Christianity through modernism. This evokes Kierkegaard, who precisely wanted to address the individual in the situation of modernity: "Christianly, one does not

---

[97]   Hansen, *Kætterbreve*, vol. 1, p. 118 (Letter to Aksel Heltoft, February 28, 1947).

[98]   *SKS* 20, 103, NB:156 / *JP* 5, 5988.

proceed from the simple in order then to become interesting, witty, profound, a poet, a philosopher etc. No, it is just the opposite; *here* one begins and becomes more and more simple, arrives at the simple."[99] One commences in the poetical ways of expression of the era, and then, so to speak, exits through the same way, through poetry, and into Christian simplicity. The content of Christianity is always the same, but the way in which thought expresses itself changes over time. One must keep this paradox in view, when one wants to convey the message of Christianity. It is at any given point in time only possible to communicate through the modes of expressions that belong to a particular zeitgeist. It does not help to return to modes of expressions of earlier times. They are no longer adequate. This also appears to be Hansen's reasoning. He wishes to impact his readers in the particular life situation in which they find themselves, and through an aesthetic language and structure that is in accordance with the times.

In the essay "At the Crossroads," Hansen writes about how it is easier to identify artistic characteristics of eras prior to the one of which you yourself are a part:

> When you read older literature, it is easier to free the poetry from the taste of the time and superficial observations. Today, this is, for instance, easily done with, say, *J.P. Jacobsen*; you strip him of naturalism, and you see that he is Protestant heretic. Like *Ibsen*, like *Pontoppidan*. Protestant rebels. And behind them, you once again see the great, dangerous, lonely—*Søren Kierkegaard*.[100]

First, it is interesting to note that Kierkegaard, according to Hansen, is the building block of J.P. Jacobsen's, Henrik Ibsen's (1828–1906), and Henrik Pontoppidan's (1857–1943) authorships, in spite of the fact that they are quite unlike him in terms of form. It is furthermore interesting that Protestantism apparently—according to Hansen—lies beneath the surface of these three great naturalistic authorships. This seems to confirm Hansen's idea that Christianity manifests itself in very opposing shapes, and that Kierkegaard is the inspiration for this realization. Finally, it is interesting to note that Hansen distances himself from naturalism. According to his account, he belongs to a more recent period, where the artistic expression is different. All this, then, seems to indicate that Hansen, in his own mind, is anything but a traditionalist. To the contrary, it appears to be one of Hansen's literary fundamental ideas that aesthetic expression is and should be constantly renewed, which again seems to be in accordance with basic modernistic tenets.

When Hansen above describes Kierkegaard as "great, dangerous" and "lonely," this can without a doubt be attributed to Kierkegaard's status in Danish literature as the first writer who in earnest insisted on a renewal of form and insisted that the form itself be subjected to reflection. Kierkegaard is dangerous and lonely, since he at all times doubts "the taste of the time and superficial observations." It is perhaps for this reason that Kierkegaard says that he himself writes about "the shoe that pinches," while H.C. Andersen writes about "the galoshes of good fortune."

However, it is not merely in terms of style that Kierkegaard is dangerous; in terms of content he also reflects on suffering, which figuratively speaking is evoked

---

[99]   *SKS* 13, 13 / *PV*, 7.
[100]   Martin A. Hansen, "Ved Korsvejen—4. Anskuelser og Syn," in *Morgenbladet*, February 21, 1946, p. 6.

when "the shoe pinches." This is undoubtedly what Hansen is referring to when he describes Kierkegaard as both dangerous and lonely; suffering in itself is a core idea in Kierkegaard's existential thinking. In this connection, Hansen's own authorship also appears to be under the influence of Kierkegaard, and one senses that he seeks to apply Kierkegaard's thoughts as principles for good poetry.

On March 8, 1948, Hansen writes to Wivel about his contemporaries:

> Is this not perhaps the first generation, the generation that acknowledges the brevity of life, and thereby life—the first generation after a series of them that were the counterfeiters of the future? But preceding this was "the single individuals." Spiraling to the bottom, expectations destroyed, only then can life be experienced in "infinite passion," with fervor, in tragedy and in joy.[101]

The expressions "the single individual" and "infinite passion" are Kierkegaard's. The single individual is, as we know, the reader whom Kierkegaard addresses in his authorship, and Hansen sees that Kierkegaard's thoughts are now breaking through the consciousness of his own generation. An entire generation seems to have received Kierkegaard's message. Hansen implies that his generation, with the help of Kierkegaard, now is positioned favorably to be able to maintain life in "infinite passion."[102] Here he refers to the famous wording about the 70,000 fathoms of water from the *Concluding Unscientific Postscript*, and thereby claims that it is only when the individual has experienced hitting rock-bottom, had his expectations destroyed, that is, felt suffering, that he can gain faith—it is first then that he can embrace life. It appears to be this realization that the generation has come to, and as we saw earlier, that gives Hansen hope that his contemporaries may be rechristened through poetry.

To Hansen, there exists an essential connection between suffering and poetry. A year earlier, he reflects on this in his diary:

> No, I return to the essence of spirit and suffering....Precisely the poet must be suffering. If he sings of joy, he has no authenticity, lest he has been suffering. All that he writes, witnesses, sings about, must have taken its toll, he must have been suffering. To me this is the eye of the needle he must pass through in order to penetrate the poem, sadness, suffering, the battle, the pain, the anxiety. To me, it is the essence of experience that he does not literally have to have experienced everything that he describes (if he were to experience everything, every moment, every nuance in this state of description—and that is something completely different than that he perhaps in experiences *can* feel: here, this was a thorn in my flesh, it stays, it becomes poetry), because regardless of how close the description lies to the experience, it transcends the private; the description then, too, is symbol; yes, something beyond, something universal, a perfection, a creation, which cannot be experienced in advance, just as it in practice cannot be repeated as an experience afterwards; this description is then as close and far from the concrete experience, which it describes, as if he instead of this description had written a drama about Caligula. In both cases, the eye of the needle of the experience leading to the poem was the suffering.[103]

---

[101]   Hansen, *Kætterbreve*, vol. 1, p. 189 (Letter to Ole Wivel, March 8, 1948).

[102]   *SKS* 7, 186 / *CUP1*, 203.

[103]   Hansen, *Dagbøger 1931–1955*, vol. 2, p. 502 ("March 7, 1947").

This section could be seen as Hansen's interpretation of the opening of Kierkegaard's "Diapsalmata" in *Either/Or*: "What is a poet? An unhappy person who conceals profound anguish in his heart but whose lips are so formed that as sighs and cries pass over them they sound like beautiful music."[104] Hansen builds his interpretation on Kierkegaard's own ideas. "A thorn in the flesh" is a direct allusion to the expression which is to be found in several places throughout Kierkegaard's works.[105] Hansen hereby not only elucidates that he views suffering as a prerequisite for writing poetry, but that he also views it as direct evidence that the poet must have found his calling in life. In addition, suffering is what elevates the poem to a level above a mere description of private experiences. Suffering makes the poem universal and gives the poet the ability to empathize; it is indeed the actual inspiration for the poem. As I have shown, Hansen identifies suffering with anxiety. In *The Concept of Anxiety*, Kierkegaard writes:

> Anxiety is freedom's possibility, and only such anxiety is through faith absolutely educative, because it consumes all finite ends and discovers all their deceptiveness. And no Grand Inquisitor has such dreadful torments in readiness as anxiety has, and no secret agent knows as cunningly as anxiety how to attack his suspect in his weakest moment or to make alluring the trap in which he will be caught, and no discerning judge understands how to interrogate and examine the accused as does anxiety, which never lets the accused escape, neither through amusement, nor by noise, nor during work, neither by day nor by night.[106]

It is this stimulation of the imagination—through anxiety—that, according to Hansen, is rendered productive in poetry, and which makes it possible for the poet to embellish reality without getting lost in private experiences. In anxiety, there is no concrete need to have experienced the embellished reality, but in "freedom's possibility," reality can be experienced so that it at once is "as close and as far from the concrete experience." In this manner, the poet, through anxiety, produces symbols that describe realistic experiences, without having to rely on concrete experiences. In anxiety, reality becomes more real, the insignificant more significant, which prompts Kierkegaard to write the following of anxiety: "If it is dismissed because it is merely a trifle, then the anxiety makes this trifle as prominent as the little place Marengo became in the history of Europe, because there the great battle of Marengo was fought."[107]

As we see, according to Hansen, suffering is the actual source of the poem. It is the source of reality. It is only in suffering that the poem gains authenticity. Kierkegaard stipulates that anxiousness in faith is educating. Kierkegaard believes in a connection between anxiety and faith which is akin to the connection between anxiety and poetry we see in Hansen's thinking. This indicates in which direction Hansen wishes to take his poetry. In a Kierkegaardian universe, anxiety only becomes

---

[104]   *SKS* 2, 27 / *EO1*, 19.
[105]   See, for instance, *SKS* 5, 317–34 / *EUD*, 327–46; *SKS* 11, 191–212 / *SUD*, 77–100; *SKS* 16, 50–123 / *PV*, 71–141.
[106]   *SKS* 4, 454 / *CA*, 155.
[107]   *SKS* 4, 459 / *CA*, 161.

authentic the moment it is contained in faith—and, according to Kierkegaard, it is only in faith that anxiety can be contained. If we follow these Kierkegaardian tracks laid out by Hansen, the poetry that springs from suffering only becomes authentic the moment it is contained in faith. With Hansen, then, there is a close connection between poetry and faith. Anxiety is the source of the poem, which is the source of faith. Through the poem, Hansen sees a possibility for inciting faith. As we have already seen, truth, seen through Hansen's optic, is identical with the truth of the gospels. Like Kierkegaard, Hansen sees suffering as the way to this truth, which can only be contained in faith, and which can only be traveled by the single individual. In poetry, Hansen sees an opportunity—through suffering—to encourage his reader, on his own, to learn existential truth.

Even as Hansen among his contemporaries sees a generation that has become conscious of the existential significance of suffering, he, in the essay "At the Crossroads," points out a growing interest in precisely Kierkegaard: "Who is now seen as the brightest star, *Saint-Beuve, Taine, Stuart Mill* or *Kierkegaard*? Kierkegaard, the stranger in the century of positivism, now rises far above all the others."[108] The progress-optimistic positivism has now been replaced by a civilization-critical Kierkegaard, and, in the essay "The Eumenides," Hansen associates the Danish philosopher with other modernistic pioneers of world literature:

> European prophets from Schopenhauer, Dostoevsky to Nietzsche and Baudelaire had augured and contributed to ensure that literature, amidst the utopian dreams of civilization, had bad nightmares. Danish intellectual society was warned early. Between 1843–46 Søren Kierkegaard published the great skeptical works, that are now read as heavyweight commentary of our situation, but which his contemporaries saw as reverie or encryption, to which the code was missing. It is not just a few in this generation who can find the code in the scars on their body....If our great dialectician's ideas could gain topicality, it is only few younger Danish writers whose ideas will be formed through Kierkegaard's influence, or through a rebellion against him, which probably could have made the hesitant acknowledgement more virile.[109]

Although only a few of Hansen's contemporary colleagues were influenced by Kierkegaard, he observes that Kierkegaard was making a quite different impression out in the wide world: "Franz Kafka's view on jurisprudence definitely stemmed from reading Kierkegaard. The flame of the Danish thinker is flaring in young France, we see. It is not a given that things will end with Christianity."[110] It is here clear that Hansen places Kierkegaard in the same category as other thinkers and poets who normally are considered groundbreaking for modernism—Friedrich Nietzsche (1844–1900), Fyodor M. Dostoevsky (1821–81), Charles Baudelaire (1821–67), and Franz Kafka (1883–1924). Since it by now should be firmly established that

---

[108]   Martin A. Hansen, "Ved Korsvejen—3. Poetisk Astrologi," in *Morgenbladet*, February 14, 1946, p. 6.
[109]   Martin A. Hansen, "Eumeniderne," in *Tanker i en Skorsten*, Copenhagen: Gyldendal 1948, p. 179.
[110]   Martin A. Hansen, "Ved Korsvejen—4. Anskuelser og Syn," in *Morgenbladet*, February 21, 1946, p. 6.

Hansen consciously applies Kierkegaard, such comments should serve as adequate evidence that Hansen, in his self-understanding, belongs to this group of modernist pioneers, which again can serve as a confirmation of the thesis that Hansen should be seen as one of Danish literature's groundbreaking modernists.

There is not much to indicate that Hansen, in his own mind, is a traditionalist or daydreams about days of old. On the contrary, he sees himself as a part of a new international movement that breaks with the simplified optimism of positivism on behalf of science, and instead looks ahead toward a more complex and nuanced world-view. Kierkegaard is one among few who, according to Hansen, has been able to foresee this development, but who, to his contemporaries, has been too forward-looking, and thereby too complicated to understand. With regard to Hansen's contemporaries, Kierkegaard's criticism has become "exciting and topical," and has won followers among the young French existentialists. Hansen, however, laments that Kierkegaard's influence is not as strong on Hansen's contemporary compatriots. As noted, Kierkegaard could have made Danish post-war poetry more virile. The core of this thought can be found in Hansen's assessment of Kierkegaard's newly-won popularity in France: "It is not a given that things will end up with Christianity." Because of Kierkegaard, French modernism is placed within a Christian interpretative framework, which, according to Hansen, makes it more virile. As mentioned, it is not a given that everything will end with Christianity, but even a rebellion against Kierkegaard would have been fruitful for Danish poetry. It lies implicit in Hansen's sentence that it is not a given, but probably desirable, that things end up with Christianity, which brings us to Hansen's place in Danish literature as a Christian modernist.

On September 12, 1947, Hansen was invited to tea at his author colleague Ole Sarvig's home (1921–81). In the gathering were a number of other Danish authors and one Swedish literature critic. One senses that the debate zeroed in on modernism, and Hansen's position in this connection as a destroyer of symbols. To Hansen's satisfaction, this discussion led to a consensus among some of the participants with regard to a remarkable viewpoint, namely that "the consequence of modernism is Christianity."[111] Hansen, however, lamented that some of those present at the gathering still had the opposing, and in his opinion, more traditional point of view.

It is controversial to unite what appears to be two incompatible elements: Christianity, that entails faith, and modernism, which is identical to doubt and division. Nevertheless, Hansen sees this as feasible, and it is for this reason that he, in his own optic, emerges as the innovator, while the others remain traditionalists.

Hansen's optic is Kierkegaardian, and it is precisely the way that Hansen applies Kierkegaard that lends meaning to the innovative statement that "the consequence of modernism is Christianity." Through the concepts of reflection and suffering, Hansen sees a union of modernism and Christianity in Kierkegaard. Among his contemporaries, Hansen sees a very advanced ailment manifest itself— reflection and despair. Objective wisdom has disintegrated from within through reflection—positivism is dead. An entire generation, an entire era in history, is

---

[111]   Hansen, *Dagbøger 1931–1955*, vol. 2, p. 582 ("September 13, 1947").

fighting in 70,000 fathoms of water; in other words, they are at the place, which according to Kierkegaard, is the actual prerequisite to enter Christianity through faith. The Passion of the modernist is so to speak contained in the Passion of the Gospels. Modernism and Christianity are therefore not incompatible, but rather prerequisites for each other's existence. The consequence of modernism is therefore Christianity.

Here it is important to underscore that it is not modernism as a collective movement that must outshine Christianity. In Kierkegaard's spirit, it is still the single individual who must attain this alone. In a setting of modernism, the single individual is, according to Hansen, particularly well equipped to leap into Christianity. For Hansen, the path definitely does not lead back to more comfortable conditions of earlier times. The path is forward, through suffering, through the reflection of modernism, and this path must be traveled by the individual alone.

On the other hand, when the single individual has made it through the suffering of modernity, there perhaps lies Christian culture waiting, in which these individuals can be united. Thereafter, Hansen predicts that Grundtvig will possibly become a man of the future, once individualized modernism has been experienced. He writes in the essay "The Belief in Knowledge":

> The path of personality is as strictly laid out with Grundtvig as with Kierkegaard. But with Grundtvig, you sense that this path is not that of individualism, but rather its opposite. With Grundtvig, the personal element cannot blossom, without it immediately transferring its seed and uniting with the personal in others. Grundtvig appears as the innovator after the three others, Luther, Kant, Kierkegaard. The latter is the Protestant accomplisher. Grundtvig represents something in a state of becoming; he transcends Protestantism, and in his world, a culture appears to be in the making.[112]

Kierkegaard is the accomplisher of Protestantism, while Grundtvig belongs to the future. In the age of modernity, which is dominated by reflection and individualism, Grundtvig's folk movement makes no sense.[113] In the age of modernity, it is not possible to establish Christian communities or Christian culture. The individual must pass through his own reflection in order to arrive at faith. He must pass through the atomization process of modernism.

Hansen lived during the era of modernism, which was the reason that it was in Kierkegaard that he found the explanations of the problems of his times. In this connection, Grundtvig could not help. Kierkegaard was Hansen's life-long source of inspiration and basis for interpretation. But where Hansen, led by Kierkegaard, predicts that the consequence of modernism is Christianity, he here, cautiously, appears to suggest that the Christianity to come might be that of Grundtvig, and thus Hansen at the same time, and in an original manner, manages to unite two traditionally opposing individuals in the history of Danish intellectual life.

---

[112]   Hansen, "Kundskabstroen," pp. 90–1.
[113]   Andersen, "Midt i en refleksionstid. Martin A. Hansens dagbøger—kristendom og modernisme," p. 18.

VIII. Conclusion

I began this article by establishing that Kierkegaard, beyond a shadow of a doubt, is a central source of inspiration in Hansen's authorship. This supposition, I hope, has been confirmed in the article, in which Hansen's own conscious and explicit affinity for Kierkegaard's philosophy is elucidated through letters, articles, and essays. Some may be left with the impression that the extent of influence that Kierkegaard had on Hansen was so exhaustive that this article only touches upon the material. Hansen's combination of Kierkegaard and Grundtvig, for instance, appears to contain enough material for an entire dissertation. The same holds true for the importance that Kierkegaard ascribes to the relation between concepts such as individualism vs. personality, remembrance vs. memory, tradition vs. modernity, and aesthetics vs. ethics in Hansen's work. In this article I have attempted to elucidate the elements that I see as the fundamental inspiration from Kierkegaard.

In the Kierkegaardian dialectic between reflection and simplicity, Hansen finds a useful tool for describing the reflection ailment that he finds prevalent among his contemporaries. Furthermore, Kierkegaard's dialectics becomes a portal for Hansen, through which he can reflect on more specific psychological phenomena such as anxiety, demonism, and despair, and thereby attempt to describe a correlation between individual psychological conditions, and more general societal and historical contours. Hansen's psychology, inspired by Kierkegaard, furthermore becomes one of the main pillars in his poetological deliberations.

To Hansen there is an underlying fundamental issue which is relevant for anyone wishing to discourse on existence. It cannot be expressed directly in language. Hansen does, in fact, explicitly concur with Kierkegaard's indirect communication strategy. The text must, to both Hansen and Kierkegaard, reflect on its own inherent inability to communicate. Furthermore, the expressive possibilities of the text continue to change over time, while the existential message that one seeks to convey remains the same. This means that the existential message must always be expressed through the means that are available at any given point in time.

To both Hansen and Kierkegaard, the existential content is, deep down, identical to Christianity, which in Hansen's interpretation of Kierkegaard has as its main tenet, through reflection, to work a way through reflection toward faith. This story must, according to Hansen, be narrated in the language of modernity, since we find ourselves in the situation of modernity. For this reason, Hansen sees no discrepancy between modernism and Christianity. Quite to the contrary, the language must reinvent itself, in accordance with the spirit of modernism, in order, again and again, to narrate the same existential content, which can never actually be defined with an adequate expression. Hansen's authorship should therefore be seen as a progressive development of a Christian modernism, which in Danish literature has been spearheaded by Kierkegaard.

In the essay "Hos 'hine Enkelte,' " Hansen wanders around Assistens Cemetery in Copenhagen, in order to inspect grave sites belonging to great personalities from the Danish Golden Age. His wanderings end at Kierkegaard's grave, and the essay concludes:

It is raining at Assistens. Now and again, the moisture captures a pallid leaf; it swirls straight down. A dark leaf has stuck to the stone, on which, in an old and simple style, Søren Aabye Kierkegaard's name stands beneath those of his two siblings, Søren Michael and Maren Kristine, who died early. Adjacent stands the stone with the parents' names. At the top, the fancier stone with the hawker's first wife, who had such a short life, had no children, had no happiness. The great thinker's self-chosen, modest place among the others, with the others, lends a warmer interpretation to his life's work about "that single individual."[114]

Through Hansen's authorship, Kierkegaard's life's work has been given a warmer interpretation. His focus is on constructive aspects of Kierkegaard's philosophy, rather than strict Christian dogmatism. To Hansen, Kierkegaard does not represent the inhuman Christian viewpoint of earlier times. On the contrary, Hansen views Kierkegaard as a forward-looking philosopher, whose thoughts contain deep human and social perspectives. With his fruitful readings, Hansen can be said to be an important transitional figure with regard to how Kierkegaard is viewed in a more complex, late modern context.

---

[114]   Hansen, "Hos 'Hine Enkelte,'" p. 147.

Bibliography

I. References to or Uses of Kierkegaard in Hansen's Corpus

Lykkelige Kristoffer, Copenhagen: Gyldendal 1945.
"Septembertaagen," in *Tornebusken*, Copenhagen: Gyldendal 1946, pp. 193–229, see p. 198; p. 210.
"Ved Korsvejen—1. Paa jagt efter en Opfattelse," in *Morgenbladet*, February 5, 1946, pp. 5–6 (reprinted in *Ved Korsvejen*, Copenhagen: Gyldendal 1968, pp. 7–33, see p. 11; p. 18; p. 21; p. 27).
"Ved Korsvejen—2. Kritik og Digtning," in *Morgenbladet*, February 8, 1946, pp. 5–6 (reprinted in *Ved Korsvejen*, Copenhagen: Gyldendal 1968, pp. 7–33, see p. 11; p. 18; p. 21; p. 27).
"Ved Korsvejen—3. Poetisk Astrologi," in *Morgenbladet*, February 14, 1946, pp. 5–6 (reprinted in *Ved Korsvejen*, Copenhagen: Gyldendal 1968, pp. 7–33, see p. 11; p. 18; p. 21; p. 27).
"Ved Korsvejen—4. Anskuelser og Syn," in *Morgenbladet*, February 21, 1946, pp. 5–6 (reprinted in *Ved Korsvejen*, Copenhagen: Gyldendal 1968, pp. 7–33, see p. 11; p. 18; p. 21; p. 27).
"Ved Korsvejen—5. Regeneration," in *Morgenbladet*, March 2, 1946, pp. 5–6 (Reprinted in *Ved Korsvejen*, Copenhagen: Gyldendal 1968, pp. 7–33, see p. 11; p. 18; p. 21; p. 27).
"Eumeniderne," in *Tanker i en Skorsten*, Copenhagen: Gyldendal 1948, pp. 178–207, see p. 179; p. 182.
"Hos 'Hine Enkelte,' " in *Tanker i en Skorsten*, Copenhagen: Gyldendal 1948, pp. 140–7, see p. 140; p. 141; pp. 145–7.
"Kundskabstroen," in *Leviathan*, Copenhagen: Gyldendal 1950, pp. 81–91, see p. 81; p. 83; p. 89; pp. 90–1.
Leviathan, Copenhagen: Gyldendal 1950.
Løgneren, Copenhagen: Gyldendal 1950.
Orm og Tyr, Copenhagen: Gyldendal 1952.
"En samtale med Martin A. Hansen," interview with Sverre Riisøen in *Aarhuus Stiftstidende*, June 4, 1954, pp. 11–2.
Dagbøger 1931–1955, vols. 1–3, ed. by Anders Thyrring Andersen og Jørgen Jørgensen, Copenhagen: Gyldendal 1999, vol. 1, p. 60 ("Taler July, 1939"); vol. 1, p. 84 ("March 7, 1940 b"); vol. 1, p. 116 ("December 5, 1940"); vol. 1, p. 134 ("February 8, 1941 a"); vol. 1, p. 137 ("February 8, 1941 c"); vol. 1, p. 154 ("April 2, 1941"); vol. 1, p. 168 ("August 5, 1941"); vol. 1, p. 202 ("January Friday 16, 1942"); vol. 1, p. 213 ("January 31, 1942 b"); vol. 1, p. 246 ("June 19, 1942"); vol. 1, p. 387 ("September 4, 1945"); vol. 1, p. 396 ("September 19,

1945 b"); vol. 1, p. 400 ("October 4, 1945"); vol. 1, p. 421 ("January 30, 1946");
vol. 1, p. 421 ("February 2, 1946"); vol. 1, p. 421 ("February 3, 1946"); vol. 1,
p. 433 ("April 2, 1946"); vol. 1, p. 436 ("April 8, 1946"); vol. 1, p. 463 ("August
11, 1946"); vol. 1, p. 466 ("August 28, not., 1946"); vol. 1, p. 468 ("September 2,
1946"); vol. 1, p. 471 ("September 13, 1946"); vol. 1, p. 472 ("September 15,
1946"); vol. 1, p. 475 ("October 10, 1946"); vol. 1, p. 479 ("November 14–15,
1946"); vol. 2, p. 479 ("February 28, 1947"); vol. 2, p. 502 ("March 7, 1947");
vol. 2, p. 506 ("March 10, 1947 b"); vol. 2, p. 528 ("March 22, 1947"); vol. 2,
p. 540 ("March 23, 1947"); vol. 2, p. 580 ("September 1, 1947"); vol. 2, p. 600
("January 17, 1948"); vol. 2, p. 618 ("May 4, 1948"); vol. 2, p. 648 ("June 30,
1948"); vol. 2, p. 658 ("July 19, 1948"); vol. 2, p. 666 ("August 8, 1948 a");
vol. 2, p. 674 ("September 20, 1948"); vol. 2, p. 677 ("October 16, 1948");
vol. 2, p. 678 ("October 26, 1948"); vol. 2, p. 679 ("November 5, 1948");
vol. 2, p. 704 ("January 24, 1949"); vol. 2, p. 839 ("May 31, 1955"); vol. 2,
p. 843 ("May 31, 1955"); vol. 2, p. 850 ("June 1, 1955"); vol. 2, p. 864 ("June 2–3,
1955").

Kætterbreve. Martin A. Hansens korrespondance med kredsen omkring Heretica,
vols. 1–3, ed. by Anders Thyrring Andersen, Copenhagen: Gyldendal 2004,
vol. 1, p. 37 (Letter to Per Arneberg, New Year, 1945–46); vol. 1, p. 62 (Letter
to Aksel Heltoft, August 5, 1946); vol. 1, p. 70 (Letter to Preben Ramløv,
September 14, 1946); vol. 1, p. 72 (Letter to Preben Ramløv, September 14,
1946); vol. 1, p. 75 (Letter to Preben Ramløv, September 14, 1946); vol. 1,
pp. 82–3 (Letter to Thorkild Bjørnvig, September 17, 1946); vol. 1, p. 85 (Letter to
Thorkild Bjørnvig, September 17, 1946); vol. 1, p. 99 (Letter to Anne-Marie and
Preben Ramløv, December 31, 1946); vol. 1, p. 106 (Letter to Bente Hammerich,
February 3, 1947); vol. 1, p. 118 (Letter to Aksel Heltoft, February 28, 1947);
vol. 1, p. 130 (Letter to Thorkild Bjørnvig, March 9, 1947); vol. 1, p. 146 (Letter
to Thorkild Bjørnvig, June 27, 1947); vol. 1, p. 160 (Letter to Bjørn Poulsen,
November 29, 1947); vol. 1, p. 180 (Letter to Thorkild Bjørnvig January 18,
1948); vol. 1, p. 189 (Letter to Ole Wivel, March 8, 1948); vol. 1, p. 194 (Letter
to Aksel Heltoft, April 4, 1948); vol. 1, p. 212 (Letter to Bente Hammerich,
August 13, 1948); vol. 1, p. 228 (Letter to Preben Ramløv, November 2–3,
1948); vol. 1, p. 249 (Letter to Ole Wivel, March 2, 1949); vol. 1, p. 318 (Letter
to Ole Wivel, September 19, 1949); vol. 1, p. 352 (Letter to Thorkild Bjørnvig,
Bjørn Poulsen, Ole Wivel, and Knud W. Jensen, December 21, 1949); vol. 1,
p. 422 (Letter to Martin A. Hansen from Paul Diderichsen, March 3, 1950);
vol. 1, p. 434 (Letter to Johannes Hohlenberg, March 13, 1950); vol. 1, p. 448
(Letter to Martin A. Hansen from Tom Kristensen, March 21, 1950); vol. 1,
p. 468 (unsent letter to Bente and Aksel Heltoft, April 4, 1950); vol. 1, p. 515
(Letter to Martin A. Hansen from Ole Wivel, June 13, 1950); vol. 1, p. 516 (Letter
to Martin A. Hansen from Ole Wivel, June 13, 1950); . vol. 1, p. 522 (Letter to
Martin A. Hansen from Torben Dijnes, June 16, 1950); vol. 1, p. 565 (Letter to
Martin A. Hansen from Ole Wivel, August 18, 1950); vol. 1, p. 594 (Letter to Ole
Wivel, September 14, 1950); vol. 1, p. 606 (Letter to Ole Wivel, September 27,
1950); vol. 1, p. 621 (Letter to Ole Wivel, October 8, 1950); vol. 1, p. 622 (Letter
to Ole Wivel, October 8, 1950); vol. 1, p. 628 (Letter to Alex Garff, October 9,

1950); vol. 2, p. 669 (Letter to Knud W. Jensen, November 2, 1950); vol. 2, p. 674 (Letter to Knud W. Jensen, November 2, 1950); vol. 2, p. 699 (Letter to A. M. Jørgensen, November 23, 1950); vol. 2, p. 762 (Letter to Thorkild Bjørnvig, January 23, 1951); vol. 2, p. 858 (Letter to Martin A. Hansen from Thorkild Bjørnvig, July 30, 1951); vol. 2, p. 936 (Letter to Heinrich Fauteck, April 19, 1952); vol. 2, p. 1005 (Letter to Knud W. Jensen, November 17, 1952); vol. 2, p. 1091 (Letter to Thorkild Bjørnvig, April 30, 1953); vol. 2, p. 1095 (Letter to Martin A. Hansen from Thorkild Bjørnvig, May 7, 1953); vol. 2, p. 1127 (Letter to Martin A. Hansen from Johannes Kirkegaard, July 10, 1953); vol. 2, p. 1131 (Letter to Tage Skou-Hansen, July 22, 1953); vol. 2, p. 1214 (Letter to Knud W. Jensen, June 25–July 1, 1954); vol. 2, p. 1258 (Letter to Ole Wivel, February 3, 1955).

II. Sources of Hansen's Knowledge of Kierkegaard

Billeskov Jansen, F.J., *Studier i Kierkegaards litterære Kunst*, Copenhagen: Rosenkilde og Bagger 1951.

Brandes, Georg, *Søren Kierkegaard. En kritisk Fremstilling i Grundrids*, Copenhagen: Gyldendal 1877.

Grønbech, Vilhelm, *Kampen om Mennesket*, Copenhagen: Jespersen og Pios Forlag 1930.

Hansen, Knud, *Søren Kierkegaard, ideens digter*, Copenhagen: Gyldendal 1954.

Henriksen, Aage, *Kierkegaards Romaner*, Copenhagen: Gyldendal 1954.

Høffding, Harald, *Søren Kierkegaard som Filosof*, Copenhagen: Det Danske Forlag 1892.

— *Religionsfilosofi*, Copenhagen: Gyldendal 1901.

— *Danske Filosofer*, Copenhagen: Gyldendal 1909.

— *Pascal og Kierkegaard*, Copenhagen: "Tilskueren" 1923.

Hohlenberg, Johannes, *Søren Kierkegaard*, Copenhagen: Aschehoug 1940.

Pedersen, Olaf, *Fra Kierkegaard til Sartre*, Copenhagen: Arne Frost-Hansens Forlag 1947.

III. Secondary Literature on Hansen's Relation to Kierkegaard

Andersen, Anders Thyrring, "Midt i en refleksionstid. Martin A. Hansens dagbøger—kristendom og modernisme," *Kritik*, vol. 118, 1995, pp. 13–23.

— "Afbrudt af en vis stor Georg—Martin A. Hansens opgør med 'det moderne gennembrud,' " in *Kritik*, vol. 135, 1998, pp. 24–34.

— "Den redigerede eksistens—i anledning af udgivelsen af Martin A. Hansens Dagbøger," in *Spring—tidsskrift for moderne dansk litteratur*, vol. 15, 1999, pp. 135–46.

— "Forførelse, Tavshed Og Uret—Kierkegaard-inspirationen i Martin A. Hansens *Løgneren*," in *Spring—tidsskrift for moderne dansk litteratur*, vol. 14, 1999, pp. 186–211.

— "Et jeg i flertal. Fiktion og dialektik i Martin A. Hansens Dagbøger," in *Efterskrifter. Omkring Martin A. Hansens dagbøger*, ed. by Anders Thyrring Andersen og Jørgen Jørgensen, Copenhagen: Gyldendal 2001, pp. 118–38.

— "'Jeg tænker ved at skrive.' Den forførende dialog i Martin A. Hansens *Heretica*-korrespondance," in *PS. Om Martin A. Hansens korrespondance med kredsen omkring Heretica*, ed. by Anders Thyrring Andersen, Copenhagen: Gyldendal 2005, pp. 117–47.

— "'Som forførere og dog sanddru.' Strategisk skrift hos Martin A. Hansen og Søren Kierkegaard," in *Sprog og forførelse. Om sandhed og løgn i religion og politik, litteratur og filosofi*, ed. by Povl Götke, Copenhagen: Forlaget Alfa 2008, pp. 31–52.

Bjørnvig, Thorkild, *Kains Alter. Martin A. Hansens Digtning og Tænkning*, Copenhagen: Gyldendal 1964, p. 105; p. 108; p. 117; p. 121; p. 137; p. 139; pp. 144–5; p. 211; p. 220; p. 270; p. 279; pp. 287–8; pp. 325–30; p. 398; p. 525; p. 529; p. 531; p. 536; p. 538; p. 547; pp. 584–5.

Bredsdorff, Thomas, *Dansk litteratur set fra månen. Om sjælen i digtningen*, Copenhagen: Gyldendal 2006, pp. 217–33.

Bukdahl, Jørgen K., "Martin A. Hansen og Grundtvig," in *Vartovbogen*, 1965, pp. 96–117.

— "Martin A. Hansen som 'genoptager af de gamles eksistenstænkning.' Om Thorkild Bjørnvigs disputats," in *Vindrosen*, vol. 3, 1965, pp. 47–59.

— "'Kains Alter' krisen—en refleksionskrise," in *Højskolebladet*, vol. 27, 1968, pp. 444–6.

Dahl, Per, *Thorkild Bjørnvigs tænkning*, Copenhagen: Gyldendal 1976, pp. 63–80.

Denman, Henrik, *Martin A. Hansen litteraturen*, Roskilde: Denmans Forlag 1990, p. 242.

Garff, Joakim, " '...da er der en, der nikker i Smug nær dig.' Om at fornemme det fremmedes medvirken i teksten—kierkegaardsk kætterbrev," in *PS. Om Martin A. Hansens korrespondance med kredsen omkring Heretica*, ed. by Anders Thyrring Andersen, Copenhagen: Gyldendal 2005, pp. 148–64.

Kingo, Anders, "Åndsfrændskab. Om ligheder og forskelle i Martin A. Hansens og Søren Kierkegaards tænkning," in *PS. Om Martin A. Hansens korrespondance med kredsen omkring Heretica*, ed. by Anders Thyrring Andersen, Copenhagen: Gyldendal 2005, pp. 165–77.

Mikkelsen, Hans Vium, "Martin A. Hansen som dialektisk teolog. Eller: Martin A. Hansen mellem Kierkegaard og Løgstrup," in *PS. Om Martin A. Hansens korrespondance med kredsen omkring Heretica*, ed. by Anders Thyrring Andersen, Copenhagen: Gyldendal 2005, pp. 178–98.

Svendsen, Erik, "Løgneren bind II-II," in *Efterskrifter. Omkring Martin A. Hansens dagbøger*, ed. by Anders Thyrring Andersen og Jørgen Jørgensen, Copenhagen: Gyldendal 2001, pp. 103–17.

Toftdahl, Helmut, *Kierkegaard først—og Grundtvig så*, Copenhagen: Arnold Busck 1969, pp. 183–90.

Jens Peter Jacobsen:

Denmark's Greatest Atheist

William Banks

Of all Danish authors of the generation following the death of Søren Kierkegaard, it is perhaps difficult to imagine a single figure *less* likely to have been significantly impacted by him than Jens Peter Jacobsen (1847–85). It is indeed true that the group of writers that the critic Georg Brandes would identify as the "Men of the Modern Breakthrough," which included the Norwegians Henrik Ibsen and Bjørnstjerne Bjørnsen as well as Danes such as Holger Drachmann and Jacobsen, made much of their status as having emerged from a virtual literary and ideological vacuum. In an essay written shortly before the "official" launching of the Breakthrough in 1871, Brandes had stressed this sense of absolute rupture, declaring that the literary epoch later termed the Danish Golden Age, that period which had produced Adam Oehlenschläger and Johan Ludvig Heiberg as well as Kierkegaard, was in effect "completed" and could no longer provide effective models for the emerging group of young writers.[1] The degree of truth in this sense of a complete break with the past remains to us, of course, subject to debate. Even Ibsen, as famously averse to the acknowledgment of influence as he was, began his cycle of world-historical plays with *Brand* (1866),[2] which by any reasonable accounting constitutes at the very least a serious entertainment of Kierkegaardian themes, in particular the power (and the peril) of religious passion. Bjørnson's less memorable response to Ibsen,

---

[1]   Writing in the November 21, 1869 issue of *Illustreret Tidende*, Brandes remarks that "there is and has already been a pause in Denmark's poetic production. A literary period lies behind us completed." Review of Vilhelm Bergsøe's novel *Fra den gamle Fabrik, Illustreret Tidende*, no. 530, p. 66. All translations from the Danish are my own unless otherwise noted.

[2]   Harold Bloom has famously noted that Ibsen "loathed influence more perhaps than anyone else," thus ensuring that future discussions of the ultimate sources of his work would be limited to speculation. *The Anxiety of Influence: A Theory of Poetry*, 2nd ed., New York: Oxford 1997, p. xxiv. That Kierkegaard's retelling of the Abraham atop Moriah story in *Fear and Trembling* served at the very least as partial inspiration for *Brand*, however, is largely irrefutable, for the central ethical conflict of the play—a fanatical rural pastor faces the impossible choice between sacrificing the needs of his flock and those of his stricken infant son—simply bears too many resemblances to that of the tale of Abraham and Isaac. Henrik Ibsen, *Brand. Et dramatisk digt*, Copenhagen: Gyldendalske Boghandel 1866.

Beyond Our Power (1883),[3] constitutes no less a direct engagement with the Danish philosopher and theologian, albeit a categorical rejection of Kierkegaard's perceived weaknesses.

With respect to the relation between Kierkegaard and Jacobsen, however, matters are much more muddled. No more than a handful of passing references may be located in the author's correspondence, and no poem, short story or novel within Jacobsen's *oeuvre* may decisively be said to bear a Kierkegaardian imprint. This dearth of direct references is further complicated but what amounts to a seemingly irremediable ideological standoff between the two writers. If we are to take the Kierkegaard of *The Point of View* and of the late polemics at his word, if we are to concede that the life of the author represents one long effort at that to which he once referred, in a moment of feigned disbelief, as "a project that amounts to neither more nor less than wanting to introduce Christianity again— into Christendom,"[4] then indeed it does appear all but inconceivable to identify any measure of common ground with a figure such as Jacobsen, accomplished man of science and committed materialist, translator, and popularizer of Darwin, unrepentant and unapologetic atheist. Over and against Kierkegaard's long effort at Christian intervention, we are faced with a personality who, according to Edvard Brandes' moving eulogy, "struggled all his life in science and literary writing for one idea: the idea of proud godlessness, the pure irreligosity, the atheism that removes all reservations."[5] If Kierkegaard stood for the renewal of the hollowed-out shell of Christendom through the reinsertion of authentic and substantial Christianity, then it seems that Jacobsen with no less fervor sought human renewal in precisely the *opposite*, in looking forward to a new horizon of possibility opened up by the death of God.

Born into a middle-class merchant family in the northwestern Jutland town of Thisted in 1847, Jens Peter Jacobsen appears to have enjoyed a relatively carefree youth marked until at least his early twenties by an abundance of possibilities. Much like Kierkegaard, the young student experienced no small measure of uncertainty over his future career path. An 1867 self-portrait recalls to a striking degree Kierkegaard's famous 1835 letter to Peter Wilhelm Lund: "I am a man with too many intellectual inclinations. I should like to study botany, arts, the history of art, mythology, and very likely much more."[6] In the end Jens Peter would settle

---

[3]		Bjørnstjerne Bjørnson's rather didactic *Over Ævne*, Copenhagen: Gyldendal 1883, sets up a situation similar to that in Brand, but with the opposite results; for example, secular ethics win out over religious passion.

[4]		*SKS* 16, 24 / *PV*, 42.

[5]		*Breve fra J.P. Jacobsen*, ed. by Edvard Brandes, Copenhagen: Gyldendal 1925, p. LVIII. English translation by Habib C. Malik, *Receiving Søren Kierkegaard: The Early Impact and Transmission of His Thought*, Washington, DC: Catholic University of America Press 1997, p. 298.

[6]		The prose sketch entitled "I" appears in Jens Peter Jacobsen, *Samlede Værker*, vols. 1–6, ed. by Frederik Nielsen, Copenhagen: Rosenkilde og Bagger 1972–74, vol. 3, p. 140. The English translation is taken from Niels Lyhne Jensen, *Jens Peter Jacobsen*, Boston: Twayne (*Twayne World Authors Series*, vol. 573) 1980, p. 19. Compare Kierkegaard's June 1, 1835 confession that he is "interested in far too many things rather than definitely in any

on a course of study in botany, his dissertation on Danish algae earning him a gold medal in 1873. Jacobsen's biological studies would, significantly, bring him into contact with Darwinism, on which he would make his authorial debut with a series of articles from 1871 in the journal *Nyt dansk Maanedsskrift*. In addition to serving as the Danish equivalent to Thomas Henry Huxley, Jacobsen would go on to publish the first translations of *On the Origin of Species* (1872) and *The Descent of Man* (1874–5) in the Danish language.[7] While Jacobsen would, in the years following the completion of his botanical studies, gravitate ever more towards his literary work, it is evident that he never entirely lost sight of his scientific work, and, moreover, remained as a writer of poems and novels throughout a committed adherent of the materialist world-view in which his botanical research was grounded.

Given the direction that the mature Jacobsen's endeavors would take, it is of some considerable interest that Jens Peter's 1867 self-portrait does not in its catalogue of possible careers include that of the poet and writer, although there is a rather offhanded mention of "a very strong penchant for transforming any experience into poetry."[8] Already while attending Thisted Realskole, the (rather lackadaisical) young student had written a poem for a self-published school newspaper as well as written and produced a comedy, and after his move to Copenhagen to attend preparatory school in 1863, he continued his literary experimentations in the self-published journal *Twigs*.[9] Jacobsen's literary pursuits appear to have taken a turn for the serious in 1868, when he compiled his first work intended for general issue, the semi-autobiographical epic cycle *Hervert Sperring*. Undeterred by publishers' rejections, the young scientist/poet proceeded to submit a selection of poems to Georg Brandes the following year, only to be turned away again. Still undaunted, Jacobsen's next major effort, the never-completed cycle *A Cactus Blooms* (1868–69), represents a substantial leap in quality. Somewhat echoing the structure of Kierkegaard's "In vino veritas," the volume portrays a circle of aspiring writers gathering round a rare cactus (as well as, not incidentally, the young daughter of the household) and sharing their work with each other. *A Cactus Blooms* (which along with *Hervert Sperring* would only see publication after the poet's death) contains the poet's first works that would, in time, acquire a significance greater than the merely national. The poem "En Arabesk" (commonly referred to as the "Pan Arabesque") occupies

---

one thing." While the young Kierkegaard goes on to elaborate his scientific interests as well as his theological, it is important to note here that Jacobsen's own reflections contain far less of the gravity that characterizes Kierkegaard's anguish over his personal calling in the famous "Gilleleje" journal entry of later that same summer. *SKS* 17, 23–30, AA:12 / *KJN* 1, 19–25.

[7]   Charles Darwin, *Om Arternes Oprindelse ved Kvalitetsvalg eller ved de heldigst stillede Formers Sejr i Kampen for Tilværelsen*, trans. by Jens Peter Jacobsen, Copenhagen: Gyldendalske Boghandel 1872; Charles Darwin, *Menneskets Afstamning og Parringsvalget*, vols. 1–2, trans. by Jens Peter Jacobsen, Copenhagen: Gyldendalske Boghandel 1874–75.

[8]   Jacobsen, *Samlede Værker*, ed. by Nielsen, vol. 3, p. 13. (Jensen, *Jens Peter Jacobsen*, p. 19.)

[9]   The full text of the poem, entitled "Fuksens Sang," as well as an excerpt from the play *Kjærlighed. Et Sørgespil*, are available in Danish in Anna Linck, *J.P. Jacobsen. Et Levnedsløb*, Copenhagen: Gyldendal 1947, pp. 12–15. Linck's summary of Jacobsen's singularly undistinguished school career is excellent.

a central place in the young poet's *oeuvre*, for it was this effort that finally earned him the coveted acknowledgment of a Brandes, in this case Edvard, who would later relate how upon hearing a reading of the poem, he was prompted to leap from a sofa and declare: "But you *are* a poet!"[10] *A Cactus Blooms* is also distinguished by the presence of a song cycle based on the medieval Danish legend of King Valdemar and Tove, which had earlier in the century been adapted by a host of Danish writers, among them Hans Christian Andersen, Johan Ludvig Heiberg, Carsten Hauch, and Bernhard Severin Ingemann. Jacobsen's "Gurresange" would, however, acquire a life far beyond national borders through the German composer Arnold Schönberg, who a generation later would set the songs to music.

Jacobsen's actual literary debut would finally arrive in 1872, the same year as his scientific dissertation was completed, when the short story "Mogens" was published in *Nyt dansk Maanedsskrift* to significant acclaim, although the ever-elusive acknowledgement from Georg Brandes was still yet to come. The following year, while touring the continent, the poet began to exhibit the first signs of the tuberculosis that would ultimately overtake him, and which very likely played a role in his decision to focus ever increasingly on his literary work at the expense of science. It is in the final twelve years of his life that Jacobsen would produce, under the most difficult of conditions, his most significant works. The second of his arabesques (also known as the "Michangelo" arabesque) from 1874 remains perhaps the most cultivated and certainly most critiqued poem in all of Danish Modernism and has over the years earned itself numerous notable admirers, most famously the German lyric poet Rainer Maria Rilke. The historical novel *Fru Marie Grubbe*, based on the legendary life of the seventeenth-century fallen Danish noblewoman, appeared in 1876 to wide acclaim and at long last earned the endorsement of Georg Brandes, who thereafter actively promoted the author as the pre-eminent stylist of the Modern Breakthrough writers.[11] Many of the novel's characters would also, curiously, reappear years later in Rilke's 1910 novel of Denmark, *Die Aufzeichnungen des Malte Laurids Brigge.* That work which remains as the crowning achievement of his career and which he had envisioned as early as the late 1860s, the semi-autobiographical *Kunstlerroman Niels Lyhne*, would reach publication in 1880,[12] five years before the poet's untimely death at the age of 38. Originally to be titled *The Atheist*, the novel was conceived as a chronicle of the difficult struggle of the previous generation of "Freethinkers"—

---

[10]   *Breve fra J.P. Jacobsen*, pp. XIV–XV. Edvard Brandes reports that Jacobsen confidently responded: "Yes, I know that well enough, and have always known it." The "Pan" poem also represents Jacobsen's first attempt in a new poetic form with which he is credited as inaugurating, that of the arabesque. Erik A. Nielsen has described the arabesque as "a poem which has its law-boundedness within itself," but not according to any "pre-existing plan," for "the plan only becomes visible when the arabesque has unfolded itself." "Naturalismens lyric," in *Lyrikere: 15 udlægninger og et digt*, Copenhagen: Forlaget Spring 2006, p. 143.

[11]   The relationship between Georg Brandes, the activist critic and advocate for literary *schools*, and Jacobsen, the seemingly irreproducible poet, was never entirely cordial. Brandes offers a tacit acknowledgmnt of this in his 1883 essay: "What young authors can and ought to learn from Jacobsen is to be themselves." Jens Peter Jacobsen, *Det moderne Gjennembruds Mænd. En Række Portræter*, Copenhagen: Gyldendal 1883, p. 207.

[12]   Jens Peter Jacobsen, *Niels Lyhne*, Copenhagen: Gyldendalske Boghandel 1880.

that generation which came of age immediately after Kierkegaard's—to shake off the cloudy phantoms of Romanticism and emerge into the clarity of a fully modern, atheist and materialist world-view. To this day the measure of Jacobsen's international renown, *Niels Lyhne* has lent itself to a myriad of critical interpretations, from the existential-heroic (Rilke) to the bourgeois decadent (Georg Lukács).

As should now be abundantly clear, hardly any Danish writers of significance would seem more fundamentally at odds than Kierkegaard and Jacobsen, and yet by no means may it be said that the former did not in some manner impact the latter. The philosopher's final and painfully public act of martyrdom was only eight years removed when the young student arrived in Copenhagen in 1863, and we may safely assume that in the far less mediated world of the nineteenth century, Kierkegaard's very loud campaign against Bishop Martensen and the national church would still have been very much alive in the intellectual circles of the capital. It is also a matter of record that Jacobsen himself claimed in a letter of 1881 that he had first read Kierkegaard in 1867 at the age of 20.[13] While the precise dating of Jacobsen's initial encounter with Kierkegaard must remain subject to a certain degree of speculation, it is of importance here to note some evidence of a slightly earlier engagement. Frederik Nielsen, in his early biography of Jacobsen, has published an incomplete poem from 1866 entitled "Phalaris," after the very same Greek tyrant employed by Kierkegaard in the first of the "Diapsalmata."[14] While the story of Phalaris and his torturous copper bull originally comes from Lucian, it has strongly been suggested that Jacobsen's particular inspiration was very likely Kierkegaard.[15] Regardless of the ultimate source, the poet would in 1868 return to the Phalaris motif in the poem, "So the world is now then a copper bull." Habib C. Malik has noted that the poet has abandoned the epic-mythological setting of the earlier treatment for a far more deeply pessimistic vision of the contemporary world over which a "cruel God the Father" reigns with impunity, interpreting this shift as evidence of a hardening of Jacobsen's rejection of Christianity.[16]

Further evidence of Jacobsen's engagement with *Either/Or* during his years as a university student may be identified in his "Diary of a Gifted Young Man," a series of journal entries composed from December 1867 to 1868. While clearly not a work of fiction, this collection of meditative self-reflections, letters, and aphorisms does indeed reveal considerable similarities in form and in spirit to Kierkegaard's "Diapsalmata." In particular, the relentless self-critique and general sense of

---

[13]   The 1881 letter (to Vilhelm Møller) contains a comprehensive listing of Jacobsen's reading from age 16 to 23 (1863–70); as a retrospective account it should of course be viewed with a degree of skepticism. For what it is worth, Jacobsen also claims to have read the Danish authors Schack Staffeldt and Hans Egede Schack as well as Feuerbach in 1867. Jacobsen, *Samlede Værker*, ed. by Nielsen, vol. 6, p. 137.

[14]   The poem appears in Danish in full in Frederik Nielsen, *J.P. Jacobsen, digteren og mennesket. En litterær undersøgelse*, Copenhagen: Gads 1953, pp. 297–303.

[15]   See Svend Ole Madsen, *J.P. Jacobsen: virkelighed og kunst. En undersøgelse af den eksistentielle erfarings transformering til kunst*, Copenhagen: Akademisk Forlag 1974, p. 78.

[16]   Malik, *Receiving Kierkegaard*, p. 292. For the full Danish text of the poem "Saa er nu da Jorden en Kobbertyr," see Jens Peter Jacobsen, *Digte og Udkast*, ed. by Edvard Brandes and Vilhelm Møller, Copenhagen: Gyldendal 1886, pp. 43–4.

Weltschmerz so ever-present in Kierkegaard's "A" seems to animate much of this brief text. Consider here the gifted young man's reflections on himself as a poet:

> Why do I write poems? To someday become famous? I would hope not. Because it is my nature, because it is necessary for me? It takes effort for me to write a poem. Because I feel I ought to use the talent I perhaps have? I am no man of responsibility. To get to know myself and the measure of my ability? Let me say: perhaps I'd rather not ask any more questions.[17]

The "Diary of a Gifted Young Man," furthermore, contains in manuscript form a note in which Jacobsen recalls "having heard something about Søren Kierkegaard" the same evening as the entry.[18] Jacobsen scholar Brita Tigerschiöld has identified further marginalia in an 1867 notebook, in which Jacobsen misquotes the "Diapsalmata": "My life is split into two conditions (or states): either I dream awake or I dream sleeping; either I wish awake and receive it as a dream, dreaming, or I receive as reality sleeping!"[19] The actual text from the "Diapsalmata"—"My time I divide as follows: the one half I sleep; the other half I dream. I never dream when I sleep; that would be a shame, because to sleep is the height of genius"—should by no means be considered as a statement of philosophical idealism; Jacobsen, at this point immersed in Feuerbach, nonetheless dismisses it as such.[20]

Any discussion of the impact of *Either/Or* on a literary figure must inevitably turn to that most literarily sophisticated of Kierkegaard's texts, namely, the diary of Johannes the Seducer, and Jacobsen appears to be no exception. Near the conclusion of "The Seducer's Diary" the narrator, in a rather mocking nod to Hegel, attempts "to consider woman categorically."[21] Situating woman in the same sphere as nature, Johannes asserts that she exists exclusively as being-for-other, existing only in a kind of vegetative dream state before she is "touched by erotic love."[22] Woman may only, according to Johannes, reach her full (albeit, of course, still severely limited) potential through the intervention of the male suitor; here Kierkegaard notes the close relationship in Danish between the adjective "free" (*fri*) and the verb "to propose" (*at frie*). And yet this act of liberation in the end amounts, of course, to the immediate exhaustion of womanly potential, for once "a girl has devoted herself completely, the whole thing is finished."[23] It is in this sense that Johannes begrudgingly confesses his respect for Diana, she who above all most jealously guarded her virginity and surely possessed "a whole bag full of all kinds of tricks."[24] Although it engages with the erotic more directly and

---

[17]   Jacobsen, *Digte og Udkast*, pp. 7–8.
[18]   The marginal note was discovered by Edvard Brandes during his preparations for the first publication of the diary, *Digte og Udkast*, p. 17.
[19]   Quoted in *J.P. Jacobsen och hans roman Niels Lyhne*, Gothenburg: Elander 1945, p. 58. (English translation by Malik in his *Receiving Kierkegaard*, p. 294.)
[20]   *SKS* 2, 37 / *EO1*, 28.
[21]   *SKS* 2, 417 / *EO1*, 429.
[22]   *SKS* 2, 418 / *EO1*, 430.
[23]   *SKS* 2, 422 / *EO1*, 435.
[24]   *SKS* 2, 423 / *EO1*, 436.

concretely—and thus in some sense prefigures the debates over female sexuality in the following decade—Jacobsen's 1868 prose sketch "A Love Relationship" does seem to reflect the presence of Johannes the Seducer on some level, and it is worth noting that nowhere in his collected works does he more closely approach the curious blend of dialectical opposition and Socratic inquiry that characterizes so much of Kierkegaard's prose. In the brief sketch, which attempts to make sense of the improbable love between a "noble youth" and a prostitute, Jacobsen qualifies woman as a "spirit which guards over a body," while man exists as "body and a coordinate spirit."[25] As has been noted, the young student at this time was very much immersed in Feuerbach, and thus the sketch seems to turn on the relation between flesh and spirit with respect to the erotic: "Can a woman then give up her body without at the same time, even in a single second, even in a slight handshake, in a lightning quick flash of the eye, in a nearly invisible trembling around the mouth give up her spirit, her very self?"[26] The answer here is wholly affirmative, and here the poet curiously begins to echo the logic of Johannes, insisting that the real basis of their love rests in an absolute belief "in something in her that had never been violated, never sold, never given up" and yet something that only he himself could call forth in her, something "which issued from him in their meeting, which filled her entirely, which illuminated her, raised her up and enchanted, delighted him."[27]

Direct textual evidence, then, clearly demonstrates that Jacobsen in his student years was familiar with the general outline of Kierkegaard's life and had at the very least devoted considerable time to the first volume of *Either/Or* by 1867 or, perhaps, a year earlier. It is likely no coincidence that these very years correspond to that which Jacobsen's biographers generally refer to as his "crisis period," ostensibly brought about by his failure to pass the university entrance examination and the consequent threats of his father to cut off his financial lifeline. Given his concurrent engagement with Kierkegaard, it is therefore tempting to see beneath the surface the kind of grand inner spiritual conflict so familiar with readers of the philosopher, all the more so when considering an 1868 poem from the unpublished collection *Hervert Sperring*:

---

[25]   The full text of the sketch "Et Kjærlighedsforhold" may be found in *Eros og døden, et J.P. Jacobsen-udvalg*, ed. by Jørgen Moestrup, Copenhagen: Gyldendal 1975, p. 14.

[26]   Jacobsen, *Eros og døden*, p. 14.

[27]   Ibid. One further note regarding the young Jacobsen's erotic/romantic leaning deserves mentioning. Frederik Nielsen has identified a couple of marginal notes written in an 1867 art history volume which would appear to suggest that Jacobsen considered his own unhappy relationship to Anna Michelson, whose offer of love he rejected, to possess certain similarities to that of Kierkegaard and Regine Olsen. In the first of the notes, Jacobsen, referencing a story in the text of a similarly unrequited love, wonders if the rejected woman had suffered more than the man. In the second, a response to a painting entitled "Psyche Receiving the First Kiss of Cupid," Jacobsen asserts that "had the exam not been so near I would write a poem about that meeting, and I as a Kierkegaard and Regine. I am a tyrant also, you know—worse luck!" Nielsen, *J.P. Jacobsen, digteren og mennesket*, pp. 65–6. (English translation in Malik, *Receiving Kierkegaard*, p. 296.)

God, do save me, it may still happen,
Still I resist,
But if I do not find salvation soon,
All my courage vanishes.
Oh, do save me, I am worthy of that,
A world lives within me,
A torrent of beauty, an army of thoughts,
Goes down without a trace.
God, do save me from the clutches of dream,
Bring the heavens down upon me,
Hurl the waves of life against my bosom,
Then I shall believe in you.[28]

A surface reading of this could identify in the figure of the tormented aesthete an attempt to bypass the ethical in an effort to reach directly the certitude and the redemption of the religious existence, and yet very little in the collection as a whole and even, to a large extent, this poem itself, would support such an interpretation. On the contrary, the poem is properly understood when emphasis is placed on the *source* of Hervert's angst—the inability to escape the life of dreams—rather than the proposed remedy, which of course is presented only in the conditional. Jacobsen here, as in countless other places in the collection, is expressing his frustration with the lingering traces of dreamy, suffocating Romantic idealism still so dominant in the intellectual life of himself and his contemporaries; in essence Hervert is re-enacting the struggle of the hero of Hans Egede Schack's 1857 novel *The Fantasts*, which we know he had read a year earlier.[29] Far less a personal religious crisis, then, Jacobsen seems in these crucial years to have shared in a kind of collective or generational inner conflict which would manifest itself in the "return to reality" characteristic of the Modern Breakthrough, the beginnings of which lay only a few years in the future.[30]

There is, indeed, every reason to agree with the received opinion that Kierkegaard had little if any role in the young student's renunciation of Christianity, which is generally dated to early 1867. Of the most significant documents of this period, neither bears the scent of the philosopher. The first, a January 1867 aesthetic manifesto entitled "On My Calling," reveals that the deity with which the young student was struggling had far more in common with earlier, pantheistic incarnations than with the God of Kierkegaard:

If I could transfer Nature's eternal laws, glories, riddles and wonders into poetry, then I would feel that my work would be more than ordinary. But the poetry would not be

---

[28]   Jens Peter Jacobsen, *Samlede Værker*, vols. 1–5, ed. by Morten Borup, Copenhagen: Gyldendal 1924–29, vol. 3, p. 18.
[29]   See the 1881 letter to Vilhelm Møller for an exhaustive review of Jacobsen's reading during the 1860s. *Samlede Værker*, ed. by Nielsen, vol. 6, p. 137.
[30]   It should be noted that Frederik Nielsen views Jacobsen's emotional crisis as rooted in a struggle against fantasies of a particularly erotic nature, concluding that the poet was subject to sadomasochistic tendencies. In support of this claim, Nielsen cites an alternate version of the poem's final strophe: "And do save me from the clutches of dream / Show me a woman / Show me, send me a lovely Maiden." Nielsen, *J.P. Jacobsen, digteren og mennesket*, p. 45.

Christian, it would treat the Bible like an Edda and not acknowledge any other works of divinity than natural law in widest extent; it would view human beings not as God's children, but as elements of Divinity, meager elements, but still elements.[31]

The single text considered to mark Jacobsen's decisive break with Christianity, his March 1867 "Letter on a Religious Standpoint," likewise evinces no real signs of intense inner struggle. After confessing that he had been but was no longer Christian, the poet likens Christianity to the Greek and Norse myths, predicting that over the course of millennia it would come to be viewed by all in such a manner. The letter even ends with the Nietzschean assertion that "Christianity began with the weak in spirit."[32]

Whatever the precise details of Jacobsen's personal engagement with Kierkegaard may have been, it is beyond contention that his initial impressions of the philosopher gathered from colleagues would have been wholly unsympathetic. While a university student Jacobsen had lodged at a boarding house owned by Marie Zoffmann, and thus became involved in what came to be called the "Zoffmann Circle," a group of young intellectuals which included the later novelist Erik Skram (1847–1923), the medical student Emanuel Fraenkel (1849–1918), the aspiring literary critic Hans Sophus Vodskov (1846–1910), and, most importantly, the theology student Poul Kierkegaard (1842–1915), the estranged son of Søren's brother Peter, the long-serving Bishop of Aalborg. Through his study of Max Stirner and of Feuerbach (as well as, of course, a strong measure of oedipal theatrics), Poul revolted against the renowned piety of his family by embracing a belligerent form of atheism; once remarking of his uncle and father as such: "My uncle became either-or, my father became both-and, and I remained neither-nor."[33] As the senior and leading figure of the group, it is likely that, as Habib C. Malik has asserted, Poul "imparted to Jacobsen some of his own personal hostility toward the religious orientation of his uncle Søren."[34]

Once Jacobsen embarked upon his literary and scientific careers proper in the early 1870s, the frequency of references to Kierkegaard in the letters and manuscripts began to decline.[35] In spite of this, Jacobsen scholars have not shied away from engaging

---

[31]   Jacobsen, *Eros og døden*, p. 9.
[32]   Ibid., p. 10.
[33]   Quoted in Malik, *Receiving Kierkegaard*, p. 292.
[34]   Ibid., p. 294.
[35]   Habib C. Malik, in his superb study of Jacobsen and Kierkegaard, has catalogued the few mentions of Kierkegaard in the 1870s. From an 1874 letter to Edvard Brandes, Jacobsen refers to Ibsen's Julian as "a young teutonic man, who has read his Kierkegaard." In an 1876 letter to fellow atheist Vilhelm Møller, the poet expresses disdain at what he takes to be "some Søren Kierkegaard words" in an anonymous essay attributed to Møller. Another note to Edvard Brandes from 1877 expresses approval of Hans Brøchner's "Reminiscences" of Kierkegaard that had recently appeared in the journal published by the brothers. Lastly, a letter to Georg Brandes of the same year indicates that Jacobsen had just read and thoroughly enjoyed Brandes' seminal 1877 study of Kierkegaard, the first book-length treatment of the philosopher. It should come as no surprise that Jacobsen received the book favorably, even indicating that the study had impacted him much more so than his previous exposure, for Brandes' view of Kierkegaard is famously slanted towards the aesthetic and against the religious. Malik, *Receiving Kierkegaard*, p. 300. (English translations by Malik.)

in speculation about the presence of the philosopher in the major works of the poet. The complex psychological framework set forth in works such as *The Concept of Anxiety* and *The Sickness unto Death* does, after all, exhibit a considerable degree of universal applicability; one of the central strengths of Kierkegaard as thinker is that his peculiar "dialectics of despair" may with some success be applied to nearly any literary work that exhibits a measurable degree of interiority. These two figures, the one a self-described martyr for authentic Christianity, the other an inveterate atheist, once again could seemingly not be more opposed to one another. And yet, in addition to the direct evidence of engagement on Jacobsen's part, consideration must also be granted to the relatively modest reach of their shared mother tongue and to the insularity of the Copenhagen literary scene, many of the central figures of whom knew both men personally. Had they been born in a larger land, perhaps Jacobsen could have gone about his business with little regard to Kierkegaard. By no means should it be asserted that Kierkegaard exercised a dominant influence upon Jacobsen, yet neither should his presence be disregarded entirely.

Of the many speculative studies of the relationship between the two writers, special consideration must be reserved for Jørn Vosmar's 1984 monograph *J.P. Jacobsens digtning*, which not only remains perhaps the most ambitious effort to link the two figures, but also deserves praise for its relative caution and for the astuteness of its close readings. While Jacobsen is known in the larger world primarily as a prose writer, his poetry retains at the very least a level of interest equal to that of his novels and poems within Scandinavia itself. The strength of Vosmar's study is accordingly to be found in his treatment of the arabesque poems, although he is alone in including the early poem "Monomanie" along with "Pan" (also known as Arabesque I) and "Michelangelo" (Arabesque II). The critic further distinguishes himself in his much more expansive view of the young poet's crisis period, which he traces back to 1865 and all the way up to 1872. The arabesque poems, according to Vosmar, should be read as a kind of inner testimony of this crisis from its first iteration in the youthful "Monomanie" on through "Pan" and finally reaching its resolution in the mature "Michelangelo."[36] While he may differ with respect to chronology, Vosmar ultimately affirms, however, Frederik Nielsen's assertion that the crisis that defined the poet's student years was fundamentally a crisis of sexual awakening. It is worth recalling here that Jacobsen, like Kierkegaard, never really came to terms with himself as a sexually mature being and most likely died a virgin.

Vosmar begins his analysis of the arabesque cycle by noting the structural similarities between "Monomanie" and "Pan." Each poem appears to invoke in the figure of the I an initial moment of innocence and relative harmony, which is then abruptly disrupted by the experience of catastrophe, in both texts set in motion by a disastrous encounter with a woman. The initial harmonious state the critic equates with Kierkegaard's notion of immediacy, while the presence of the sexual encounter

---

[36]   It should be noted here that the "Pan" arabesque (1868) actually predates "Monomanie" (1869), although all manuscript evidence suggests that the two poems were worked on simultaneously, in addition to the fact the poet himself considered the former far superior to the latter. The "Michelangelo" arabesque is dated 1874. Jørn Vosmar, *J.P. Jacobsens digtning*, Copenhagen: Gyldendal 1984, p. 149.

with woman as the initiator of the process of inner transformation he associates with the philosopher's emphasis on the role of the erotic in the transition from innocence to guilt, that very first step in the long journey toward Kierkegaardian selfhood. Jacobsen's notion of catastrophe and its subsequent fallout, furthermore, is likened to the Kierkegaardian sense that it is through the experience of despair that individual inner growth is made possible, and yet here the two arabesques begin to diverge. The inner storm from which the I recoils in the wake of catastrophe in "Monomanie" is, curiously, identified as the "thought of God, his powerful, clear thought."[37] The presence of the godhead in this poem completed fully two years after the author's renunciation of Christianity may only be explained, according to Vosmar, with reference to Jacobsen's continued engagement with Kierkegaard. Of particular significance here is the Kierkegaardian conception of the demonic, defined in *The Concept of Anxiety* as "anxiety about the good" and as an "unfreedom that wants to close itself off."[38] Qualified in *The Sickness unto Death* as a form of despair to which the poets are particularly susceptible, the demonic places the individual in a state of tension between the more powerful need for inclosing reserve, which is a function of the fear of freedom, and the subordinated desire for disclosure.[39] Vosmar points to a similar sense in the first strophe of the poem: "I am mad and now I will sing/ But I know that I am dumb/ And that the strings I pluck/ Are iron bars for my cell."[40] The crisis at this early stage is a crisis of poetic communication as well as a sexual crisis.

The presence of the God-figure in "Monomanie" Vosmar interprets as a lingering sense in the poet of the possibility of a religious solution to his personal crisis; in the "Pan" arabesque, however, any such remedy has been entirely abandoned, and the general tone of the text is therefore all the more characterized by a tone of futility and hopelessness. The critic notes that figure of woman who initiates the catastrophe, relatively shrouded in obscurity in "Monomanie," is here presented in a starkly concrete manner:

> There was a sigh in her laughter,
> Jubilation in her crying;
> Before her everyone must bend,
> Only two dared cross her,
> Her own eyes.[41]

Whereas in the earlier poem the poet appears to have clung to the possibility of a religious solution to his crisis, he has now placed his hopes in redemption through a kind of romantic idyll, and yet, echoing Schopenhauer, the promise of salvation through woman proves to be all the more illusory, as is abundantly clear in the poem's fourth strophe ("The Toast"):

---

37   Jacobsen, *Samlede Værker*, ed. by Nielsen, vol. 4, p. 125.
38   *SKS* 4, 424 / *CA*, 123.
39   *SKS* 11, 186 / *SUD*, 72.
40   Jacobsen, *Samlede Værker*, ed. by Nielsen, vol. 4, pp. 123–4.
41   Jacobsen, *Digte og Udkast*, p. 61.

From the poisonous lily's
Dazzling chalk
She drank to me;
To him who is dead
And him who now kneels at her feet.
With us all she drank
—And then her gaze was obedient—
The cup of promise of unfailing fidelity
From the poisonous lily's
Dazzling chalk.[42]

This is the very moment of the dissolution of the dream of romantic love, at which the figure of woman is suddenly transformed into an image of unimaginable cruelty, the inspiration for which Vosmar locates in the musings of Johannes the Seducer toward the end of his diary. Here Johannes ponders the impact of woman, who is by nature being-for-another, attempting to assert herself as genuine autonomous subject, as endeavoring to relate to another as being-for-it. In such rare occurrences, woman "assumes the quality of abstract cruelty" to a degree wholly unfathomable to the male half of the species, for it must be said that "a man can never be as cruel as a woman."[43] Whereas Bluebeard kills off his suitors without pleasure, Johannes asserts, the same may not be said of his numerous female counterparts in folk literature.

If the "Pan" poem represents the crisis in the poet at its most intense, then the "Michangelo" arabesque of 1874 is to be understood as its resolution. Structurally, the later poem is a major departure. The initial strophes describe in immense, almost naturalistic detail the journey of a wave, here a symbol of human longing, from its origin out in the sea and then across a vaguely Mediterranean landscape. As the wave, initially evocative of the purity of human will, progresses across the land, it is gradually pulled down by the corrupting influence of the earthly before it ultimately disintegrates among grapevines, that most sensual of fruits. In the poem's middle section, the exhausted human will revels in an earthly bacchanalia, a kind of grotesque caricature of its original nobility. In a breakdown of time–space continuity, the poet figure, never much of a concrete presence in the text before, is then abruptly deposited before an Italian villa, on the balcony of which there appears the figure of a woman, presumably one and the same as she who is referred to in the poem's full title: "Arabesque to a Drawing by Michelangelo: Woman with Sunken Gaze in the Uffizi." The poet figure proceeds to project a series of deeply pessimistic reflections on the human condition into to the mind of the mysterious woman, which Vosmar loosely correlates with the futilitarian variant of Darwinism then coming into vogue, but the speculations of the poet appear to be disproven, for the poem concludes with a kind of triumphant vision of the woman who "Has no words, no sigh, no complaint, / Silhouetted against the dark air / Like a sword through the heart of the night."[44]

---

[42]   Ibid., p. 62.

[43]   *SKS* 2, 419 / *EO1*, 432.

[44]   Jacobsen, *Digte og Udkast*, p. 159.

The "Michelangelo" arabesque has been read as a deeply pessimistic poem, most famously by Rilke, and yet Vosmar has indeed done much to rescue this most famous of Danish poems from the depths of despair and futility, although in doing so he begins to depart from Kierkegaard. His analysis begins by distinguishing the text from the earlier arabesques, both of which locate the source of corruption in the human will in the erotic longing for woman. Here the corrupting force appears to be placed within the human will itself, independent of any external object of desire. The wave of longing in the opening lines, crucially, dissipates at the foot of the balcony *before* the woman makes her appearance. The woman figure, in absolute contrast to the earlier poems, is here represented as "the atheistic, Sartrean existential hero," who has "lived through and suffered through the degrading circumstances" of human existence and acquired a measure of hard-won indifference to them.[45] She is to be understood, according to Vosmar, as a representative of "the highest form of self-mastery, as the spirit that carries out the [Kierkegaardian] synthesis" of the finite and the infinite.[46] That the woman-figure is depicted in a visionary haze, outside the time–space plan of the poem, is taken as evidence by Vosmar that Jacobsen is employing "the modernistic effect"[47] of veiling the distinction between reality and irreality, permitting the poet-figure to transcend the seemingly "insurmountable"[48] gulf between himself and the woman-figure.

With regard to the major prose works, numerous scholars have attempted to establish concordances between Jacobsen's *Fru Marie Grubbe* and Kierkegaard, but the majority of such speculations lack firm grounding.[49] Jacobsen's preoccupations in this naturalist historical novel are really quite distant from those of Kierkegaard, and, moreover, far more interesting models for the work may easily be identified. Instead, we must turn to *Niels Lyhne*, which again represents not only the summation of the poet's authorship, but also offers the most lucrative territory for Kierkegaard scholarship—at least on a speculative basis. Caution must certainly be observed here, for we are, after all, attempting to detect the presence of the thought of "Denmark's greatest Christian" in the work of no less than Denmark's greatest atheist, and in a novel originally to be titled *The Atheist* at that. It is likely a bit of an overreach to suggest, as Habib C. Malik has, that "what Flaubert's Emma Bovary was to Marie Grubbe, Kierkegaard was to *Niels Lyhne*."[50] And yet it must be understood that Jacobsen by no means conceived of his novel as an expression of the kind of aggressive atheist triumphalism that began to appear in the decades after Darwin and which once again has found its proponents in our current age. In absolute contrast, the poet had in an 1878 letter to Georg Brandes clearly indicated that the novel would portray the ultimate *failure* of the first generation of Danish freethinkers:

---

[45]   Vosmar, *J.P. Jacobsens digtning*, p. 164.

[46]   Ibid.

[47]   Ibid.

[48]   Ibid., p 165.

[49]   For a summary of *Fru Marie Grubbe* scholarship, see Malik, *Receiving Kierkegaard*, pp. 300–2.

[50]   Ibid., p. 302.

This is the young generation that grow up, love, rant, betray, fight, get disillusioned and leveled down in my story, showing through their virtues and vices, their cowardice and failure, how difficult it is to be freethinkers with the siren voices of tradition and childhood memories on one side, and the thunder of condemnation from society on the other.[51]

Jacobsen here in effect historicizes his novel, suggesting that the eponymous hero is to be understood as a necessary sacrifice in a longer historical struggle against superstition and irreason. It is worth noting here that the eponymous hero of the novel himself acknowledges, in the pivotal exchange with his skeptical interlocutor Dr. Hjerrild, that the struggle against the false consolation of Christianity will itself play out over many generations and that in the beginning "most will fall in the struggle."[52]

It is for this reason that Malik considers *Niels Lyhne* to be fundamentally a *transitional* work, a "rare literary bridge between Kierkegaard's writings, with their promise of spiritual solace amidst the bleak despair they so exquisitely portray, and the absurdism of 'no exit' writers like Sartre and Camus."[53] In the aforementioned conversation with Dr. Hjerrild, a young Niels Lyhne had dared to imagine a kind of future post-Christian utopia:

The day that humanity can freely cry: there is no God, on that day a new heaven and a new earth will be created as if by magic. Only then will heaven become the free, infinite place instead of a threatening, watchful eye. Only then will the earth belong to us and we to the earth….That enormous stream of love, which now rises up toward that God who is believed in, will bend back over the earth when heaven is empty, with loving steps toward all the beautiful, human traits and talents with which we have empowered and adorned God in order to make God worthy of our love.[54]

That this rather naïve and uncomplicated dream would prove to be illusory within the novel, to say nothing of the historical unfolding of modernity itself, is painfully evident to the reader. Malik accordingly qualifies Niels as "Kierkegaard minus faith in God,"[55] left adrift in a world thoroughly disenchanted, yet entirely devoid of the inner reserves necessary to fashion an inwardly harmonious post-Christian selfhood, reserves which would only become available to the existentialists of the mid-twentieth century. Jacobsen, in turn, may be understood as the first in a long line of readers who, wholly internalizing Kierkegaard's diagnosis of the crisis of Christian civilization, find comfort in neither the promise of post-Christian renewal nor in the prescribed Kierkegaardian religious solution.

There is much that is appealing in this essentially historical reading of Niels Lyhne; indeed, no less a luminary than Lukács would affirm this view in his

---

[51]   Quoted in Jensen, *Jens Peter Jacobsen*, p. 70. (English translation by Niels Lyhne Jensen.)
[52]   Jacobsen, *Niels Lyhne*, p. 186. (English translation from *Niels Lyhne*, trans. by Tiina Nunnally, Seattle: Fjord 1990, p. 118.)
[53]   Malik, *Receiving Kierkegaard*, p. 305.
[54]   Jacobsen, *Niels Lyhne*, pp. 184–5. (*Niels Lyhne*, trans. by Nunnally, pp. 117–18.)
[55]   Malik, *Receiving Kierkegaard*, p. 303.

(in)-famous commentary on Jacobsen in his 1920 *Theory of the Novel*. Himself a "lapsed" Kierkegaardian, Lukács dismisses the novel as perhaps the pre-eminent example of *fin de siècle desillusionerung*:

> Jacobsen's novel of disillusion, which expresses in wonderful lyric images the author's melancholy over a world "in which there's so much that is senselessly exquisite," breaks down and disintegrates completely; and the author's attempt to find a desperate positiveness in Niels Lyhne's heroic atheism, his courageous acceptance of his necessary loneliness, strikes us as an aid brought in from outside the actual work.[56]

Both of these efforts, Malik's attempt to identify the novel as a kind of missing link between Kierkegaard's preliminary explorations and the mature standpoint of the French existentialist school, as well as Lukács' Marxist insistence on the retirement of the novel altogether, in essence result in the significant *diminishing* of the author's accomplishment in addition to, significantly, the degree of his engagement with Kierkegaard. In the first respect, it is important to understand that Jacobsen has not, as Malik would seem to imply, delivered on his promise to deliver a generational portrait of Europe's first non-believers. Jacobsen's abandonment of the original title was by no means coincidental, for *Niels Lyhne* is in every way a drama of the inner life of one single individual, the aforementioned *social* impediments to non-belief never really playing a part in the narrative. That Niels should not be taken as a representative figure of his generation is evident in the hero's initial renunciation of God itself, a consequence of the death of his first (and most hopeless) love, Edele: "There are those for whom grief is a violence directed against them, a cruelty that they never learn to regard as a test or merely as simple fate. For them it is a manifestation of tyranny, something personally hateful, and there will always be a thorn left in their hearts. *It is not often that children grieve like this, but Niels Lyhne did.*"[57]

There is also additional evidence, particularly in the hero's relation to the Kierkegaardian categories of the ethical and the religious, that Jacobsen's engagement with the philosopher runs far deeper than has been assumed. In his famous discourse on the question of a teleological suspension of the ethical, Kierkegaard had demonstrated how, at the moment of crisis, the ethical itself had functioned for Abraham as a temptation "which would hold him back from doing God's will."[58] In the novel the author at several points appears to entertain this theme, most prominently in the hero's relationship with his wife Gerda and their young child. His wife a relatively unreflective soul in comparison to himself, Niels at first does not have the heart "to take her God away from her, to exile all those white flocks of angels who hover, singing, all day in heaven and then come back down to earth in the evening, spreading themselves out from bed to bed in a faithful vigil."[59] Here the ethical, in its broadest and warmest sense, appears to intervene against the higher claim of the religious, albeit its negation. It is only at the insistence of Gerda

---

[56]   Georg Lukács, *The Theory of the Novel*, trans. by Anna Bostock, Cambridge, Massachusetts: MIT Press 1971, pp. 119–20.

[57]   Jacobsen, *Niels Lyhne*, p. 65. (*Niels Lyhne*, trans. by Nunnally, p. 44.)

[58]   *SKS* 4, 153 / *FT*, 60.

[59]   Jacobsen, *Niels Lyhne*, p. 304. (*Niels Lyhne*, trans. by Nunnally, p. 192.)

herself that Niels brings her around to his views, although as so often is the case, Gerda relents at the final moment of her passing. Niels obediently calls for a pastor and, significantly, it is remarked by the narrator that "the *right* desire won out in her heart—the deep submission before the almighty, judging God; the bitter tears of remorse before the forsaken, blasphemed, and tortured God; and the humble, bold yearning for the new pact of bread and wine with the inscrutable God."[60]

The non-belief of Niels himself survives the early death of his wife, but the same cannot be said regarding the almost unimaginably cruel death of their child, following ever so closely on the heels of Gerda. At the child's deathbed Niels at last can no longer resist the desire for succor, and yet his prayer is a far cry from that he offered as a child in the final moment of Edele's passing: "He threw himself to his knees on the floor and prayed to that Lord who is in heaven, who keeps the kingdom of earth in fear with trials and admonitions, who sends poverty and sickness, suffering and death, who wants everyone's knees to bend with trembling, and from whom no escape is possible, not to the farthest ocean nor down in the abyss."[61] That this is not the prayer of one who genuinely believes that the possibility of recompense is all too apparent; instead, Niels' relapse may only properly be understood, once again, as a kind of temptation, a curious reworking of Kierkegaard's retelling of the Moriah legend in which it is the *religious* that plays the role of tempter over against that of the higher principle of atheism: "In the midst of his despair, he had known what he was doing. He had been tempted and had fallen; it was a fall from grace, a fall away from himself and the Idea….He had not been able to endure life as it was; he had been in the struggle for Greatness, and in the violence of the battle he had forsaken the banner to which he was sworn."[62]

The crisis of non-belief that had afflicted Niels upon the death of his child is shortly resolved by his decision to volunteer for service in Denmark's futile 1864 war against Prussia, and it is not long before the tortured life of the hero mercifully meets it close. Dying of wounds in a field hospital, Niels is again visited by his old friend Hjerrild, and in some sense atones for his earlier lapse by rejecting the offer of a pastor. It is the skeptic Hjerrild, curiously enough, who offers the novel's final statement on belief and non-belief: "Let's be honest—we can be whatever we may call it, but we can never completely remove that God from heaven; our minds have imagined Him up there too many times, it has been chimed into us and sung into us ever since we were very small."[63] The doctor's words of consolation appear to suggest, commensurate with Malik's reading of the novel as a transitional work, that future individuals, gradually released of the iron grip of religious indoctrination, might some day finally be able to cast away the illusion of God altogether. And yet it can hardly be said of Niels himself that he had been subjected to much in the way of a religious education. The twin poles of his childhood are to be found in the earthbound humility of his father and in the romantic flights of fancy of his mother, the Lyhne household marked in no way by excessive piety. In contrast, Hjerrild's

---

[60] Jacobsen, *Niels Lyhne*, pp. 312–13. (*Niels Lyhne*, trans. by Nunnally, p. 197.)
[61] Jacobsen, *Niels Lyhne*, pp. 315–16. (*Niels Lyhne*, trans. by Nunnally, p. 199.)
[62] Jacobsen, *Niels Lyhne*, pp. 317–18. (*Niels Lyhne*, trans. by Nunnally, p. 201.)
[63] Jacobsen, *Niels Lyhne*, p. 322. (*Niels Lyhne*, trans. by Nunnally, p. 204.)

contention should be understood as a recognition that the individual struggle between belief and non-belief is in essence an eternal and ongoing struggle, to be inwardly enacted within the soul of each single individual, never reaching any kind of historical conclusion. If, once again, we may take the Kierkegaard of *The Point of View* at his word, then we must acknowledge that his single lifelong preoccupation was the effort to undermine the illusion of Christendom, to devote himself entirely to the contention that there can be no progress in the individual life of the spirit, that each and every individual must in her own lifespan re-enact the whole of the drama of Christian belief. In this way "Denmark's greatest Christian" and her "greatest atheist" acquire a curious form of reconciliation, the essential teaching of *Niels Lyhne* would seem to suggest, in the end, that the drama of non-belief is subject to no lesser measure of rigor.

Bibliography

I. References to or Uses of Kierkegaard in Jacobsen's Corpus

"En begavet ung Mands Dagbog" and "Saa er nu da Jorden en Kobbertyr," in his *Digte og Udkast*, ed. by Edvard Brandes and Vilhelm Møller, Copenhagen: Gyldendal 1886, pp. 1–22; pp. 43–4.

Breve fra J.P. Jacobsen, ed. by Edvard Brandes, Copenhagen: Gyldendal 1899, pp. 45–6.

"Et Kjærlighedsforhold," in his *Samlede Værker*, vols. 1–5, ed. by Morten Borup, Copenhagen: Gyldendal 1924–29, vol. 3, pp. 35–8.

Georg og Edvard Brandes. Brevveksling med nordiske Forfattere og Videnskabsmænd, vols. 1–8, ed. by Morten Borup, Copenhagen: Gyldendal 1939–42, vol. 2, p. 261; vol. 3, pp. 126–9.

Letter to Vilhelm Møller, in *Samlede Værker*, vols. 1–6, ed. by Frederik Nielsen, Copenhagen: Rosenkilde og Bagger 1972–74, vol. 5, pp. 153–5.

Letter to Vilhelm Møller, in *Samlede Værker*, vols. 1–6, ed. by Frederik Nielsen, Copenhagen: Rosenkilde og Bagger 1972–74, vol. 6, pp. 135–7.

II. Sources of Jacobsen's Knowledge of Kierkegaard

Brandes, Georg, *Søren Kierkegaard. En kritisk Fremstilling i Grundrids*, Copenhagen: Gyldendal 1877.

Brøchner, Hans, "Erindringer om Søren Kierkegaard," *Det Nittende Aarhundrede*, vol. 5, March 1877, pp. 337–74.

Goldschmidt, Meir, *Livs Erindringer og Resultater*, vols. 1–2, Copenhagen: Gyldendal 1877, vol. 1, pp. 395–440.

Vodskov, Hans Sophus, "En krise i Søren Kierkegaards liv," *Illustreret Tidende*, vol. 22, 1881, nos. 1118–20.

III. Secondary Literature on Jacobsen's Relation to Kierkegaard

Capecci, Giorgio, "Aspettando un temporale, ovvero *Niels Lyhne* e *La Ripetizione*," *Studi Nordici*, vol. 11, 2004, pp. 11–21.

Durand, Frédéric, *Jens Peter Jacobsen ou la Gravitation d'une Solitude*, Paris: Faculté des letters et sciences humaines de l'Université 1968, p. 45; pp. 74–5.

Helland, Frode, "En analyse av J.P. Jacobsens roman *Niels Lyhne* i lys av Kierkegaards *Om Begrebet Ironi*, 2. del," *Norskrift*, vol. 92, 1996, pp. 69–89.

Jensen, Niels Lyhne, *Jens Peter Jacobsen*, Boston: Twayne 1980 (*Twayne World Authors Series*, vol. 573), p. 19; p. 25; p. 56; p. 92.

Kühle, Sejer, "Fra J.P. Jacobsens Kreds," in *Fund og Forskning i det Kongelige Biblioteks Samlinger*, vol. 4, 1957, pp. 120–37.

Linck, Anna, *J.P. Jacobsen. Et Levnedsløb*, Copenhagen: Gyldendal 1947, p. 41; p. 68.

Madsen, Carsten, *Om læsning. Kierkegaard, Kafka, Mallarmé og Jacobsen*, Århus: Aarhus Universitetsforlag 1995.

Madsen, Svend Ole, *J.P. Jacobsen: Virkelighed og Kunst. En undersøgelse af den eksistentielle erfarings transformering til kunst*, Copenhagen: Akademisk Forlag 1974, p. 41; p. 51.

Malik, Habib C., *Receiving Søren Kierkegaard: The Early Impact and Transmission of His Thought*, Washington, DC: Catholic University of America Press 1997, pp. 290–306.

Nielsen, Frederik, *J.P. Jacobsen: Digteren og Mennesket. En Litterær Undersøgelse*, Copenhagen: Gads 1953, p. 62; p. 66; p. 94.

Ostenfeld, Ib, *Poul Kierkegaard. En skæbne og andre studier over religion og ateisme*, Copenhagen: Nyt Nordisk Forlag 1957, pp. 36–48.

Rehm, Walter, "Jacobsen und die Schwermut," in *Experimentum Medietatis. Studien zur Geistes- und Literaturgeschichte des 19. Jahrhunderts*, Munich: Rinn 1947, pp. 184–239.

— *Gontscharow und Jacobsen, oder Langweile und Schwermut*, Göttingen: Vandenhoeck & Ruprecht 1963.

Tigerschiöld, Brita, *J.P. Jacobsen och hans Roman Niels Lyhne*, Gothenburg: Elander 1945, pp. 46–7; p. 58.

Vosmar, Jørn, *J.P. Jacobsens digtning*, Copenhagen: Gyldendal 1984, pp. 135–72.

Harald Kidde:

"A Widely Traveled Stay-at-Home"

Poul Houe

I. General Introduction

The Danish author Harald Kidde was born in 1878 in the east Jutland county seat of Vejle. The son of the county road surveyor and his thirty-year younger wife, Kidde had an older sister who died prematurely from tuberculosis, and a younger brother whose political career as a conservative member of the Danish parliament was cut short by the Spanish flu in 1918. Harald himself had died of the same disease a month earlier. A half-brother, born out of wedlock to a woman his father knew before marrying Harald's mother, served as a school teacher on the same remote island where Harald's mother had spent an important part of her childhood; both of these connections to life on an isolated island became crucial sources of inspiration—along with Søren Kierkegaard—when Harald Kidde penned his principal work of fiction, the novel *The Hero* (1912).[1]

Kidde's home in provincial Vejle had a cultivated bourgeois atmosphere that was conducive to his artistic dreams. But before his son's graduation from high school, the elderly father died, and Harald and his brother had to abandon their adolescent comfort zone for Copenhagen, where they settled with their mother, and where the serious young poet now cultivated his fledgling creative aspirations concurrently with university studies in theology. He left academe without a degree in order to embark on a full-time existence as an independent man of letters, and after commencing his authorial career with (two collections of) short prose sketches around 1900, his artistic voice developed through years of experiments with longer novelistic formats. Meanwhile, in 1906 he married the former musician and future author Astrid Ehrencron-Müller (1874–1960), who would survive her spouse by more than forty years. The childless couple shared an itinerant life of spiritual intimacy, including a lengthy professional sojourn during World War I in a province of Sweden.

As an author, Kidde was never a popular figure. His earnest, profound existential and artistic passion did not curry favor with the masses, though it secured him a small circle of ardent, if by no means uncritical, fin-de-siècle admirers, including the pre-eminent critic Valdemar Vedel (1865–1942). Post-mortem, one of Kidde's

---

[1]   Harald Kidde, *Helten*, Copenhagen: Gyldendal 1918; see also the reprint of the first edition, *Helten*, ed. by Jørgen Bonde Jensen, Copenhagen: Gyldendal 1963, cited here.

novels, the aforementioned *The Hero*, saw a renaissance and has since defended its position as a classic work of twentieth-century Danish literature; and Kidde's last work, a monstrosity of a novel called *The Iron* (1918),[2] published shortly before his death as the only finished part of an ambitiously planned tetralogy, is a *tour de force* through Swedish socio-cultural history and a complicated mix of spirituality and materiality, genres and styles, that in many ways prefigures major achievements in European modernism. This cusp of his career was, for better and worse, an unparalleled achievement in Danish letters.

"Epochal symbolistic or allegorical Jugend style,"[3] was the trademark of Kidde's first book of short prose, *Symbols* (1900).[4] The same mode of writing extends well into the subsequent collection, *Castles in the Air* (1904),[5] whose short and legend-like pieces even furnish the genre with secular if not blasphemous topsy-turvy renditions of Norse and Old Testament, as well as classical Greek and New Testament, tales.[6] Between these collections appears *Aage and Else* (1902–03),[7] Kidde's first and "most consistent novel."[8] The long text of lyrically charged prose is divided into two parts, "Death" and "Life," and like the medieval ballad that has offset its title, it concerns the strife between fixations to memories and the past, on the one hand, and the challenge of *carpe diem*, on the other. The dilemma, which consumes the male protagonist Tue and his psyche, is also one between outreach and "inreach," accentuated by the fact that out there, where life is for real, struggle and egotism prevails, whereas in here, where home is, there is only living death.[9] If the truth be told, Tue's rejection of life here and now is just about as selfish as the way of life he rejects. But when he finally arrives at that insight himself, it is too late for his choice of existence to come to fruition,[10] a melancholy outcome that is foregrounded in many Danish novels, including those of Jens Peter Jacobsen (1847–85) to whose stylistic idioms Kidde's novel debut is heavily indebted.

---

[2]   Harald Kidde, *Jærnet: Roman om Järnbäraland*, Copenhagen: Aschehoug 1918; see also the critical edition, *Jærnet: Roman om Järnbäraland*, ed. by Knud Bjarne Gjesing and Thomas Riis, Copenhagen: Danske Klassikere/DSL/Borgen 1990.

[3]   Knud Bjarne Gjesing, "Harald Kidde," in *Danske digtere i det 20. århundrede, 1*, 4th ed., ed. by Anne-Marie Mai, Copenhagen: Gad 2001, p. 171.

[4]   Harald Kidde, *Sindbilleder*, Copenhagen: Det nordiske Forlag 1900.

[5]   Harald Kidde, *Luftslotte*, Copenhagen: Gyldendal/Nordisk Forlag 1904.

[6]   Ibid.

[7]   Harald Kidde, *Aage og Else*, Copenhagen: Det nordiske Forlag 1902–03.

[8]   Johannes Møllehave, "Religiøs tydning og protest [Harald Kidde]," in *Danske digtere i det 20. Århundrede, Bind 1: Tiden fra Johannes V. Jensen til første verdenskrig*, 2nd ed., ed. by Frederik Nielsen and Ole Restrup, Copenhagen: Gad 1965, p. 209.

[9]   Christian Kock, "Harald Kidde," *Danske digtere i det 20. århundrede, 1: Fra Johs. V. Jensen til Martin Andersen Nexø*, 3rd ed., ed. by Torben Brostrøm and Mette Winge, Copenhagen: Gad 1980, p. 264.

[10]   See also Gjesing, "Harald Kidde," p. 172.

In four subsequent novels, *The Blind* (1906),[11] *The Law* (1908),[12] *The Other* (1909),[13] and *The Blessed* (1910),[14] the conflict between acceptance and rejection of life is subjected to a variety of artistic experiments leading up to Kidde's breakthrough with *The Hero*. Here the physical setting of the earlier texts, more or less the environment of the author's boyhood city of Vejle, has receded in favor of a remote and desolate island to which *The Hero*'s protagonist migrates as a young man to spend the rest of his life.

A recurrent narrative pattern in most of Kidde's novels is a triangle in which a virtuous, but introverted, emotionally distant, and sexually inhibited male protagonist, bound to home, mother, and bygone days, fails to reciprocate the feelings of a bright and spirited female soul mate. Instead, this male character gets overwhelmed by the living force and dark sensuality of a more erotic woman, or ends up being out-competed by a lowly, sensuous man. Only in *The Blessed*, the last of the early novels, is a healing of the leading male's divided self in the offing—on the condition that sexuality, as a key to life, be completely and whole-heartedly rejected. To elaborate the critic Henrik Schovsbo's point about *The Blessed*, one might say that the thematic stalemate and traumatic bindings to the past that dominated Kidde's earliest works have finally been loosened. However, both life and selfhood in this author's universe will henceforth depend entirely on an erotically charged Platonism if they are to keep spirit and memory intact; and that is a scheme of things in which critics like Villy Sørensen have little confidence.[15]

That said, while the question about human existence in the future is raised on this basis, it is taken to a new level in Kidde's *The Hero*. After discussing the novel's early part about Clemens Bek's upbringing in a Copenhagen whorehouse under the tutelage of the German émigré and Kierkegaardian Pietist Eberhard, Schovsbo writes: "The question which the rest of the narrative will address after this colorful prelude, is: Can one achieve a valid life, in Kierkegaard's sense become a witness to the truth, when one is escaping life such as Clemens does?"[16] The answer afforded by Clemens' example is indeed a Pietist one, writes Schovsbo, for Clemens achieves his self by deadening it, that is, by following *the path of suffering*—to cite the title of a novel by Ernesto Dalgas (1871–99), published posthumously in 1903—in a spirit of non-sexual Eros.[17]

Finally—to stay for a moment with Schovsbo's depiction—in 1918 the process of purification undergone by *The Hero*'s most pivotal character becomes itself "the central entity" in *The Iron*, as this novel shows a nation (Sweden) perpetually in the throes of war and death and an old industrial (Swedish) culture in irreversible

---

[11]   Harald Kidde, *De Blinde*, Copenhagen: Gyldendal/Nordisk Forlag 1906.
[12]   Harald Kidde, *Loven*, Copenhagen: Gyldendal/Nordisk Forlag 1908.
[13]   Harald Kidde, *Den Anden*, Copenhagen: Gyldendal/Nordisk Forlag 1909.
[14]   Harald Kidde, *De Salige*, Copenhagen: Gyldendal/Nordisk Forlag 1910.
[15]   Henrik Schovsbo, "Harald Kidde," *Arkiv for Dansk Litteratur*, accessed February 5, 2011. http://adl.dk.
[16]   Ibid., p. 11.
[17]   Ibid., p. 12.

decline and fall.[18] The novel clearly "points in the direction of the transpersonal and postindividual,"[19] where life in the individual sense yields the right of way to life as an open-ended, perhaps utopian, impersonal process. Christian Kock considers the volume an opaque but fascinating work of great symbolic and symbolistic power, albeit torn by both thematic and formal conflicts,[20] and Johannes Møllehave sums up his impression of the text by calling it linguistically and stylistically "a religious incantation of the reality to which the characters of [Kidde's] other works succumb."[21]

II. Kierkegaard in Harald Kidde's Works

As could be expected in any *corpus* of fiction, specific references to, or uses of, named sources of influence on Kidde's *oeuvre*—be they sources of literary, theological, or philosophical import—are few and far between; *explicit* allusions to Kierkegaard are thus in evidence in merely two of Kidde's—mid-career—novels and sparsely so in both.[22]

The title of *The Blessed* reflects this novel's motto, which is culled from the first of Kierkegaard's *Three Upbuilding Discourses* about a multitude of sins (1843). The quotation resurfaces later in the novel's main text when Henning Norden, its protagonist, uses it in an exchange with Enevold Rosen:

> Don't you remember, Enevold, Kierkegaard's words in the first discourse about "a multitude of sins": "Happy the person who saw the world in all its perfection when everything was still very good; happy the person who with God was witness to the glory of creation. More blessed the soul that was God's co-worker in love; blessed the love that hides a multitude of sins."[23]

Henning opposes his mother's law-abiding idealism because it is a menace to life itself; but as he seeks to salvage the passion for life that falls victim to her attitude, by removing this passion from the impure sphere of human desires, he actually engages in a dubious idealism of his own. A living dead man, or an exile in life here and now, Henning evokes Kierkegaard's loving alternative to the law of retribution. But as Enevold's dreamy irresponsibility illustrates, such a poetic gesture may be well-intended yet misguided at the same time, and so the conflict between life and law as Henning sees it remains unresolved and deadening. Indeed, the law of life *is* retribution—and hence as counterproductive as sheer lawlessness.

---

[18]   Schovsbo, "Harald Kidde."
[19]   Ibid.
[20]   Kock, "Harald Kidde," pp. 271–3.
[21]   Møllehave, "Religiøs tydning og protest [Harald Kidde]," p. 217.
[22]   The fact that the female character Riborg in Kidde's novel *Den Anden* "personifies ties to the past, a *demonic* symbol—the demonic being precisely the emotional ties to that which is considered negative (love of evil) or angst for that which is considered positive (Kierkegaard's 'angst for the good')," is entirely the judgment of the critic Villy Sørensen in his *Digtere og dæmoner. Fortolkninger og vurderinger*, Copenhagen: Gyldendal 1959, pp. 71–2; for a mention of Sørensen's reading of Kidde's entire work, see also note 15 above.
[23]   Kidde, *De Salige*, p. [vii], p. 116; cf. *SKS* 5, 72 / *EUD*, 62.

The only viable alternative is the law of the human heart, that is, mercy and grace. This is not life in place of the law; it is human law in place of life's law of retribution, which, again, is lawlessness. Neither idealistic condemnation nor superficial empathy, but only life lived to its utmost consequence, in bottomless suffering, at once fettered by the law and erupting in blessed freedom, reconstitutes idealism and reclaims its value. Instead of safely escaping from life, being unselfishly at its mercy or lost therein amounts to an idealism that is priceless in its hope to receive life anew from those expelled by its law. In short, judgment becomes subservient, and blind idealism sighted and conscious of a life resurrected beyond the law and its verdicts. The way Kierkegaard informs the title and motto of *The Blessed*, and Henning Norden's retort to Enevold Rosen as well, make it plain that gratuitous dreams of human perfection pale in comparison with God's boundless love of the imperfect from which resurrection and a new and truer life obtains.

Only one more passage in this novel refers directly to Kierkegaard—and it drives the same point home.[24] Henning has just reflected on his mother's asexuality (and his father's turning to a mistress in return) and found it congruent with his own; to him as well, it is bliss to escape from sexuality and life and to be subjected to the law in exile and solitude instead. Confessing his past romantic inclinations for Terese to his mother, he notices the unforgettable sight of the old woman sinking back in her chair and the "all too heavy volume of Kierkegaard falling from her slender hands." After that he begs her not to leave him. "And I was hers alone again.…And the two of us were alone in the world."[25] Kierkegaard's calls for personal choice and sacrifice have not gone unheeded.

The Blessed marks the climax of Kidde's juvenilia—the early poetic prose works of short parables, chronologically framing the author's bulky first novel about death and life, and, subsequently, the series of four more or less autobiographical, more or less experimental, more or less schematic novels—as it leads up to his most mature and lasting literary work: the novel *The Hero*. It is worth noting that *The Blessed* as a gateway to this artistic achievement puts Kidde's fullest exposition of Kierkegaard on display. It is, not surprisingly, an intertextual reference aimed at transcending its own focus: not a narrow dogmatic marker, but the sign of an all-embracing Christian spirit. Kidde made the point in his own words in a letter to Valdemar Vedel. Citing his novel's motto (and musing about its relation to its title), the author explains its meaning:

> It can't be pretentious, can it, to preface it with these words? They say so precisely what I wanted the book to articulate. They have contributed to it, all in all Kierkegaard has contributed to the transmutation I feel in my being. His high degree of patience, his humble mildness, his deep passion, which I see most beautifully in his "Discourses."[26]

---

24   Kidde, *De Salige*, p. 97.
25   Ibid.
26   Letter from Harald Kidde to Valdemar Vedel, April 27, 1910 (The Royal Library, NKS 4465, 4): "*Det kan vel ikke synes pretentiøst at stille de Ord foran? De siger så nøje, hvad jeg vilde, Bogen skulde give Text til. De har virket med til den, Kierkegaard har i det Hele virket med til den Forskydning, jeg føler i mit Væsen. Hans høje Tålmod, hans ydmyge Mildhed, hans inderlige Lidenskab, sådan jeg ser den smukkest i hans 'Taler.'*"

At its core the passage emphasizes Kierkegaard's contribution to the transformation
and enrichment of Kidde as a human being. Thanks in part to this inspiration, the
young author accommodates a wider, deeper, and taller sense of self than he had
known before. Kierkegaard's combination of humble mildness and passionate
intensity is key to the spiritual renewal awaiting the later Kidde's artistic universe.
Few critics have elaborated specifically on this impact on *The Blessed*, and when
Knud Bjarne Gjesing does so in a recent literary history, even he broadens his take
on this particular novel so as to include Kierkegaard's overall influence on the author.
In fact, his reading conforms to Kidde's own comments to Vedel: "[Kidde] was an
empathetic reader of Kierkegaard; however, his understanding was not concerned
with the refined theological dogmas on the paradox and the hidden nature of faith,
but rather with the later *corpus*' straightforward demand to imitate Christ."[27]

There is a direct connection between the two expositions, especially Kidde's own
formulations in the letter to Vedel, and the one (lengthy) passage in *The Hero* where
Kierkegaard is mentioned explicitly. Young Clemens Bek, the novel's unworldly and
bereft protagonist, who has just lost his estranged biological father and his German-
born Pietist mentor and spiritual father Mr. Eberhard on the same day, declares
that "nothing was mine—let alone life."[28] Distraught by despair he joins two old
classmates on a visit to the gregarious Copenhagen students' union, where lively
debates about current affairs in culture and politics, matters completely unknown
to the solitary Clemens, fill the air. As a stranger among strangers, his thoughts and
feelings begin wandering back to the brothel where he was raised as an orphan, and
where the prostitutes were as agitated by the turbulent national fervor in the wake of
the First Schleswig War as are the young men now crowding the student union. One
student in particular utters polemically, in a voice "trembling from anger or fear,"[29]
the name Søren Aabye Kierkegaard. And suddenly the vision returns to Clemens of
this historical character whom his mentor Eberhard had shown him in the streets
and described to him in a voice trembling not from anger or fear, but from awe and
admiration, as "this country's only truthful man."[30] The despised and caricatured
philosopher who so repelled the young theology student—Mr. Either/Or, scorned by
street urchins as a limping peripatetic with uneven legs and a broken engagement
to his discredit—was embraced by the emigrant German Pietist in "devotion and
gratitude,"[31] especially for his various articles against official Christendom in *The
Moment*. To underscore Kierkegaard's role as yet a third father figure for Clemens
Bek, we are told that he, "the great dangerous one, was now dead, only few days
after Eberhard" (and Clemens' biological father).[32]

Knud Bjarne Gjesing, whom I cited earlier, picks up on the latter point in a
separate analysis of *The Hero*, and recognizes in Eberhard's derogatory words
about, and Clemens's more subdued contempt for, Danish church officials, "the

---

[27]   Gjesing, "Harald Kidde," pp. 174–5.
[28]   Kidde, *Helten*, p. 139.
[29]   Ibid., p. 141.
[30]   Ibid., p. 142.
[31]   Ibid.
[32]   Ibid.

provocative tone of the polemical writings which Kierkegaard in the last year of his life directed against the state church."[33] Stating that Eberhard's confrontation of Lutheran orthodoxy with Pietism amounts to a theology that is more practically and morally attuned to the epistle of James than it is to the theology of the epistles of Paul, Gjesing writes: "The resemblance which interpreters most often detect between Kierkegaard and the notion of Christianity in *The Hero* applies in no way to his teaching about the concealment of faith in, e.g., *Fear and Trembling* (1843), but it does indeed apply to the passionate demand to imitate Christ that obtains in the last part of the *corpus*."[34]

Jørgen Bukdahl, an older critic, wrote a book chapter as early as 1931 on Kidde as the epitome of "The moral breakthrough," in which he claims that Eberhard in *The Hero*

> is a revolutionary, a church subverter, a man who in his fiery conviction is cast in armor and metal sheet. Kidde has here drilled himself into the spirit of pietism that Kierkegaard set free; it is overthrowing church and society....What Kidde wanted to achieve through Clemens Bek was to vitalize the moral sum total of Christianity, the imitation [of Christ], the suffering, the Kierkegaardian idea of dying from the world.[35]

Stressing Clemens' imitation of Christ has remained a staple for critics to this day, as both of Gjesing's readings illustrated. But otherwise critics have recently been less inclined to see Clemens taking the moral high road on Kidde's behalf, and more inclined to highlight his grappling with self-realization. Christian Kock, in a 1976 study of "The Meaning of *Helten*," cites *The Sickness unto Death* to illustrate how Bek comes to his island "despairingly willing to be his abstract self," which really means: despairingly unwilling to be his true self;[36] the fact that his resignation to death and eternity is being reversed in the course of the novel leads him to an appreciation of being and living where he actually is, and thus marks a transformation of outlook that is key to the entire novel.[37] According to Kock, it can also be described, in the terms of *Works of Love*, as the fact that the flesh in Christianity is only symbolically a matter of sexuality; rather than indicating sensuousness, it indicates selfishness, and instead of advocating resignation, the educational process undertaken by the hero of Kidde's novel points away from selfish longing for, and preoccupation with, better places than the place where one actually lives—that is, away from preferential love and the whole center–periphery model of thinking and feeling. An actual and consequential self-realization here and now must not be forfeited.[38]

---

[33]   Knud Bjarne Gjesing, "De nedrige steder: Harald Kidde, *Helten*," in *Læsninger i dansk litteratur: Tredje bind 1900–1940*, 2nd ed., ed. by Povl Schmidt et al., Odense: Odense Universitetsforlag 2001 (1997), p. 152.
[34]   Ibid., p. 160.
[35]   Jørgen Bukdahl, "Det moralske gennembrud: Harald Kidde," in his *Det moderne Danmark*, Copenhagen: Aschehoug 1931, p. 235.
[36]   Christian Kock, "Meningen med *Helten*: En studie i symbolik," *Danske Studier*, 1976, pp. 55–6.
[37]   Ibid., pp. 62–4.
[38]   Ibid., pp. 73–5.

In his later discussion of Kidde's entire work, Kock reiterates the points he made about *The Hero* by saying that Clemens escapes in "selfish resignation" to his island, and once again his act of despair is construed in the terms of *The Sickness unto Death*'s "despair to will to make the eternal suffice, and thereby to be able to defy or ignore suffering in the earthly and the temporal."[39] But while Clemens believed he could escape the destructive forces of extroverted desire in this way, he gradually comes to realize that accepting and living *with* this desire is the way to avoid succumbing to it. Though desire in Christian terms is sheer selfishness, it is a fact, according to *Works of Love*, that Christianity does not lay blame on humans for harboring this trait, which they have not chosen for themselves any more than they have chosen their need for food and drink.

It should be noted here that it is Kock the interpreter of Kidde and his work, and not the novelist or *his* interpretation of the human condition, who calls specific attention to Kierkegaard and his input. Not surprisingly, given the nature of artistic writing, this is how narrative fiction and philosophical discourse are typically linked to one another. Except for the few explicit references to Kierkegaard in Kidde's work that I mentioned previously, the older philosopher's presence in the younger novelist's universe is but a plausible critical construction, or an implicit fact brought explicitly to the fore in critical expositions. The ultimate case in point is Niels Kofoed's discussion of the nostalgic dimension in *The Hero*, the only book-length study of this work and a major scholarly treatment of Kidde overall.

It is telling here that Kofoed refers directly and approvingly to Kock and his claim that living, either at the center or the periphery, in *The Hero* is insignificant compared to the dictum "despairingly not willing to be oneself."[40] Kofoed even goes on to say that "the author [Kidde] focuses on the spiritual development of his protagonist, which he interprets in light of Kierkegaard's *Works of Love*."[41] Then he continues on his own by asserting that "just like in Kierkegaard's *Either/Or*, there is a relation between [*The Hero*'s] two parts, which shows that the second part is written first, so that the work's innermost intention is expressed in the last part."[42] Polemicizing against Kidde's friend and biographer Niels Jeppesen (1882–1962), Kofoed further submits that the author of *The Hero* deliberately makes Kierkegaard's attack upon the Danish State Church "a turning point in the novel," whereas "the role which Kierkegaard may have played as a historical figure in Kidde's imagination has more to do with Eberhard than with the boy Clemens."[43] Kidde writes in a letter to Jeppesen that "characters like [Hamann] and Kierkegaard's father I have melted together with memories of old people in our family, my paternal grandmother's brothers, who immigrated to Denmark from Westphalia, and whose old, sacred books I pondered over as a child: Eberhard originated from all this."[44]

---

[39]   Kock, "Harald Kidde," pp. 270–1; cf. *SKS* 11, 184 / *SUD*, 70.

[40]   Niels Kofoed, *Den nostalgiske dimension. En værkgennemgang af Harald Kiddes roman Helten*, Copenhagen: Akademisk Forlag 1980, pp. 17–18.

[41]   Ibid., p. 18.

[42]   Ibid., p. 26.

[43]   Ibid., p. 32.

[44]   Ibid., pp. 32–3.

The parallel between Clemens' upbringing and that of Kierkegaard "is quite clear," according to Kofoed, "but unlike circumstances in Kierkegaard's home, [in Clemens' case] the isolation is not the result of a despotic father's whims, but dictated by bitter destitution."[45] Finally, in Kofoed's judgment, "the immoral bookkeeping with double entries in the Copenhagen of the postwar period [sc. the Schleswig War] and the year of the cholera is thrown into strong relief by Kierkegaard's attack upon the Church and official Christendom in 1854–55."[46]

Most recently, Børge Kristiansen has compared the theme of identity, "becoming one's self and being one's self," in *The Hero* with comparable manifestations in Henrik Pontoppidan's novel *Lucky Per*—all in light of Kierkegaard. In both novels, longing for other places and conditions than the ones in which one is situated is pivotal to the loss of self and selfhood. Conversely, accepting one's meager circumstances, be it Per's rural Jutland or Clemens' desolate island, is key to attaining self and selfhood, to being in "truth" by dint of a choice that redeems the individual from the prison house of existence, as Clemens Bek describes it. In both instances it is a negative move, rejecting social life as an empty illusion that only serves to conceal that the true human condition is isolation. It is, however, a negativity which takes a redeeming dialectical turn toward the utmost positivity. Kristiansen might have labeled it a truly splendid isolation! In Pontoppidan's (and Nietzsche's) case, he sees the positive outcome grounded solely in "the self's relation to itself,"[47] whereas in Kidde's case the outcome rests upon the same relation being ultimately grounded in a relation to God. In both authors, " 'the secret road to redemption' (Novalis) leads into the self and not away from the self into the world, as the world can only be conquered after one has found peace in oneself."[48]

III. General Interpretation

Of the critics cited thus far for their comments on Kierkegaard's particular relevance to Kidde's *The Hero*, several suggested the probability of a wider influence of the philosopher upon Kidde and his literary production, or suggested conversely that such an alleged influence was too farfetched to be credible. Bukdahl, for instance, submits a general comparison between Kidde and Kierkegaard's style:

> Paludan-Müller is said to have once advised Kierkegaard to go to Rome to learn form. Kierkegaard meant he could be clear without being classical. His style meant more to him than a living skin around an affected content; it was the sound of his soul, the vivid air of his ideas, with the combination of oxygen and nitrogen which only he knew how to combine. His style was like the sharp, lapped mirrors of a lighthouse lantern, and the end result was a cone of light of unusually concentrated strength; not so in Kidde (whose

---

[45] Ibid., p. 54.

[46] Ibid., p. 66.

[47] Børge Kristiansen, "Om identitet: Selvet hos Kidde, Pontoppidan og Frisch i lyset af Kierkegaard," *Kritik*, vol. 182, 2006, p. 131.

[48] Ibid.

densely expressionistic and associative style tragically and desperately attempted to make the word utter "what his imagination reflected and his heart whispered").[49]

Positing a possible connection between Kidde and Kierkegaard only to reject it, as it happened in this quotation, was not what Knud Bjarne Gjesing did when he directed our attention, in both of his treatments, to *The Hero*'s representation of the Kierkegaardian demand to imitate Christ. To Gjesing there was indeed a significant resemblance between Kierkegaard's and *The Hero*'s Christianity, but it is one that is more restricted than many interpreters will have it.

Even Johannes Møllehave, who writes about Kidde as a mouthpiece for religious interpretation and protest, goes along with this tempered claim. But only to a point. Beyond that, he questions the overall relevance of Kierkegaard to Kidde: "He [Kidde] read Kierkegaard—especially *Works of Love*—and used on a single occasion a quotation from him as motto for a novel (*The Blessed*), but it is a matter of controversy how much Kierkegaard has otherwise influenced him."[50] In fact,

> in his understanding of what it means to be a Christian, Kidde is decidedly un-Lutheran, and with respect to Kierkegaard, Kidde only pursues this one idea, the "imitation" (of Christ), while he does not even brush on the idea of "admission" (i.e., the individual's admission that the imitation is an impossibility and that one receives God's grace undeservedly).[51]

Kofoed's general remarks are similarly skeptical and reserved: "There is…no reason to place Kidde within the Kierkegaardian tradition, although Kierkegaard is among his favorite authors. In his novels' exposition of life, Kidde is never in line with the sin–grace axis, but is often in line with the guilt–destiny axis."[52] Less reserved claims about a Kierkegaard–Kidde connection usually issue from writers outside the scholarly community who tend to make sweeping summary assessments that are not anchored in thorough readings of particular texts. Kidde's older friend, the novelist and dramatist Henri Nathansen (1868–1944), in his portrait of the author delivers an object lesson in this respect by writing that Kidde was most profoundly attracted to remote and lonely natures: the German Romantics, Paludan-Müller, and "Kierkegaard's dialectic monologues and tragic passion plays between Eros and ethos, irony and pathos."[53] Another example obtains from Jacob Paludan (1896–1975), a younger author of fiction and essays, who states that like others of his turn-of-the-century generation of writers, Kidde cultivated unhappiness, especially in love, as he—Kidde—and they consummate, "in the mode of Kierkegaard, what they presumably deep down have wished for: the blessed suffering."[54]

---

[49]   Bukdahl, "Det moralske gennembrud: Harald Kidde," p. 238.

[50]   Møllehave, "Religiøs tydning og protest [Harald Kidde]," p. 202.

[51]   Ibid., pp. 213–4.

[52]   Kofoed, *Den nostalgiske dimension. En værkgennemgang af Harald Kiddes roman Helten*, p. 15.

[53]   Henri Nathansen, "Harald Kidde," in his *Portrætstudier*, Copenhagen: Nyt Nordisk Forlag/Busck 1930, p. 91.

[54]   Jacob Paludan, "Lysstraalen fra Anholt," in his *Litterært Selskab*, Copenhagen: Hasselbalch 1956, p. 18.

In three cases such blanket statements about a Kierkegaardian influence (or lack thereof) on Kidde teeter on biographical discourse. Jens Marinus Jensen asserts that Kierkegaard was discussed by members of the young Kidde's circle of friends, and that Kidde "was influenced by Kierkegaard and rejected official Christianity";[55] Kidde continues Kierkegaard's work by promulgating that "faith is dead without acts of faith, and to be a true disciple entails acting in the spirit of the master."[56] Christian Rimestad in his biographical treatment reads Kidde's circle of friends differently, but elaborates on Kidde's own religiosity in the same vein as Jensen. Unlike his comrades, says Rimestad, Kidde struggled with "the most difficult religious problems: right up to his death Kierkegaard remained his favorite reading";[57] as much as he admired and loved true Christianity, he showed "an uncompromising contempt for the leveling of Christianity which official Christendom had entailed";[58] indeed, this "distortion and falsification of the supreme doctrine, he abhorred and despised with a fanaticism that was no less than that expressed by Kierkegaard himself";[59] moreover, Kidde's negative sentiments "were also directed against the upper echelon of this world, the social climbers, worshippers of mammon, the cusp of society."[60]

By contrast, in a third biographically based account of Kidde and his work, Niels Jeppesen diverges from both Jensen and Rimestad, and from Bukdahl as well, when these critics allege a significant connection between Kidde and Kierkegaard.[61] As mentioned earlier, Jeppesen has been taken to task by Niels Kofoed for lack of analytical rigor, but even a lack of consistency must be added to this grievance. Jeppesen, who knew the young Kidde personally, admits that he had Kierkegaard's picture on his wall, but insists that it was the philosopher's beautiful profile he found attractive, not the man's (dubious) character and certainly not his theology. Neither the religious paradox, "the central point in Kierkegaard's *oeuvre*," nor the dialectical mode of thinking resonated with Kidde's mental make-up.[62] And while "Kierkegaard scoffed at the official church, Kidde cancelled his membership."[63] Accordingly, "Kidde is not to be found on the line between Kierkegaard and Dostoevsky, he was much closer to the Grundtvig–Tolstoy line."[64]

This distinction is blurred, however, when Jeppesen less than one page later claims that "Pietism was much closer to his [Kidde's] heart than was Grundtvigianism."[65] And on the note of piety (if not Pietism), Jeppesen goes on to claim that Kidde's

---

[55]   Jens Marinus Jensen, *Harald Kidde. Bidrag til en Biografi*, rev. ed., Aarhus: Aros 1948 (1924), pp. 67, 84.

[56]   Jensen, *Harald Kidde. Bidrag til en Biografi* (1924), p. 96.

[57]   Christian Rimestad, "Efterskrift," in Harald Kidde, *Vandringer*, Copenhagen: Aschehoug 1920, p. 172.

[58]   Rimestad, "Efterskrift," p. 179.

[59]   Ibid.

[60]   Ibid.

[61]   Niels Jeppesen, *Harald Kidde og hans Digtning*, Copenhagen: Levin & Munksgaard 1934.

[62]   Ibid., pp. 9–10.

[63]   Ibid., p. 10.

[64]   Ibid., pp. 9–10.

[65]   Ibid., p 10.

absolute fidelity to the dead parallels the fact that Kierkegaard's ultimate fidelity to his father came about after the old man's death.[66] On other occasions as well, Jeppesen seems at odds with his own rejection of Kierkegaard's influence on Kidde. The latter's portrayal of Jesus is compared with Kierkegaard's way of probing *Ecce homo!* "with the whole passion of his soul";[67] and while there may be little in the order of dialectics in *The Hero*'s composition, Jeppesen concedes that the development of Kidde's writing "corresponds to Kierkegaard's three stages: the aesthetic, the ethical, and the religious."[68]

As to the model behind this novel's protagonist, Jeppesen is no less ambiguous. First he makes the point that "Harald Plesner, Harald Kidde's half-brother, is the real model for *The Hero*," and that Clemens Bek "was no Søren Kierkegaard; that was never Kidde's intention, and he has never mentioned it in a letter to me."[69] However, when Kidde's mother is mentioned for writing that Clemens personifies "her son's idea of a Christian human being," this parenthesis is added: "(influenced by S. Kierkegaard)."[70]

Somewhat more credible, and interesting, is Jeppesen's take on Kidde's reading of Kierkegaard, because it is supposedly based on the biographer's close-up observations. He adamantly disputes what others have claimed to be Kidde's predilection for Kierkegaard's texts; books by Kierkegaard "could not be found on [Kidde's] desk," which for years was filled with the Norwegian author Jonas Lie's collected works.[71] Jeppesen notes the rather few and short direct Kierkegaard quotations (from *Works of Love* and the first of the *Three Upbuilding Discourses*) and references (to passages in *The Hero* inspired by *The Moment*) in Kidde's publications and continues by saying that "he has probably not studied much more of Kierkegaard; *Works of Love* was the only book of his that he liked."[72] Maybe so. Yet the putative authority of an eyewitness account should not lead to suspension of critical judgment. Jeppesen's testimony about Kidde and Kierkegaard is flawed.

A far more measured view of the matter is given by Henrik Schovsbo in his online portrait for *Arkiv for Dansk Litteratur*. Here, too, the Kierkegaardian leanings of Eberhard in Kidde's *The Hero* are mentioned, on which Rimestad, for one—in the Postscript to Kidde's *Vandringer*—based his claim that Kidde himself was a Kierkegaardian; but unlike Eberhard and his religious affinity to Kierkegaard, Kidde's own religiosity is "emotional and diffuse."[73] Even when Schovsbo earlier found *The Hero*'s narrative exploring Clemens' potential as a Kierkegaardian witness to the truth,[74] he was quite nuanced, extracting a general question from a concrete reading of a specific text, and implying an answer in tune with scholarly and critical consensus. The outcome does admit a larger Kierkegaardian strain in

---

[66] Ibid., p. 14.
[67] Ibid., p. 72.
[68] Ibid., p. 106.
[69] Ibid., p. 113 and p. 115, respectively.
[70] Ibid., p. 115.
[71] Ibid., p. 10.
[72] Ibid., p. 9.
[73] Schovsbo, "Harald Kidde."
[74] Ibid.

Kidde's writing than some readers will acknowledge, but it does not exaggerate the scope of this dimension, as others tend to do.

Yet the precise nature of Schovsbo's middle ground remains a bit elusive. That the answer to his question is in the affirmative is attributable to the fact that Clemens on his island is only seemingly escaping life. In reality, the remote and desolate location that appears to be the ideal destination for an escapist is rather the site for the epitome of a life condensed and relieved of all distractions and frills. When Kidde in an autobiographical piece about "How I became an author" calls himself "a widely traveled stay-at home,"[75] he may inadvertently have produced the clue to his dependence on Kierkegaard. For in admitting to being a traveler on location, who brings his home along on his journey, he clearly parallels Clemens Bek, his most Kierkegaardian fictive character, who so desperately sought to escape life as he knew it but only found more of it at the end of his journey than he had left behind at his point of departure.

As others, witness Paludan, Nathansen—and Gjesing in particular[76]—have intimated, Kidde was a transitory writer: torn between the nineteenth and twentieth century, between traditional provincial rootedness and modern urban homelessness, between a secular worldliness deprived of existential redemption and a religious passion tainted by officialdom. A product of a bourgeoisie with its future behind it, he boldly embraced modernistic stances and artistic forms; low-keyed in his personal demeanor, yet attuned to the social diversity of modern city life, he retained a sensibility for the purity of nature; and equally beholden to realist and symbolist idioms, he eventually embarked on a colossal novel project in which "the realistic and symbolistic tendency of his work would combine into a sort of symbolistic documentarism."[77] Suspended throughout his authorial life between these poles, if not stuck in their traumatic interregnum, he persistently upped the existential antes in his work and found, not surprisingly, at least occasional inspiration in (or elected affinity to) the "dialectic monologues and tragic passion plays between Eros and ethos, irony and pathos" and "the blessed suffering" in Kierkegaard's mode of living, thinking, and writing.[78]

---

[75]   Harald Kidde, "Hvorledes jeg blev digter," in his *Artikler og Breve*, ed. by Jens Marinus Jensen, Copenhagen: Woels Forlag 1928, p. 16.

[76]   Cf. Gjesing, "Harald Kidde," p. 170.

[77]   Ibid., p. 175.

[78]   For these indications, by Nathansen and Paludan, respectively, of impulses that Kidde may have received from Kierkegaard, see notes 53 and 54.

Bibliography

I. References to or Uses of Kierkegaard in Kidde's Corpus

De Salige, Copenhagen: Gyldendal/Nordisk Forlag 1910, p. [vii]; p. 97; p. 116.
Helten, Copenhagen: Gyldendal 1912, pp. 144–5; reprint ed. with Postscript by Jørgen Bonde Jensen, Copenhagen: Gyldendal 1963, pp. 141–2.

II. Sources of Kidde's Knowledge of Kierkegaard

Kierkegaard, Søren, *Enten-Eller. Et Livs-Fragment*, vols. 1–2, Copenhagen: C.A. Reitzel 1843.
— *Tre opbyggelige Taler*, Copenhagen: Bianco Luno 1843.
— *Kjerlighedens Gjerninger. Nogle christelige Overveielser i Talers Form*, Copenhagen: C.A. Reitzel 1847.
— *Sygdommen til Døden. En christelig psychologisk Udvikling til Opbyggelse og Opvækkelse*, Copenhagen: C.A. Reitzel 1849.
— *Øieblikket*, Copenhagen: C.A. Reitzel 1877.

III. Secondary Literature on Kiddes's Relation to Kierkegaard

Bukdahl, Jørgen, "Det moralske gennembrud: Harald Kidde," in his *Det moderne Danmark*, Copenhagen: Aschehoug 1931, pp. 222–39; see p. 235; p. 238.
Gjesing, Knud Bjarne, "De nedrige steder: Harald Kidde, *Helten*," in *Læsninger i dansk litteratur: Tredje bind 1900–1940*, 2nd ed., ed. by Povl Schmidt et al., Odense: Odense Universitetsforlag 2001 (1997), pp. 146–63; see p. 148; p. 152; p. 160.
— "Harald Kidde," in *Danske digtere i det 20. århundrede, 1*, 4th ed., ed. by Anne-Marie Mai, Copenhagen: Gad 2001, pp. 170–6; see p. 175.
Jensen, Jens Marinus, *Harald Kidde. Bidrag til en Biografi*, rev. ed., Aarhus: Aros 1948 (1924), p. 67; p. 84; p. 96.
Jeppesen, Niels, *Harald Kidde og hans Digtning*, Copenhagen: Levin & Munksgaard 1934, pp. 8–10; p. 14; p. 72; p. 106; p. 115.
Kock, Christian, "Meningen med *Helten*: En studie i symbolik," *Danske Studier*, 1976, pp. 49–75; see pp. 55–6; pp. 62–4; pp. 73–4.
— "Harald Kidde," in *Danske digtere i det 20. århundrede, 1: Fra Johs. V. Jensen til Martin Andersen Nexø*, 3rd ed., ed. by Torben Brostrøm and Mette Winge, Copenhagen: Gad 1980, pp. 259–74; see p. 259; pp. 270–1.

Kofoed, Niels, *Den nostalgiske dimension. En værkgennemgang af Harald Kiddes roman Helten*, Copenhagen: Akademisk Forlag 1980, p. 15; p. 18; p. 26; pp. 32–3; p. 54; p. 66; p. 91; p. 105.

Kristiansen, Børge, "Om identitet. Selvet hos Kidde, Pontoppidan og Frisch i lyset af Kierkegaard," *Kritik*, vol. 182, 2006, pp. 128–36; see pp. 129–31.

Møllehave, Johannes, "Religiøs tydning og protest [Harald Kidde]," in *Danske digtere i det 20. århundrede, Bind 1: Tiden fra Johannes V. Jensen til første verdenskrig*, 2nd ed., ed. by Frederik Nielsen and Ole Restrup, Copenhagen: Gad 1965, pp. 202–17; see p. 202; pp. 213–14.

Nathansen, Henri, "Harald Kidde," in his *Portrætstudier*, Copenhagen: Nyt Nordisk Forlag/Busck 1930, pp. 86–104; see p. 91.

Paludan, Jacob, "Lysstraalen fra Anholt," in his *Litterært Selskab*, Copenhagen: Hasselbalch 1956, pp. 16–23; see p. 18.

Rimestad, Christian, "Efterskrift," in Harald Kidde, *Vandringer*, Copenhagen: Aschehoug 1920, pp. 166–82; see p. 172; p. 179.

Schovsbo, Henrik, "Harald Kidde: Forfatterskabet," *Arkiv for Dansk Litteratur*, accessed February 5, 2011. http://adl.dk.

Sørensen, Villy, "Erindringens digter: Harald Kidde," in his *Digtere og dæmoner: Fortolkninger og vurderinger*, Copenhagen: Gyldendal 1959, pp. 46–96; see pp. 71–2.

Henrik Pontoppidan:

Inspiration and Hesitation

Peter Tudvad

In an age when it has become fashionable to declare oneself a Christian and when Søren Kierkegaard has become a good *brand*, used for more or less anything at all, it is once more appropriate to bring out the big critics of religion. In this context it is interesting to consider what use the Danish author Henrik Pontoppidan (1857–1943) made of his reading of Kierkegaard, who not only counts as a religious poet but also as an energetic critic of the church. Thus Pontoppidan's speech about *The Church and Its Men* from 1914 sounds like an echo of Kierkegaard's struggle against the State Church's "official Christianity" in 1855.[1]

However, the common criticism of the church also represents a fork in the road, which, for Pontoppidan, leads away from the Christianity which Kierkegaard wants instead to proclaim with all the strength that the church has deprived it of. Pontoppidan can certainly respect this kind of passion and honesty vis-à-vis the "tradesmen-like" clergy's opportunism, but in his authorship one also seems to find a criticism aimed against Kierkegaard's melancholy troll nature.

The objective of this article is therefore to investigate what knowledge Pontoppidan had of Kierkegaard's work and life, and how this knowledge can be traced in Pontoppidan's authorship, albeit limited to his autobiographies and his great novels, where Kierkegaardian character traits can be found in, among others, the figures Emanuel Hansted, Per Sidenius and Pastor Fjaltring, Jytte Abildgaard, and Mads Vestrup.

I. Pontoppidan's Knowledge of Kierkegaard

The first time that Pontoppidan threw himself into Kierkegaard's authorship was apparently in the winter of 1880–81. In *Inheritance and Debt* (1938) he says that during the course of the winter he read industriously, among other things, the works of Kierkegaard "and many other authors who are difficult to digest."[2] It is not clear exactly which works of Kierkegaard he is referring to, but this can be determined

---

[1]   Henrik Pontoppidan, *Kirken og dens Mænd. Et Foredrag*, Copenhagen and Kristiania: Gyldendalske Boghandel, Nordisk Forlag 1914.

[2]   Henrik Pontoppidan, *Arv og Gæld*, Copenhagen: Gyldendal, Nordisk Forlag 1938, p. 41.

based on the records from the libraries in Copenhagen where Pontoppidan says that he borrowed them.

In spite of the difficulty of digesting him, Pontoppidan did not entirely lose his appetite for Kierkegaard; from 1893 and for the next few years he regularly borrowed diverse works by him from the University Library. This is documented in Flemming Behrendt's investigation of the records of the library, which reveal that from March 1893 to May 1896 Pontoppidan borrowed the following works by Kierkegaard: in 1893 *Stages on Life's Way*, the next year *The Moment* and *Fear and Trembling*, in 1895 *Prefaces*, *Practice in Christianity*, *Concluding Unscientific Postscript*, *Philosophical Fragments* along with *Works of Love*, and finally in 1896 *Repetition*.[3]

This is a quite extensive study since one can certainly assume that Pontoppidan in fact read the books that he borrowed. Otherwise it is difficult to see why he would have continued to borrow new books at such regular intervals. The first works that he borrowed can perhaps, as Behrendt assumes, be the result of a wish to familiarize himself with the life of the character which he was in the course of developing in *The Promised Land*, namely, Emanuel Hansted.

In the third part of *Stages on Life's Way*, which by virtue of its title alone must have tempted Pontoppidan, he could have found much that was relevant for his description of Hansted's melancholy character. In Kierkegaard's text we follow a certain *Quidam*, who just like his author, has dissolved an engagement, allegedly due to the melancholy which he suffers from, a melancholy which prevents him from becoming a competent husband but by the same token disposes him to Christianity, which is supposed to be a comfort for those who grieve (Matthew 5:4).

As is well known, *The Moment* is a journal that Kierkegaard published in 1855 as the organ for his violent and rhetorically exuberant struggle against the church and its proclamation of what counted as Christianity, a comfortable watered-down version of the Christianity that Kierkegaard believed that he found in the New Testament. This kind of lemonade Christianity, as Kierkegaard called it,[4] Hansted finds among the Grundtvigians and other "good people" in the "Society of Friends," and it is towards them that he developed an increasing opposition in the course of his development. His Christian development is, in his own words, a path of trial, and this trial is the cornerstone in the faith that Kierkegaard presents in *Fear and Trembling*, which Pontoppidan could also have managed to read before he had Hansted go to ruin in the final book of *The Promised Land*.

It is more doubtful whether he was able to make use of the works he borrowed in 1895 before he finished the novel. The short satirical work *Prefaces* is likewise not of any relevance in this context, while *Philosophical Fragments* might have been of more interest with its dogmatic determinations of what Christianity is. Everything stands and falls here with the divinity of Jesus, which Kierkegaard can only conceive as something inconceivable, as an absolute paradox and a stumbling block for the

---

[3]   Cf. Flemming Behrendt's master's thesis, "Pontoppidans værksted," note 14, which is available at www.henrikpontoppidan.dk.
[4]   See *SKS* 13, 396 / *M*, 332. *SKS* 13, 305 / *M*, 249.

understanding, which is, to put it mildly, in blatant opposition to the clever people in the "Society of Friends," who quickly dismiss everything inconceivable.

Works of Love, like the *Concluding Unscientific Postscript*, is a quite extensive work, which takes a long time to read. To a greater degree than in the other works, there are here practical instructions about how the Christian might manifest his faith in daily action, but I do not think that Pontoppidan could have found anything particularly relevant for his work in this relatively uncontroversial book.

By contrast, he presumably found *Practice in Christianity* worth reading with all the book's radicality and poorly hidden criticism of the church's preaching. If nothing else, the work was recommended in an unusually warm manner by Georg Brandes (1842–1927) in his biography on Kierkegaard from 1877, *Søren Kierkegaard: A Critical Exposition in Outline*. Here Brandes writes as follows: "I regard this book as one of his greatest writings, and it is in general an outstanding work due to its acuity and love of truth. The person who does not have time to read much from the final phase of Kierkegaard's life ought to read it thoroughly and can then find in it his entire way of thinking and emotional life."[5] Pontoppidan would hardly have overlooked such a demand, even less so since he in fact seems to have read Brandes' biography. In a letter to his publisher Frederik Hegel (1817–87) dated February 2, 1884, Pontoppidan asked if he could be sent the biography together with a number of other books by Brandes.[6] A few days earlier, on January 25, Pontoppidan had met Brandes for the first time and on that occasion received recognition for his novel *The Polar Bear*.[7]

Brandes' portrayal of "The Figure of Christ," as he calls the section on *Practice in Christianity*, could well have served Pontoppidan as a description of Emanuel Hansted. With a series of well-chosen quotations, Brandes describes the Kierkegaardian Christ as a humiliated and humble person, who surrounds himself with sinners, tax collectors, lepers and insane, sick and miserable people, just as he in general rejects the existing order and all its power and knowledge. Yet, despite his rejection, Christ dares to offer everyone who works and is troubled, rest and consolation (Matthew 11:28).

On his behalf the pastor in the church now offers the same thing, "an elegant man in silk,"[8] as Brandes writes, quoting Kierkegaard; but when *he* says it, all contradiction between Christ's humiliation and elevation is eliminated such that he instead offers the community his protection as a king. One would have to be straightforwardly stupid not to accept this offer when one also receives it on such favorable conditions as is the case in the Protestant Church and perhaps above all in the Danish Church. The task is, therefore, if it is meaningful to speak of the gospel as a stumbling block for the understanding, to make the community contemporary with

---

5   Georg Brandes, *Søren Kierkegaard. En kritisk Fremstilling i Grundrids*, in *Samlede Skrifter*, vols. 1–3, 2nd ed., Copenhagen: Gyldendal 1919, vol. 2, p. 349.

6   According to an article by Carl Henrik Clemmensen in *Dagens Nyheder* on February 21, 1927, Pontoppidan later referred to the biography as Brandes' "superb treatise on Søren Kierkegaard."

7   Henrik Pontoppidan, *Isbjørnen. Et Portræt*, Copenhagen: Gyldendal 1887.

8   Brandes, *Søren Kierkegaard. En kritisk Fremstilling i Grundrids*, p. 349.

the historical Christ, so that one does not receive salvation cheaply, which would mean not receiving it at all.

In Brandes' Kierkegaard biography there are many other observations which Pontoppidan might have read with interest and made use of in his authorship. I am not saying that these observations are therefore necessarily the source for this or that passage in Pontoppidan's authorship, since most often one must be satisfied with showing a more or less striking parallelism. For example, Lucky Per's belief in being able to do what he wants is not far away from Kierkegaard's view, which Brandes makes clear with a quotation from his posthumous self-reflections, *The Point of View for My Work as an Author*. Kierkegaard writes there, it "never occurred to me at any time that I would not be victorious, even if I would have attempted something utterly rash."[9]

This sounds in its own way very reasonable and almost like that happy son of nature, namely, Oehlenschläger's Aladdin, whom Kierkegaard was so crazy about due to his foolhardiness. But Brandes has a good eye for what is sickly in Kierkegaard's genius, which he gives an admonishing portrayal of in connection with his analysis of the publication of Kierkegaard's first book, *From the Papers of One Still Living*. This work is a long cutting down of Hans Christian Andersen on occasion of his novel, *Only a Fiddler*, which, according to Kierkegaard, taught a doctrine of the genius as dependent on the warm attention and loving care of his surroundings—a doctrine which stood in radical opposition to Kierkegaard's own belief that the genius could prevail due to his own will. But it is a very special kind of genius that Kierkegaard, in Brandes' words, possesses, one with a desire for pain.[10] This lust for pain, which, according to Brandes, is special for the Kierkegaardian genius, is also special for many of Pontoppidan's over-sized enthusiasts, be they religious geniuses such as Emanuel Hansted and Mads Vestrup or mundane geniuses such as Lucky Per. Figures such as these have something epochal about them, but above all they are ideal types, which expose a special Danish character trait, namely, melancholy, depression, and darkness. Thus in a letter to Richardt Gandrup from 1924 Pontoppidan mentions Kierkegaard as one of Danish literature's "great melancholics."[11]

Pontoppidan himself knew melancholy and certainly also knew that it could be a literary stimulus, but nonetheless he constantly diagnosed it as something unhealthy, which should yield to a happy and powerful enthusiasm for life. He did not find this kind of healthiness in Kierkegaard but rather in Nietzsche. About his first reading of the German philosopher, around the turn of the century, he writes in *Underway to Myself* (1943), that he "frequently during the reading compared…him with our own philosophical celebrity, the dark man with the name so characteristic of a self-tortured religious person, Kierkegaard [sc. Churchyard]."[12] In *Family Life* (1940)

---

[9]   Ibid., vol. 2, p. 254. The passage quoted corresponds to *SKS* 16, 60 / *PV*, 81.

[10]   Brandes, *Søren Kierkegaard. En kritisk Fremstilling i Grundrids*, pp. 254–5.

[11]   *Henrik Pontoppidans breve*, vols. 1–2, ed. and annotated by Carl Erik Bay and Elias Bredsdorff, Copenhagen: Gyldendal 1997, vol. 2, p. 152.

[12]   Henrik Pontoppidan, *Undervejs til mig selv. Et Tilbageblik*, Copenhagen: Gyldendal, Nordisk Forlag 1943, p. 172.

it is made a bit clearer what the point is in the comparison with Nietzsche. Here Pontoppidan writes:

> I must confess that he really was a creative spirit, a spirit with albatross wings in comparison, for example, with Kierkegaard, whose criticism of the age and its people had struck me through and through as being quite small-minded, and whose highly admired style all too often led me to think of his sad name with its traces of death and the grave.[13]

Kierkegaard himself writes that he cannot live without an idea, but when he only wastes away with the ideas, then he becomes precisely the kind of ghost existence that Pontoppidan describes. Even if Kierkegaard must be respected for his honest insistence not least on Christianity's idea without any ecclesial trappings, then he also becomes a dangerous extremist, who places the idea above the given actuality. For this reason Pontoppidan in a letter to Vilhelm Andersen (1864–1953) in 1915—with explicit reference to Kierkegaard and a few other authors of the nineteenth century—denies that the Danes, in Ludvig Holberg's words, are a people, who "rarely fall into extremes"; for this reason a great Norwegian such as Henrik Ibsen seems almost "bourgeois and clerical in comparison with his teacher Kierkegaard."[14]

Six years later Pontoppidan wrote something similar in a letter to Harald Høffding (1843–1931), saying that Danes lack an ear for the intermediate tones, for which reason "the good citizen" in literature since Holberg has almost exclusively been "an object of satire"; in any case he could not sense a preference for the golden mean, since "from the young Grundtvig's visionary judgment day tones to Drachmann's radical, devil-may-care attitude runs in actuality a path of pain from the one extreme to the other (Søren Kierkegaard, Paludan-Müller and their opposite Georg Brandes)."[15]

Now one could almost be suspicious that Pontoppidan himself becomes somewhat "small-minded" in his anxiety for the extremes, but his refusal is due only to the fact that he consistently insists that even the extremists must earn a living and not only the idea. Nonetheless he must, of course, praise the lack of consideration—understood as indifference towards the surrounding world's judgment—which these extremists show. In 1910 he refers to Kierkegaard, when he, in a letter to Harald Nielsen (1879–1957), chastises him for fishing for recognition. "Least of all can a castigator expect to enjoy appreciation," he writes. "Think of the indifference, with which a man like Søren Kierkegaard raised his tower of Babel....Does one dare squint at the results of one's activity?"[16]

Kierkegaard is thus an extremist, but Pontoppidan, as already mentioned, seems to conceive his extremism as honest in a purely theological context, namely, in relation to the State Church's self-interested pastors, who dishonestly seek to make Christianity into an appetizing repast for a consumer bourgeois class, which is

---

13   Henrik Pontoppidan, *Familjeliv*, Copenhagen: Gyldendal 1940, p. 80.
14   *Henrik Pontoppidans breve*, vol. 2, p. 17.
15   Ibid., vol. 2, pp. 128–9.
16   Ibid., vol. 1, p. 320.

interested just as little as the clergy in their eternal salvation but all the more in appearing in public as morally correct.

Just like Brandes, who likewise did not care much for Kierkegaard, Pontoppidan must thus concede to him that in relation to the church and its proclamation he represents what he himself in *The Moment* called "human honesty."[17] Thus in a letter from February 16, 1912, Pontoppidan describes to Brandes his childhood pastors from the area around Randers as wholly mundane. The situation that he refers to is more or less the same throughout the country, where, in spite of "Kierkegaard" and a few other champions, one finds among hundreds of pastors hardly more than ten "truly reliable workers in the vineyard."[18] Two years later Pontoppidan confirms his agreement with Kierkegaard's criticism in *The Church and Its Men*, and again in *Boyhood Years* (1933) he refers to the rationalist and opportunist pastors of the Randers countryside: "In spite of Mynster and Grundtvig, in spite of Kierkegaard and Martensen it was the barn and the field, the gaming board and the rum bottle which seized the time and thoughts of these ecclesial large landholders."[19] Pontoppidan's wrestling with Kierkegaard ends with what one could ultimately call a sympathetic–antipathetic relation—at once sympathy with his honest and fearless one-man struggle against the church and antipathy towards his life-denying character and proclamation.

Before I go over to an account of the three long novels and the lecture critical of the church, I want to mention an important figure in the autobiography, who seems to illustrate Pontoppidan's relation to Kierkegaard in a clearer and more personal manner. I refer here to one of Pontoppidan's fellow students at the Polytechnical School, a certain Hansen-Schaffalitzsky or merely Schaff, who called himself a "Kierkegaardian to the 8th degree."[20]

No one has managed to identify this curious figure, and so he must doubtless be understood as a literary construction. This makes him no less interesting in this context; on the contrary, since it means that Pontoppidan, due to a lack of actual knowledge, had to make up a fictional Kierkegaardian in his biography in order to be able to give an account of certain decisive trends in his development. In any case Schaff is an important component in his autobiographical reconstruction.

We learn about Schaff in *Sloughing* (1936), where it is said that he is somewhat older than Pontoppidan and his fellow students at the Polytechnic School. He had previously studied theology, and later he drops his polytechnic studies for philology. Schaff has an excellent mind but is also, writes Pontoppidan, "a devil of contradiction, whom not even our teachers can get to shut up."[21] After he changed his field of studies—which must have been around 1875—Pontoppidan meets him in a café with a view of the Church of Our Lady:

---

[17]   *SKS* 13, 213 / *M*, 165.

[18]   *Henrik Pontoppidans breve*, vol. 1, pp. 349–50.

[19]   Henrik Pontoppidan, *Drengeaar*, Copenhagen: Gyldendal, Nordisk Forlag 1933, pp. 79–80.

[20]   Henrik Pontoppidan, *Hamskifte*, Copenhagen: Gyldendal, Nordisk Forlag 1936, p. 54.

[21]   Ibid., p. 52.

I had to think of what he once told me with the same grimace, namely, that he sometimes would experience sentimental relapses to his theological past, indeed, would truly regret that originally he gave up growing a stomach in a rural life of a pastor together with a pretty and pious wife and a nest full of children. In order to explain his falling away from the church, he quoted in his own manner Matthew: "No one sews a piece of unshrunk cloth on an old cloak." And he called the church a great patching business, where officious pastors, each in their own way, seek to mend the faith's moth-eaten raiment. I knew that he called himself a Kierkegaardian, even to the 8th degree; but I only had a poor idea of what that was supposed to mean.[22]

Since Schaff is apparently fictional, already five years before he himself begins to read Kierkegaard, Pontoppidan seems to be spontaneously drawn by the Kierkegaardian criticism of the church. Schaff gives a wonderful example of this, when he and Pontoppidan from the café catch a glimpse of a young pastor wearing his vestments on his way across Frue Plads with his wife or girlfriend under his arm, a view which Schaff comments upon thus:

> Just look at him there! An inoffensive fellow without a thought in his head, probably the future bishop of Zealand. Now he is going in to preach for the penitent in silk and ermine. One can be certain that the people will afterwards leave the church in the most edified mood; but on the way home they will storm into the bakeries and, with their mouths watering, will inspect the pastries on display in order to take the most delicious pieces home with them for Sunday coffee. Isn't that touching? But what does the Scripture say? It is written that when the master had spoken on the mount, his listeners went away deeply shaken, and many were offended by him. You see, that was a somewhat different kind of talk. How should good people understand this?[23]

In other words, Schaff might have sharpened Pontoppidan's view for the church hypocrisy, which Kierkegaard, with drums beating and flags flying, presented in *The Moment*. After the meeting in the café Pontoppidan ruminates about what it was with this unpleasant person, Schaff alias Kierkegaard, "who against my will attracted me and in an almost demonic manner occupied my thoughts."[24] Pontoppidan adds that some more time would have to pass before he understood it; but he never discloses to the reader what kind of understanding he reaches. On the contrary, he seems later to annul his claim to have ever come to an understanding. He continues to visit Schaff and also quotes, even after his death, many of his brief and pointed statements. But Pontoppidan writes the following about his visit to him when Schaff was on his deathbed in Vesterbro: "Many confused memories streamed into me, and I had a presentiment at that moment that the memory of him would perhaps always be alive in me and would occupy my thoughts. But would I ever manage to be successful at fathoming myself in relation to this mysterious person? I doubted it."[25] What nonetheless can be said about Pontoppidan's relation to Schaff is that it

---

[22]   Ibid., p. 54. Reference is made to Matthew 9:16: "No one sews a piece of unshrunk cloth on an old cloak; for the patch pulls away from the cloak, and a worse tear is made."
[23]   Pontoppidan, *Hamskifte*, p. 55.
[24]   Ibid., p. 56.
[25]   Ibid., p. 124.

recalls somewhat Lucky Per's relation to Pastor Fjaltring. Schaff is a Kierkegaardian to the 8ᵗʰ degree, and Fjaltring is also a Kierkegaardian to some degree or another. For Per, Fjaltring becomes the catalyst for the decisive choice between genuine faith and serious doubt and, moreover, for how he can honestly manage his melancholy. One can, therefore, ask whether Schaff alias Søren Kierkegaard, in the end and in spite of Pontoppidan's dislike of him, contributes in a similar manner to his own self-understanding? To give a qualified answer to this question would have to be the task for Pontoppidan's biographer.

II. Traces of Kierkegaard in Pontoppidan's Authorship

A. The Promised Land

I turn now to Pontoppidan's authorship in order to look for possible traces of his occupation with Kierkegaard. Before and during his work on the first of his long novels, *The Promised Land* (1891–95),[26] Pontoppidan, as I have also mentioned, read a number of Kierkegaard's works, which above all could have contributed to the portrayal of the novel's tragic main character, Emanuel Hansted. In addition to Emanuel there are also other characters and situations which might have been inspired in part by his reading of Kierkegaard, not least of all the almost caricatured description of the Grundtvigians alias the "Society of Friends" and the new version of the ethical pseudonym from *Either/Or* and *Stages on Life's Way*, namely, Judge William, who here appears as "Pastor Petersen." Here I will, for the most part, confine myself to Emanuel.

As Emanuel is presented to us, he has certain characteristics in common with Kierkegaard, including melancholy and a preference for the heath, loneliness, and books, but in the first part of the novel, *Soil* (1891), it is more the differences that immediately capture one's attention. Kierkegaard would not judge his enthusiastic relation to the peasants any differently than Ragnhild Tønnesen, who criticizes him for wanting, with self-important missionary zeal, to be "the prophet of the new times, to found parties and lead riots, according to the fashion of these days!"[27] She and Kierkegaard would also be in agreement about ridiculing Emanuel, when he, in

---

[26]   Originally this was three novels, *Muld. Et Tidsbillede*, Copenhagen: P.G. Philipsen 1891 (English translation: *Emanuel or Children of the Soil*, trans. by Mrs. Edgar Lucas, London: J.M. Dent & Co., Aldine House 1896), *Det forjættede Land*, Copenhagen: P.G. Philipsen 1892 (English translation: *The Promised Land*, trans. by Mrs. Edgar Lucas, London: J.M. Dent 1896), and *Dommens Dag*, Copenhagen: P.G. Philipsen 1895. Then later the trilogy was rewritten and edited considerably, and the title of part two became the title of the entire work. The standard modern edition is *Det forjættede Land*, ed. by Esther Kielberg and Lars Peter Rømhild, vols. 1–2 (text and commentary), Copenhagen: Gyldendal 1997 (Det Danske Sprog- og Litteraturselskab).

[27]   Henrik Pontoppidan, *Det forjættede land*, 11ᵗʰ ed., vols. 1–3, Copenhagen: Gyldendal 1993, vol. 1, p. 120. (*Emanuel or Children of the Soil*, p. 193.) Since Pontoppidan made substantial revisions to the original edition, I will, in the following be using the later, more complete 11ᵗʰ edition referenced above.

a Grundtvigian manner, courts the common people by taking on their manners and attitudes.

Moreover, it is the congregation or even the collective that Emanuel Hansted wants to reform and not the individual. This takes place cunningly when the bishop comes on a visit to the parsonage because Emanuel's boss, Pastor Tønnesen, has complained about his curate. Fortunately for the curate, that is, Emanuel, the bishop is one of the old national liberals who thinks that the political reform of the social order and the breaking down of class difference corresponds more or less to walking in the footsteps of Jesus. Emanuel listens with enthusiasm and finds himself confirmed in the view that "he now walked in his Master's footsteps, and was helping to create a kingdom of happiness which the Christian brotherhood would one day spread over the whole earth."[28]

The bishop is certainly modeled on the national liberal father of the constitution and former minister of culture and prime minister Ditlev Gothard Monrad (1811–87), whom Kierkegaard had just as little respect for as Pontoppidan and also for the same reason, namely, his unholy blending of Christianity and politics. It is, however, not the bishop who becomes Emanuel's model but Christ himself, just as Kierkegaard prescribes for the person who really wants to be a Christian. The outline of such a Kierkegaardian character begins to take shape in the second part of the novel, *The Promised Land* (1892).

The decisive driving force in that which can be described as Emanuel's development or rather retrograde development—the force which drives him from the one stage to the next on the road of life denial—is the trial. The first great trial, which is supposed to prepare him to become a Christian in the Kierkegaardian sense, is the death of his son, Gutten. His son had been ill previously, but Emanuel initially believed that the boy would be able to overcome it by virtue of the robust health that he ascribes to him, and later by virtue of his prayers. When neither of these seems to work, his wife Hansine tempts him to seek help from the doctor. He should have been called long before and struggles in vain for Gutten's life.

"The Lord gave, and the Lord hath taken away; blessed be the name of the Lord," says Emanuel with the well-known words of Job, when his son dies in his arms.[29] Pontoppidan had himself experienced the loss of a child, his oldest daughter, and so he had known Emanuel's despairing attempt to find meaning in the midst of his grief and pain. Moreover, he might have known Kierkegaard's enthusiastic treatment of Job in *Repetition*, which he later borrowed from the University Library, but had already read in the winter of 1880–81. He might also have known *Fear and Trembling*, which to a higher degree than *Repetition* gives an account of the trial as a religious category. In any case the description of Emanuel's scruples after the boy's death sounds like reminiscences of such a reading:

> In his shaken state of mind, he conceived of the boy's illness as a trial, that God had sent to him, and the death of the child as a punishment from heaven because his faith

---

28   Pontoppidan, *Det forjættede land*, 11th ed., vol. 1, p. 166. (*Emanuel or Children of the Soil*, p. 266.)
29   Pontoppidan, *Det forjættede land*, 11th ed., vol. 2, p. 70.

had failed in the hour of need, and he in his weakness had called upon the help of people against the inexorable will of providence. Every time he thought of that night when he, from the mound of earth in the garden, had stared out into the darkness after the lantern light from the doctor's wagon and in his perplexed despair even denied the heavenly light, he hid his shameful face from God. In his deep remorse he had entrusted himself to Hansine; but also on this occasion he had found missing something of the correct seriousness in her and felt alone and misunderstood in his grief. She had heard his confession in silence, had merely said that God certainly would not disapprove of his grief for the boy, and then went out again to work in the kitchen.[30]

In *Fear and Trembling* Kierkegaard describes how Abraham, on the strength of the double movement of faith, receives Isaac back again even if God had unambiguously given him the command to sacrifice him. The first movement is the infinite relinquishing of Isaac, the resignation, which anyone in principle is capable of doing with his own help; the second movement is, by contrast, only possible on the strength of the absurd, namely, to believe contrary to the understanding, that God, even if he demands the sacrifice of Isaac, will restore him again—and that not only in the beyond but already in this life.

This is the kind of faith that Abraham, due to God's testing of him, shows himself to have, but the test which God thus gives to him is also a test that Abraham himself chooses. He could indeed have refused to comply with God's command and could, instead of taking the journey to Mount Moria, have remained at home in his safe Mamrelund together with Isaac and Sarah. Now he takes the trial upon himself and passes the test and receives Isaac back.

The death of his son can also be interpreted as a trial of this kind, for Emanuel could indeed have chosen not to call the doctor, just as Abraham refused the possibility of remaining at home with Isaac. Emanuel interprets the death of his son in precisely this manner. His son's death was not due to the father's failure to act in the face of his son's failing health, but his lack of faith in the midst of the trial. Had Emanuel had faith, his son would have been alive and God would thereby have confirmed that Emanuel had lived up to his name, which means, "God be with us!"

Abraham continues to pass the test not merely as the father of faith, as he is called in the three monotheistic religions, but also as "the heir to the finite," as Kierkegaard writes in *Fear and Trembling*.[31] He belongs to this sphere and continues to belong to the blessed finite after his trial. The situation is different with Emanuel, who after the death of his son in despair seeks to see the trial as an arrival at the beyond. "From that day things began to fall apart," one reads later in Hansine's recollections. "With the death of the boy Emanuel lost the dauntless hope, the unconditioned certainty that is confident assurance of being escorted by God's blessing, which up until then had born him safely through all disappointments."[32]

So in spite of all the trials that Emanuel later undertakes to come to resemble Abraham, he ends up as something wholly different, namely, a Christian. Kierkegaard notes in 1853, ten years after the publication of *Fear and Trembling*,

---

[30]   Ibid., vol. 2, p. 71.

[31]   *SKS* 4, 144 / *FT*, 50.

[32]   Pontoppidan, *Det forjættede land*, 11th ed., vol. 3, p. 72.

that Abraham does not count as a Christian model since, by receiving his son back in this life, he shows himself rather to be what he already was, namely Jewish.[33] The Christian solution would, according to the later Kierkegaard, have been such that he only in the beyond would have received Isaac back, while he here in this life would have despaired as Christ did on the cross—"My God, my God, why have you abandoned me!"—in order to find his joy in the resurrection. This is the brutal twist that Pontoppidan sees as the consistent conclusion of Emanuel's zealous process of conversion, which perhaps also explains his sympathy for Judaism, such as it comes to expression in *Lucky Per*.

Many times after the death of his son Emanuel speaks of the trial and, with a very Kierkegaardian word, "self-examination." "Test me—and test me again, I pray you, Father,"[34] says Emanuel in his secret closet after having been all too close to being tempted by this world. When he finally believes that he has received "the calling of God," he explains to his sister Betty that he finally has understood "how God himself chooses his servants…disciplines them with hard tests and makes them into obedient executors of his will."[35]

For this reason he also dares to say to Betty: "Look, God has taken your child and your husband from you, moreover wealth, honor, respect and the admiration of the world….have you remembered to thank him for this?"[36] Kierkegaard would have said the same thing to her as he says, for example to his readers in one of his edifying discourses:

> And when people wronged you and insulted you, did you thank God? We are not saying that their wrong thereby ceased to be wrong—what would be the use of such pernicious and foolish talk! It is up to you to decide whether it was wrong; but have you taken the wrong and insult to God and by your thanksgiving received it from his hand as a good and a perfect gift?[37]

It is not merely the trial (*prøvelsen*) or self-trial or self-examination (*selvprøvelsen*), which stamp *The Promised Land* as Kierkegaardian categories, but also "the hidden inwardness," that is, that according to *Fear and Trembling* there is no external sign or mark of faith. "*There* I went about so self-confident, so completely certain in the consciousness of walking in the footsteps of Jesus," says Emanuel to Betty, "and did not realize that I followed them in the wrong direction, outward to temporality with all its desires, worries and never satisfied demands, instead of inward toward the small, the low and the narrow door of the heart, which Christ has opened for us with the words: My kingdom is not of this world!"[38]

Similarly, he later explains to Pastor Petersen that he has not been able to apply for a post in the State Church, "in it I have found more of the outwardness

---

[33] *SKS* 25, 248–9, NB28:41 / *JP* 2, 2223. *SKS* 25, 32–4, NB26:25 / *JP* 2, 2222.

[34] Pontoppidan, *Det forjættede land*, 11th ed., vol. 2, p. 110.

[35] Ibid., vol. 3, pp. 81–2.

[36] Ibid., vol. 3, p. 84.

[37] *SKS* 5, 51 / *EUD*, 43.

[38] Pontoppidan, *Det forjættede land*, 11th ed., vol. 3, pp. 22–3.

of paganism than the inwardness of Christianity."[39] Emanuel seems almost to have
read Kierkegaard, a fact that pastor Petersen then also notes when he in a slightly
patriarchal manner refers to his more advanced age and consequently greater
experience:

> I will tell you first—what you will perhaps find a bit difficult to understand—that also
> I once in my younger days was investigating, with toil and tears, Meister Eckhart,
> Johannes Tauler, Søren Kierkegaard, and whatever all the other canonized *salto mortale*
> acrobats are called, who in older and more recent times have dazed a nervous public.[40]

Pastor Petersen has certainly read Kierkegaard, but even if he cannot appreciate his
theological acrobatics, he seems all the more to appreciate his ethical pseudonym
from *Either/Or* and *Stages on Life's Way*, that is, Judge William, who constantly
argues for the universal and criticizes the exceptions. Thus he remarks to Ragnhild
Tønnesen that we all nowadays "have a sick tendency to make ourselves exceptions
and interesting phenomena. At the cost of the common human being, we meticulously
cultivate our small idiosyncrasies, cultivate with industry some small oddity, some
fixed idea, merely for fear of becoming 'like all the other people'—the worst thing
that one knows."[41] Recalling what Pontoppidan himself wrote in 1915 and 1921
to, respectively, Vilhelm Andersen and Harald Høffding about the Danish authors'
tendency towards extremism, one dares assume a quite marked sympathy for the
ethical pseudonym in Kierkegaard's authorship.

   In spite of the religious suspension of the ethical, which Kierkegaard gives an
account of in *Fear and Trembling*, it nonetheless happens in his authorship that the
heretofore hidden inwardness must reveal itself, namely, in the imitation of Christ.
The same thing happens for Emanuel, who, after having fortified his faith inwardly,
asserts himself as an imitation of Christ in the way Kierkegaard prescribes it in
Practice in Christianity.

   The ethical aspect of imitation is evident in his interaction with the poor and the
reprobate, not least of all "black Trine," who quickly becomes his disciple, and the
sick as he proclaims what Kierkegaard, with one of his favorite phrases, calls "the
gospel of suffering." "When he sat at their bed," as it is written about Emanuel, "he
spoke about their illness as a great favor and called their sufferings 'God's caress,'
for which they should be happy and thankful."[42]

   The purely Christian aspect of imitation is evident in the—let us call it—
martyrdom with which Emanuel ends his life. The imitation of Christ reaches its
highest point as a tragic parody when Emanuel constantly puts the savior's words in
his own mouth,[43] until he apparently is cast out by God when he, from the lectern of
the school, waits in vain for the word to reveal itself to him. The only thing that he
can say is again a simple repetition of the words of the gospel: "My God! My God!

---

[39]   Ibid., vol. 3, p. 38.
[40]   Ibid.
[41]   Ibid., vol. 3, p. 66.
[42]   Ibid., vol. 3, p. 58.
[43]   Ibid., vol. 3, p. 84 ("And why do you want to anger me?"), p. 84 ("Judgment day is
near!"), and p. 106 ("You have so many worries, Betty. Only one worry is necessary!").

Why have you abandoned me?"[44] In despair he is led away and shortly thereafter he ends his life in a hospital.

In spite of Emanuel's sad fate, it is perhaps wrong to assume that Pontoppidan intended to show that the imitation failed, for actually it is consistently done right up until the final words. The point is then that the success of imitation cannot be evaluated since the model itself fails. It is, Pontoppidan must also admit, a question of faith, and therefore he willingly has a little group of Emanuel's disciples gather at his grave and call him "God's lamb."[45] Thus Pontoppidan has retold the history of Christianity, and he ends it by giving to Caesar what is Caesar's—and to the meek the sympathy that they deserve. "They all live quietly and peacefully," he writes, "since they strive humbly to become equal to Emanuel in all his perfections."[46]

B. Lucky Per

Also in *Lucky Per* (1898–1904),[47] which I now pass over to, the main character seems to suffer a kind of happy martyrdom, although not for religion but for the self or the subject. In spite of a temporary relation to Christianity, Per has no plans of becoming a Christian but rather of overcoming the world by the strength of his iron will.[48] However, he decides not to be such a world conqueror and must even give up the little bit of the promise which he has realized in the form of a wife and three children. After thus having given up the world he discloses in the concluding conversation with Inger, before she leaves him, that he has likewise not been able to find happiness in God: "Everywhere I sought him, I have only found myself. And for the one who has become truly conscious of himself, a God is superfluous."[49] Formally Per has merely become what he was in the way he already at the beginning of the novel proudly proclaimed to Alexander Neergaard: "I am only myself."[50] In fact, he has become something different, or more correctly, he has become what he, on the strength of his nationality and his family, was disposed to become, namely, the kind of life-denying and shady hill troll which he was taught by Neergaard to see in the majority of his countrymen. I will soon return to this, but after first having noted a striking similarity between Per's retrospective understanding of life—everywhere

---

44   Ibid., vol. 3, p. 110.

45   Ibid.

46   Ibid., vol. 3, p. 134.

47   Henrik Pontoppidan, *Lykke-Per. Hans Ungdom*, Copenhagen: Det Nordiske Forlag 1898; *Lykke-Per finder Skatten*, Copenhagen: Det Nordiske Forlag 1898; *Lykke-Per. Hans Kærlighed*, Copenhagen: Det Nordiske Forlag 1899; *Lykke-Per i det fremmede*, Copenhagen: Det Nordiske Forlag 1899; *Lykke-Per. Hans store Værk*, Copenhagen: Det Nordiske Forlag 1901; *Lykke-Per og hans Kæreste*, Copenhagen: Det Nordiske Forlag 1902; *Lykke-Per. Hans Rejse til Amerika*, Copenhagen: Det Nordiske Forlag 1903; and *Lykke-Per. Hans sidste Kamp*, Copenhagen: Gyldendal 1904. Since this cycle of novels was also constantly revised in various editions by Pontoppidan, I will use the modern edition in the following: *Lykke-Per*, vols. 1–2, Copenhagen: Gyldendal 1984, 15th ed.

48   Pers motto: "Jeg vil," Cf. Pontoppidan, *Lykke-Per*, vol. 1, p. 256.

49   Ibid., vol. 2, p. 396.

50   Ibid., vol. 1, p. 84.

one seeks God only to find oneself—and Georg Brandes' account of what Kierkegaard in *his* way sought and found. Brandes writes, "When Kierkegaard abandoned the old naive path to faith, did he find on that ship which he himself had built, the untrodden path of brooding to it? No, in the moment when he saw land, it was in actuality not the India of tradition that he had reached but the America of the personality, of the great passion, and great independence."[51] But, as Brandes adds, Kierkegaard would admit no more than Columbus that it was the tradition's old wonderful country— India alias the promised Christianity—that he had arrived at. He believed that "the single individual" coincided in everything with "the Christian," but Pontoppidan only allows Per to suffer from this illusion momentarily. During his final years as assistant highway engineer among the dunes and people of western Jutland, one never sees him in church, whereas he likes to explain to the school teacher that the greatest human happiness is "to become fully and clearly conscious of oneself."[52]

This formulation is merely a variation of many similar ones in the novel, which involuntarily leads one to think of Kierkegaard's ethicist, Judge William, who zealously repeats that what matters is becoming conscious of one's *eternal* self. The difference from Kierkegaard's ethicist that Pontoppidan thus seems to want to expose with frequent repetition, and from Christian dogmatics, is therefore that the self is and becomes temporal, not eternal.

Similarly, Per's previous fiancée, Jakobe Salomon, wants to fight against the "inheritance handed down from the fathers."[53] This expression might also refer to Kierkegaard, who in the *Concluding Unscientific Postscript* claims in his authorship to have read "the original text of individual human existence-relationships, the old familiar text handed down from the fathers."[54] Brandes analyzes and thoroughly rejects this reverence (*pietet*) in his Kierkegaard biography.[55] It is also rejected by Jakobe, who to the heir, claims "what is universally human in us."[56] What this is, Per explains to the school teacher, namely, the instinct to self-unfolding, which is deposited in everything created, and to which we must fearlessly commend ourselves.

However, Per has himself come to know fear as a part of the troll nature that he first believes he is free of, but later decides as his own "inheritance from the fathers." As a young polytechnic student, he does not believe that he is included in this inheritance but with so much more disdain notices it in others, for example, Fritjof, who zealously parades his indifference to others but, abandoned by the noisy surroundings immediately becomes terrified of death and loneliness and shows himself to be a real Danish troll: "a subterranean being, whose innermost soul wanders

---

[51]   Brandes, *Søren Kierkegaard. En kritisk Fremstilling i Grundrids*, p. 285.
[52]   Pontoppidan, *Lykke-Per*, vol. 2, p. 402.
[53]   Ibid., vol. 1, p. 397.
[54]   *SKS* 7, 573 / *CUP1*, 629–30.
[55]   Brandes, *Søren Kierkegaard. En kritisk Fremstilling i Grundrids*, p. 251: "reverence [*Pieteten*] is something very different from piety [*Fromhed*], although these words literally mean the same thing: piety is immediately grasped, it trustingly folds its hands. Reverence does not want to use criticism, it continually breaks its critical instruments. Kierkegaard had a little piety but much reverence."
[56]   Pontoppidan, *Lykke-Per*, vol. 1, p. 398.

in the realm of shadows, circled the grave and the judges of the beyond—terrified by the powers of the light which he a moment ago had so arrogantly invoked."[57]

One aspect of this troll nature is conscience,[58] which the young Per is assaulted by, when he refuses to marry the plain Francisca, whom he has flirted with for a long time, but who cannot serve his enormous ambitions. However, he quickly manages to free himself from the remorse which not only would bind him to the girl but also to his entire past as the son of Johannes Sidenius. Like conscience and remorse, the scruples[59] also belong to the characteristics of the troll nature and—if one follows Kierkegaard—to the discipline of the Christian.

As antipode to trolls Pontoppidan places, with certain reservations, Georg Brandes alias Dr. Nathan. "Compared with homegrown characters such as Grundtvig or Kierkegaard, he could...seem to lack deeper characteristic traits," Pontoppidan writes. "He had been too impatient to hatch any independent world-view, too occupied with life and lust for life for such a tough, light-shunning, spiderlike spinning out of the content of one's own personality, during which even those with lesser abilities can stumble across making more or less matchless discoveries."[60]

The matchless discoveries of course refer to Grundtvig, who not least thanks to Kierkegaard's satirical pen almost became synonymous with these somewhat dubious goods; but the "tough, light-shunning, spiderlike spinning out of the content of one's own personality" is just as obviously stamped by Brandes' and Pontoppidan's—and before them P.L. Møller's and M.A. Goldschmidt's—understanding of Kierkegaard's troll nature.

Just like Kierkegaard, Per inherited his melancholy troll nature from his father, and in spite of his energetic attempts, he is unsuccessful in escaping this paternal inheritance. He eventually makes up his mind just like Kierkegaard, but only so late that in order to spare others from the hereditary infection he must not only leave a fiancée but a wife and three children. When he does so, his justification for his actions sounds like an echo of Kierkegaard's actions, which Pontoppidan could have known from the *Efterladte Papirer*, the pseudonymous retelling of the breaking of the engagement in *Stages on Life's Way* and Brandes' biography:[61]

> The paternal curse, which hung over his life, and which made him a stranger and restless here on earth must not be allowed to pass to his children. And Inger! Now when he had become fully conscious of his invincible shyness of life, how could he then continue to justify allowing her to share his fate? Poor child! She still did not know her misfortune. She did not yet understand that she was bound to a changeling, subterranean being, who went blind in the light and was killed by happiness. And should also her eyes once be

---

[57]   Ibid., p. 61.

[58]   Ibid., vol. 1, p. 128. Conscience is here described as "that indeterminate, ghostlike thing, which suddenly places before one's eyes a troll mirror, in which one saw oneself in an ugly, distorted form."

[59]   Ibid., vol. 1, p. 358.

[60]   Ibid., vol. 2, pp. 66–7.

[61]   Brandes, *Søren Kierkegaard. En kritisk Fremstilling i Grundrids*, pp. 264–73, especially pp. 268–9.

opened with the love of another—she would keep his secret as if it were a mortal sin, wither away and die without even having confessed it to herself.[62]

Kierkegaard can likewise describe himself as a changeling, but in several letters to his then fiancée, Regine Olsen, he plays the role of a merman in order to give her an allegorical representation of their mutual disparity. He uses the same allegory in *Fear and Trembling*, where the tragic in the disparity between the merman and the young girl lies in the fact that he can only get her by making himself a human or making his beloved a mermaid; but his nature prevents him from doing the former, and his love for the innocent girl from doing the latter.

Therefore the merman, after having led her to the sea, must sacrifice his love, but, to be sure, in such a way that she believes that she has been deceived by him so she, unbound by his love, can enter into a relationship with another. This is precisely what Kierkegaard does when he pushes Regine to break the engagement and thereafter pretends that she was a matter of complete indifference to him. Two years later she became engaged to another, and six years later she was married.

In *Lucky Per* the relation of Kierkegaard, the merman, to Regine is retold in the troll Per's relation to Inger. "But *she* was not troll," he realizes. "Therefore she must and should be given back to life and the light."[63] Just like Kierkegaard, Per discovers one of her old loves which he then prepares Inger to return to, after which he creates a break by making her believe that he does not love *her*, but someone else. Thus one reads: "Without any compelling reasons she, however, would never accept a legal divorce, and it should be precisely his goal to bring her to hate and disdain him; all the more quickly would she forget him. And when he was giving up so much, he could just as well sacrifice his honor as well."[64] Kierkegaard writes the same thing both via his pseudonym in *Stages on Life's Way* and in his own name in his posthumous papers,[65] that is, that he must bring his former fiancée to hate and disdain him, even if it costs him his honor. Nevertheless, he has no doubts that he is acting nobly towards Regine; and Brandes, too, has apparently no doubts about this. In any case he writes in his biography that there is not "the slightest reason to condemn him, but every good reason to understand him in accordance with his abilities."[66] Pontoppidan does not disregard this challenge, but in *Lucky Per* gives as sympathetic a portrait of trolls and mermen as possible. Even Inger ends by expressing her gratitude to Per for the sacrifice that he has made for her.[67]

Another and just as significant troll nature in *Lucky Per* is, of course, Pastor Fjaltring, whom Per also refers to in his justification for leaving Inger. He tells her that Fjaltring's wife presumably has been of a wholly different nature than him, but during her life with him she has been destroyed "because he has kept her back in a shadow life, which had the effect of maturing and liberating *him*, while *she* had to be

---

[62]   Pontoppidan, *Lykke-Per*, vol. 2, p. 380.
[63]   Ibid., vol. 2, p. 394.
[64]   Ibid., vol. 2, p. 399.
[65]   See, for example, *SKS* 19, 229, Not8:15 / *KJN* 3, 224–5. *SKS* 6, 331 / *SLW*, 356.
[66]   Brandes, *Søren Kierkegaard. En kritisk Fremstilling i Grundrids*, p. 267.
[67]   Pontoppidan, *Lykke-Per*, vol. 2, p. 411.

destroyed."[68] Shortly after her death, Fjaltring commits suicide, which Per interprets as an expression of a guilty conscience about the "murder of the soul" that he had committed.[69]

In other words, Pontoppidan's portrait of Fjaltring might also have been inspired by the Kierkegaardian troll nature, which is made probable by a long series of correspondences with regard to the view of the church and Christianity. Like Kierkegaard, Fjaltring is a true dialectician who is not satisfied with simple answers to the decisive questions about sin and grace. In opposition to the carefree and popular Grundtvigian, Pastor Blomberg, he does not sell grace at a bargain price but demands, just like Kierkegaard, that the Christian have concrete experiences with sin so that the knowledge of sin as a presupposition for grace does not become an abstract tirade. "You should sin some more," he is supposed to have said, to Blomberg's irritation, to one of his virtuous parishioner. "With the life you lead, you can never become a convinced Christian."[70]

Just as the Christian's life in Blomberg's view is cheerful and energetic, carefree and harmonious, by contrast it is in Fjaltring's view ideal suffering and struggle, self-examination and contradiction. "I believe fully and firmly both in God and the Devil," he says; "I am only not always equally certain which of the two is most against me?"[71] Kierkegaard was likewise not certain, but he leaned most to the view that it must be God, inasmuch as his kingdom was not of this world, for which reason the proclamation must always be polemical against the mundane views about a light and happy existence.

Symptomatic of Blomberg's followers is the wife of the master of the royal hunt, who is "grateful to him that she so relatively easily and painlessly has been freed from her guilt of sin."[72] A differently serious matter is the remorse for Per, who suffers from it but by the same token also becomes a different human being in this ordeal. "There was in his awakening remorse and pain the same wonderfully impressive element as in the pains of a woman in labor—pains which announce that a new life is coming with new hopes and new promises."[73] Thus it is described when Per travels across the Kattegat as guard of honor for his mother's dead body. Similarly, in *The Concept of Anxiety* Kierkegaard calls remorse as "the embryo of the highest life."[74]

Even if remorse, as the Christian faith's midwife, is later described in *Lucky Per* as "the dictate of the frightened conscience,"[75] there is thus something honest about it in opposition to "the Blombergian condition of innocence."[76] It is nonetheless what attracts people, since Blomberg, of course must win many followers with such

---

68   Ibid., vol. 2, p. 397.
69   Ibid.
70   Pontoppidan, *Lykke-Per*, vol. 2, p. 192.
71   Ibid., vol. 2, p. 180.
72   Ibid., vol. 2, p. 147.
73   Ibid., vol. 2, p. 139.
74   *SKS* 4, 418 / *CA*, 117.
75   Ibid., vol. 2, p. 253.
76   Ibid., vol. 2, p. 327.

a "comfortable everyday gospel, which does not demand insurmountable sacrifices with regard to life's amenities."[77]

For this reason Pastor Fjaltring very fittingly calls his beneficent colleague "the merchant,"[78] since he, entirely in the spirit of the times, "has made religion into a market commodity" and predictably has enticed people to "the shops where they buy indulgences most cheaply."[79] Similarly, Kierkegaard calls churches "boutiques and booths"[80] in *The Moment*, where he also taunts the pastors for having achieved "amazing feats of mimicry,"[81] such that instead of the imitation of Christ they get "the holy monkey tricks."[82] The pastors generally lack the passion of faith, which Per also notes as Fjaltring's view: "Faith as a passion, and where it does not exist, one plays a monkey's game with our Lord."[83]

Pontoppidan might well have borrowed such a formulation from *The Moment* and put it in the mouth of Fjaltring, but he undoubtedly also was helped by Brandes, who in his biography focuses on passion as the decisive element in Kierkegaard's understanding of Christianity. Brandes astutely remarks that in the course of Kierkegaard's authorship there is a sliding from the theoretical interest in Christianity to the practical, such that *"The paradox gives way to passion."*[84] Relevant to Per's story of suffering—and incidentally also that of Emanuel Hansted in *The Promised Land*—Brandes writes further: "A truth outside us does not exist; for the truth is inwardness, and since no more passionate inwardness can be thought than that which belongs to wanting to lay down one's life for one's conviction, [Kierkegaard] arrives consequently at martyrdom as the truth's actual witness."[85] Thus Per deliberates his "instinctual sense that it was in loneliness that his soul had its home, that it was grief and pain his life belonged to."[86] But this is not due to the Christian "inwardness" which Kierkegaard prescribes and which Emanuel Hansted practices, but, by contrast, due to Per's "enclosedness" (*indesluttethed*)[87] and "melancholy,"[88] purely psychological character traits that he shares with Kierkegaard. "The great happiness that he had blindly sought, was the great suffering," Pontoppidan writes about Per, "it was that incurable lack that Pastor Fjaltring had so often praised him for and called the chosen person's divine gift of grace."[89] For Per, however, God does not exist, and for this reason he ends up, so to speak, as a consistent *Kierkegaardian*

---

[77]   Ibid., vol. 2, p. 147.
[78]   Ibid., vol. 2, p. 222.
[79]   Ibid., vol. 2, p. 334.
[80]   *SKS* 13, 206 / *M*, 158.
[81]   *SKS* 13, 379 / *M*, 316.
[82]   *SKS* 13, 379 / *M*, 317.
[83]   Pontoppidan, *Lykke-Per*, vol. 2, p. 334.
[84]   Brandes, *Søren Kierkegaard. En kritisk Fremstilling i Grundrids*, p. 346.
[85]   Ibid., p. 330. Brandes writes of Kierkegaard's emotional life, "he actually did not feel pleasure before it approached and changed into pain—pain became a pleasure for him." Ibid., p. 288.
[86]   Pontoppidan, *Lykke-Per*, vol. 2, p. 379.
[87]   Ibid., vol. 2, p. 350.
[88]   Ibid., vol. 2, p. 374, cf. p. 362.
[89]   Ibid., vol. 2, p. 379.

without Christianity. He writes thus in his posthumous papers: "the life and story of Christ teach us in actuality nothing beyond this (which is an old wisdom), that there is only one thing that overcomes suffering, and that is passion."[90] In other words, Per's martyrdom is a martyrdom of a wholly different order than that of Emanuel Hansted, and in general one ought to be satisfied—like Per himself—with calling it a passion. As far as it goes, Per has dissolved his polemical relation to his surroundings in suffering itself, in that rather than as a martyr, who stands in a relation of opposition to the external world, he is in absolute identity with the internal. As such, Per has undertaken the first part of what Kierkegaard in *Fear and Trembling* called the double movement of faith, namely, resignation, and he is fully satisfied with this.

C. The Realm of the Dead

Also in *The Realm of the Dead* (1912–16) we find a troll nature along the lines of that of Per, now in the form of the despairing Torben Dihmer.[91] I will not dwell on him but merely remark that he, just like Per, in the course of the novel finds his way back to himself, a self, which can be classified as neither Christian nor bourgeois. In a Kierkegaardian typology he is rather an honest aesthete, who has got rid of his illusions in order to live instead as what he is, namely, in despair.

Kierkegaard likes to designate despair, to use the title of one of his main works, as *The Sickness unto Death*. Torben is sick, physically so sick that at the beginning of the novel he wishes "that you should all think of me as a dead person—since that is what I am in reality."[92] However, through the intervention of his friend and doctor Asmus Hagen, he receives the hope of being able to live without the symptoms of the sickness, but he ends up renouncing such a dishonest existence.

I do not know whether one dares to understand Hagen's medicine as an allegory for Kierkegaard's medicine, namely, faith, which alone is supposed to be able to rid one of existential despair. But it is again fitting to see Pontoppidan as a corrective to Kierkegaard, when the latter—according to Pontoppidan—dishonestly induces the person to believe in a salvation from despair by means of faith. Thus Torben first becomes happy and cheerful when he stops taking Hagen's medicine, and the symptoms of the sickness again become evident. "If I should tell you my opinion," he says to Hagen, as he intends to refuse to obey his doctor, "then I rather believe

---

[90]   Ibid., vol. 2, p. 412.

[91]   Henrik Pontoppidan, *Torben og Jytte. En Fortælling-Kres I*, Copenhagen: Gyldendal, Nordisk Forlag 1912; *Storeholt. En Fortælling-Kres II*, Copenhagen: Gyldendal, Nordisk Forlag 1913; *Toldere og Syndere. En Fortælling-Kres III*, Copenhagen: Gyldendal, Nordisk Forlag 1914; *Enslevs Død. En Fortælling-Kres IV*, Copenhagen: Gyldendal, Nordisk Forlag 1915; *Favsingholm. En Fortælling-Kres V*, Copenhagen: Gyldendal, Nordisk Forlag 1916. Like his other great novels, Pontoppidan reworked this one, and for this reason I refer in the following to the later edition: Henrik Pontoppidan, *De dødes rige*, vols. 1–2, ed. by Thorkild Skjerbæk, 9th ed., Copenhagen: Gyldendal 1992.

[92]   Pontoppidan, *De dødes rige*, 9th ed., vol. 1, p. 12.

that I will feel as if I had returned to the sun and the real life—after a long journey in the realm of the dead."[93]

Torben's former fiancée, Jytte Abildgaard, certainly also has a part of the troll nature in her. This is presented to the reader when she, at the beginning of the novel, rather impetuously becomes engaged to Torben, and she now expects that he will love her as she is, together with all of her demons. It can be difficult, one must understand from a self-observation, which is as if taken from the aphorisms, "Διαψαλματα," which introduce the aesthete's contribution to *Either/Or*: "As soon as she herself sought to penetrate into the deep primal forest of her being, she was gripped by a kind of panic fear. There was neither road nor path there but the place was full of ghosts and wandering shades. And wild, red predator eyes stared out from the darkness."[94] The Kierkegaardian aesthete A explains along similar lines that he certainly has courage to doubt but not to acknowledge anything since he must confront "the pale, bloodless, tenacious-of-life nocturnal forms with which I battle and to which I myself give life and existence."[95] Moved by such demons, Jytte in great haste annuls her engagement with Torben perhaps because she realizes the truth of what Judge William teaches A about, namely, that the person who cannot reveal himself cannot love—and, Jytte could add, likewise cannot be loved—and for this reason is the unhappiest of all.[96]

Just as Kierkegaard broke with Regine, so also Jytte with Torben. "Now she should again live in her memory as a beautiful memory, and it was best so."[97] For only what is lost is owned eternally, as Kierkegaard is fond of saying. Just as Kierkegaard is constantly rehashing the memory of Regine and trying to explain himself to her in one more subtle manner after the next, so also Jytte tries to explain herself to Torben. Predictably she becomes caught in her own inwardness and ends up burning the letter she wrote to him, for "the more seriously she tried to explore her own inwardness, the darker and more impassable it became."[98]

Jytte is without illusions and without religion, more or less a universal critic along the lines of Kierkegaard's aesthete from *Either/Or*. With dialectical acuity she sees the hypocrisy that Pastor Johannes Gaardbo makes himself guilty of when he seeks to manipulate the despair that he senses lies behind her denial of Christianity: "I know that you, like all sincere people, bear a longing in your soul," he says to her. "Your eyes and all your speech bear witness to a lack which you have not even understood yourself and therefore prefer to deny. If I did not know it to be unerringly certain, I would have never spoken to you as I have done here."[99] The pastoral dictate and spiritual patronizing has no effect on Jytte, who promptly remarks that his hope of improving her is not in harmony with his claim to like her as she is.

---

[93]   Ibid., vol. 2, p. 102.
[94]   Ibid., vol. 1, p. 58–9.
[95]   *SKS* 2, 32 / *EO1*, 23.
[96]   *SKS* 3, 158 / *EO2*, 160.
[97]   Pontoppidan, *De dødes rige*, 9th ed., vol. 1, p. 92.
[98]   Ibid., vol. 1, p. 133.
[99]   Ibid., vol. 1, p. 208.

"It is so comical that I can only laugh at it," she responds to him; "but after all I ought probably to feel insulted."[100]

Gaardbo is rejected thoroughly by Jytte, who is merely confirmed in her suspicion about the infinite emptiness of existence and the vanity of human beings. Instead, she surrounds herself with the dubious company of actors and artists, whom she likes because they do not take life more seriously than it deserves. Her development is of concern to her mother, Bertha, who gives her this judgment:

> It was with the same uncanny self-command that her brother Ebbe approached his downfall. It was the same inconceivable indifference, the same shameless giving up on oneself! Just like Ebbe, she stopped having fun; but when she came home from the theater or the sports grounds, she found the whole thing so stupid. She, who once loved to read, now never opened a book, and at best looked at a western novel of the worst kind in order to kill an evening. One could hardly understand that it was the same person, who as half-adult carried heavy scholarly works home from the libraries and sat with her fingers in her ears and read Søren Kierkegaard.[101]

One should hardly place any great weight on it, but I will nonetheless note that Pontoppidan uses more or less the same formulation about his own reading of Kierkegaard when he as a 23-year-old, according to *Inheritance and Debt*, brought his writings "to life with my fingers placed in my ears."[102]

In her rampant nihilism Jytte comes together with the painter and womanizer Karsten From, who without shame curries the favor of his ignorant customers. Suddenly one day in his atelier Jytte seems to understand the meaning of this. "When people are so overjoyed at being deceived, why then begrudge them this happiness?"[103] The world wants to be deceived, and so let it be deceived—"*Mundus vult decipi; ergo decipiatur*"—she adds with a saying that she ascribes to a pope, but which she could also have read in Kierkegaard.[104]

Jytte, however, thinks that she is not deceived since she has no illusions about her engagement with Karsten From. "The conviction that has taken root in her since her seventeenth year that when she gave herself to love, she also dedicated herself to unhappiness and death—this conviction she had not got rid of."[105] Kierkegaard had the same conviction. He again and again has his pseudonymous authors ponder over such a tragic disposition in, for example, *Either/Or* and *Fear and Trembling*.

Karsten From like Jytte is very Kierkegaardian, but in the absence of the tragic element also a more cynical aesthete. Like her, he reminds one of the aesthete A, whom he even seems to plagiarize from. "No man lays himself bare except for the beloved," he says to Jytte at a ball, right before he declares to her his dubious love. "Life is a great masquerade."[106] Kierkegaard's aesthete says the same thing

---

[100]   Ibid., vol. 1, p. 209.
[101]   Ibid., vol. 2, pp. 11–12.
[102]   Pontoppidan, *Arv og Gæld*, p. 41.
[103]   Pontoppidan, *De dødes rige*, 9th ed., vol. 2, p. 15.
[104]   See, for example, *SKS* 1, 292 / *CI*, 253. *SKS* 6, 316 / *SLW*, 340. *SKS* 12, 46 / *PC*, 32.
[105]   Pontoppidan, *De dødes rige*, 9th ed., vol. 2, p. 96.
[106]   Ibid., vol. 2, p. 90.

according to Judge William's quotation of him in the second part of *Either/Or*: "Life is a masquerade."[107]

Like the aesthete, Jytte also differs from Karsten From in another way: when she on the strength of her (broken) will lays herself bare, she has an affinity to the ethical. In opposition to him, she does not have the intention of dissolving all of existence into a game of fools and a masquerade. While she sees through the illusions, he takes them into his service. For this reason it is also only him, whom Judge William would be able to refer to with his well-known words to A: "Are you not aware that there comes a midnight hour when everyone must unmask; do you believe that life will always allow itself to be trifled with; do you believe that one can sneak away just before midnight in order to avoid it?"[108]

In *The Realm of the Dead*—just as in *The Promised Land* and *Lucky Per*—it is not only the aesthete that one recognizes from Kierkegaard's typology of personalities, but also a single religious person, namely, the itinerant pastor Mads Vestrup. In many aspects he reminds one of Pastor Fjaltring, but with one essential distinction, namely, that Vestrup has not been able to give up the illusion that it could be worthwhile to be a missionary in Denmark, "to proclaim Christianity in Christendom," as Kierkegaard formulates it.[109]

As a missionary, Vestrup has the potential to become a martyr, but in the meeting with the entire clergy and all of its political schemes he comes up short. The scene is nothing less than gruesome, where one of these wanabe-politicus pastors convinces him that he is an enemy of God merely by writing in an anticlerical journal and thus breaks him. It is like seeing the cold bishop Martensen intimidate the unruly Kierkegaard in order to finally force him in under the auspices of the church—as a clerk in the bishop's palace.

Previously Vestrup had chastised the church and its men, which Pontoppidan also at more or less the same time did in his own name in his lecture in Aalborg and Horsens at the beginning of 1914. Thus Vestrup sneers at "the power-crazy church, for whom all means are equally good, just so long as they produce respect and authority in this poor world."[110] Kierkegaard exposed the same view during his attack on the church in 1854–55, from which Vestrup, when taken on the whole, seems to take a good part of his rhetorical ammunition, such as when after being thrown out of the State Church, he confesses his immoral relation to a sweetheart of youth in front of his congregation:

> He spoke with a loud voice, confessed with merciless openness his offense before the congregation, which on this occasion was present in such large numbers that many people had to stand up in the middle aisles. But then he turned against the clergy, which had cast him off. He said what he now knew, that his sin, as ugly as it was, in God's eyes was less in comparison to the shamelessness with which virtually all of God's servants betray his church and falsify the gospel. He declared that Our Lord preferred to see drunkards, fornicators, indeed even thieves and murderers stand at the country's pulpits

---

[107]	*SKS* 3, 157 / *EO2*, 159.
[108]	*SKS* 3, 157 / *EO2*, 160.
[109]	See, for example, *The Moment*, no. 2: *SKS* 13, 145–68 / *M*, 103–26.
[110]	Pontoppidan, *De dødes rige*, 9th ed., vol. 1, p. 194.

than these foolish and morbid pastors, who fornicated with the world and gratified the ears of the ungodly with loose chatter about the highest things.[111]

Also, when Vestrup seeks to awaken the slack peasants and comfortable citizens to a more serious relation to Christ than the merely titular, one senses that Kierkegaard might be the source of inspiration. "In the footsteps [of Christ] anxiety and despair arose, and the pious hearts trembled,"[112] he thus explains in polemic against the church's coquettish lemonade Christianity. According to Vestrup, God must ask everyone of all these happy Christians, "Where is your trembling heart?" "Where are the tears you have cried for yourself? Where is your anxiety and the grief of your nights?"[113] Thus Vestrup cries for himself and departs, after which the reaction is, as it should be, according to Kierkegaard, if this is a case of true preaching: "Was that a madman or a prophet? Or was it merely a comic actor?"[114]

Vestrup shows himself ultimately to be neither the one nor the other, but a poor man who honestly believed in his ruined mission. While Emanuel Hansted in *The Promised Land* had an ambiguous fate, where one cannot without further ado determine whether he was a madman or a witness to the truth, there is no doubt in *The Realm of the Dead*. Here it is the existing order both in politics and in the church that has become so prosaic that there is no possibility for staging passion. Thus Vestrup ends up neither as an institutionalized pauper nor as a martyr, but as a shy hermit in the midst of the crowd.

If one were to summarize Pontoppidan's three big novels, one might well dare to claim that, in spite of his maintenance of ethics' golden mean between the eccentric attempts of aesthetics and religion to master existential despair, he portrays the despairing escapists at the loss of the exemplary citizens. The same thing is the case in Kierkegaard's authorship, where the ethicist Judge William stands as a sole support among an abundance of aesthetes and religious figures, who are all concerned to confront bourgeois society with their doubt and faith. One recalls here Brandes' words about Kierkegaard's authorship:

> Characteristically he was not successful in giving other personalities some kind of visibility than the apostles of despair. This was due to the fact that in spite of his attempt to wedge the ethical sphere between the aesthetic and the religious, he in reality only believed in two possibilities: the doctrine of desire or renunciation, the life of pleasure or abstinence; both forms of life grew before his eyes to such strength that they pressed to death the natural human form of being that lay between them.[115]

There is a descriptive agreement between Kierkegaard and Pontoppidan in their conception of despair, but normatively they are not in agreement. This lack of agreement appears most clearly at the end of *The Realm of the Dead*, where the until then so Pharisee-like Pastor Johannes Gaardbo finally renounces his dictatorial

---

111   Ibid., vol. 1, pp. 43–4.
112   Ibid., vol. 1, p. 194.
113   Ibid., vol. 1, p. 196.
114   Ibid., vol. 1, p. 197.
115   Brandes, *Søren Kierkegaard. En kritisk Fremstilling i Grundrids*, p. 307.

gospel and travels to Jutland in order to be reconciled with his brother Povl Gaardbo, and thus promises us a healthier human race without the seed of fanaticism and extremism—that is, with Brandes' words, "the natural human form of being that lay between them."

D. The Church and Its Men

As mentioned, Pontoppidan gives, in the figure of Mads Vestrup, a sharp criticism of the state-authorized clergy, but in *The Realm of the Dead* the criticism is represented to a greater degree by the old liberal politician, Enslev. However, their focus is not the same, for while Vestrup's criticism aims at the preaching pastors, Enslev's aims at the politicizing pastors or—as he calls them—the "ornately dressed politicians."[116] The two perspectives on the pastors' actions, the theological and the political, are, however, brought together in Pontoppidan's lecture *The Church and Its Men*, which he gave in 1914, while he was still working on *The Realm of the Dead*.[117]

The lecture, which shortly thereafter appeared in print, is introduced with a fanfare, which Pontoppidan could hardly have doubted would be understood as a reference to Kierkegaard's notorious attack on the church sixty years earlier:

> We have here in our country eleven hundred acting pastors, who Sunday after Sunday stand at the pulpit and speak zealously against people who think differently. I have thought that they should now and again meet a critical response, and I believe that it is useful for our age, also for the Church itself, that this relation be elucidated from as many sides as possible. My words are intended to be a humble contribution to this.[118]

In his articles in the attack on the church Kierkegaard likes to refer in a similar manner to the pastors as "the thousands of tradesmen officials,"[119] who seem more concerned with criticizing anyone who challenges their authority than with preaching the Christianity of the New Testament. Under the title "The Religious Situation" in the newspaper *Fædrelandet* he writes, for example,

> We have, if you please, a full staff of bishops, deans, pastors. Learned, exceptionally learned, talented, gifted, humanly well-intentioned, they all declaim—well, very well, exceptionally well, or fairly well, poorly, badly—but not one of them is in the character of the Christianity of the New Testament any more than in the character of striving towards the Christianity of the New Testament.[120]

Pontoppidan likewise challenges the authority of the pastors because they also, according to his view, lack the spirit that they are speaking about; "if they had a faith as firm as a rock, which made the mind rich and created great pathos," says

---

[116]   Pontoppidan, *De dødes rige*, 9th ed., vol. 1, p. 186.
[117]   Pontoppidan, *Kirken og dens Mænd. Et Foredrag.*
[118]   Ibid., p. 5.
[119]   Kierkegaard uses this phrase or some variant of it repeatedly in his articles in *The Moment*. See, for example, *SKS* 13, 133 / *M*, 95. *SKS* 13, 149 / *M*, 107. *SKS* 13, 151 / *M*, 109. *SKS* 13, 264 / *M*, 210.
[120]   *SKS* 14, 163 / *M*, 35.

Pontoppidan, "indeed, then one could, if necessary, understand that they have preserved their privileged so untouched."[121]

Instead of passionate Christians they have become learned theologians, who dispute about Christianity as a doctrine, which is precisely what it is not, according to Kierkegaard, at least only understood as a doctrine of existence, which communicates itself by means of the paradoxical existence of the God-man, who, for the Christian, is supposed to be the object of faith and imitation.

The pastors have become tradespeople like those pastors in the district of Randers in Pontoppidan's childhood; "in spite of Mynster and Grundtvig," Pontoppidan explains in his lecture, "in spite of Søren Kierkegaard and Martensen, in spite of the uninterrupted ringing and clanging, which has sounded from Copenhagen for more than a half century, most of the places were the cowshed and the field, the pigsty and the dung heap, which occupied the pastors' daily thoughts."[122]

In spite of Pontoppidan's own dislike for Kierkegaard's troll nature, one must understand here that he places him far above these prosaic pastors, which is confirmed by a hidden, but nonetheless clear reference to him shortly thereafter. "What we hear in the churches for the most part," he explains, "is thoughtful people's pious *observations* or sermons with a dominant moralizing tendency."[123] In the printed edition of the lecture the word "observations" is in italics, which one can hardly understand otherwise than as a reference to Kierkegaard, who often chastises the pastors for presenting distancing "observations" instead of awakening the congregation to self-examination and stimulating them to imitation. Pontoppidan presumably knew this criticism from *Practice in Christianity*, which Brandes recommended in his biography and which he himself borrowed from the University Library in 1895. Kierkegaard writes, for example:

> Soon it will have gone so far that even though sermons are often enough preached about or rather, "observations" are made about what it means to follow Christ, what it is to be a follower of Christ, etc., this talk still produces, if it evokes any effect at all, only this, that it strengthens admirers in admiring Christianity, and once in a while it wins a new admirer. But in the strictest sense the admirer is indeed not the true Christian; only the imitator is that.[124]

In *Practice in Christianity* Pontoppidan could also find the passionate interest for Christianity as a decisive and transforming factor in the existence of the individual, as he explains in the lecture. He complains that one as auditor in the churches on Sundays does not hear a single word "which tells about an independent inward experience of significance or merely a truly deep, personal emotion."[125] The same thing is true for the most part of the church literature, of which Pontoppidan gives this assessment:

---

121   Pontoppidan, *Kirken og dens Mænd. Et Foredrag*, p. 12.
122   Ibid., p. 13.
123   Ibid., p. 16.
124   *SKS* 11, 249 / *PC*, 257.
125   Pontoppidan, *Kirken og dens Mænd. Et Foredrag*, p. 16.

It is well-meant and often well-written books, sometimes in a fictional form, and with literary or scholarly pretensions. But most rarely does one stumble upon a personality, which bears the marks of a crucifixion of the soul or the flesh, or upon an expression of true joy, the genuine and profound joy, which alone is won through struggle and suffering. Most of these writings seem to have come to the world in all coziness with a tobacco pipe and a cup of tea. I am still not at all thinking about the flood of devotional books and collections of sermons, which is purely mercantile speculation, an industry in blatherskite.[126]

This sarcastic tirade also doubtless has its root in Kierkegaard's attack on the church, which Pontoppidan knows from *The Moment*. Not least of all the word "blatherskite" Kierkegaard likes to use about the pastors' good-humored Sunday sermons and the trivializing interpretation of the gospel. One protects oneself against the demands of the gospels by talking nonsense: "be a blatherskite, and you will see, all difficulties vanish!"[127]

Pontoppidan also sees blather in the fact that a pastor, from whom one ought to be able to expect a passionate faith relation, is not shaken by the fact that philology, history, and science shake the fundamental dogmas of faith, but coolly takes note, as if it had nothing at all to do with something so decisive as his eternal happiness. Kierkegaard describes the same phenomenon by comparing how such a pastor would have raised an outcry and had sweat on his brow, if someone instead had doubted the genuineness of the hundred rix-dollar bill that he had in his pocket.

Pontoppidan uses more or less the same analogy by comparing the blasé pastor with a man who has lived comfortably by his means, but one day gets the news that the better part of his securities have lost their value due to a bank crash. In such a case one would certainly be able to notice the catastrophe weighing on the man, but one cannot do this with the pastor, even if it is his eternal happiness that is at stake, and not just his temporal welfare.[128]

Pontoppidan, moreover, rails against the ordinations and all the ceremony they are endowed with. "Here the bishop himself steps toward them in golden apparel,"[129] Pontoppidan writes as an echo of Kierkegaard, who liked to refer to the bishop as a "man in silk" due to his dress, which seems to indicate his lordship's disdain for the congregation's ability to understand the New Testament's warning to watch out for men in soft clothes.

Just like Kierkegaard in his time—and incidentally also like Schaff in the autobiography—Pontoppidan has an eye for the baroque, that the young pastors come to the ordination with their wives or girlfriends on their arms, so that already beyond Vor Frue Kirke's magnificence one sees the comfortable parish with a stork's nest on the roof and a bunch of children inside. "The earnestness of life is not this pressure of finitude and busyness with livelihood, job, office, and procreation," as Kierkegaard writes in *Practice in Christianity*.[130]

---

[126]   Ibid., p. 17.
[127]   *SKS* 13, 381 / *M*, 319.
[128]   Pontoppidan, *Kirken og dens Mænd. Et Foredrag*, pp. 22–3.
[129]   Ibid., p. 6.
[130]   *SKS* 11, 189 / *PC*, 189–90.

Pontoppidan also takes up Kierkegaard's question about what a "witness to the truth"[131] is for a renewed consideration in his lecture. He thinks that a pastor formerly—and this means more or less before the Reformation—could count as such a witness to the truth, when he preached the truth with the entire church's thousand-year authority. But when this truth no longer is present as one, when the pastor in the Denmark of the day—and as already in Grundtvig's and Kierkegaard's time—"turns the pulpit into a lectern for his own private opinions,"[132] then for these opinions there is no other basis for authority than the pastor's own personal basis. In this way Pontoppidan sees a discrepancy between the subjective stamp of preaching and the nimbus of objective truth, which the church with all its time-honored authority, veneration, and decor is endowed with.

Pontoppidan concludes the lecture *The Church and Its Men* with an allegory on the pastors' loss of authority. He imagines that their ruffs are halos, "which have fallen down upon their necks because their heads were too small."[133] Then he refers to a scene in Oehlenschläger's tragedy, *Hakon Jarl*, where the earl tries on the king's crown, which is made for the old king's size. Unfortunately the earl does not have the same size, and the crown slips down over his eyes. Then the smith exclaims: "He bears the crown who has grown to the size of the crown!"[134]

Pontoppidan certainly did not regard Kierkegaard as a saint, but on the contrary, like Brandes, believed that there was more reverence (*pietet*) than piety (*fromhed*) in his relation to Christianity. By the same token Pontoppidan was able to respect Kierkegaard for the fact that he was, with Brandes' words, "disinclined...to call himself a Christian and was more seeking in the Christian direction than actually certain of his faith."[135] This is what Kierkegaard himself calls "honesty" (*Redelighed*), and which in extension of Pontoppidan's allegory can be expressed by saying that he did not make a demand for a crown which he knew well he could not wear.

Translated by Jon Stewart

---

[131]   Pontoppidan, *Kirken og dens Mænd. Et Foredrag*, p. 8.

[132]   Ibid., p. 8.

[133]   Ibid., p. 29.

[134]   Ibid., p. 30.

[135]   Brandes, *Søren Kierkegaard. En kritisk Fremstilling i Grundrids*, p. 336.

Bibliography

I. References to or Uses of Kierkegaard in Pontoppidan's Corpus

Kirken og dens Mænd. Et Foredrag, Copenhagen and Kristiania: Gyldendalske Boghandel, Nordisk Forlag 1914, p. 13.
Drengeaar, Copenhagen: Gyldendal, Nordisk Forlag 1933, pp. 79–80.
Hamskifte, Copenhagen: Copenhagen: Gyldendal, Nordisk Forlag 1936, p. 54.
Arv og Gæld, Copenhagen Gyldendal, Nordisk Forlag 1938, p. 41.
Familjeliv, Copenhagen: Gyldendal 1940, p. 80.
Undervejs til mig selv. Et Tilbageblik, Copenhagen: Gyldendal, Nordisk Forlag 1943, p. 7; p. 172.
De dødes rige, vols. 1–2, ed. by Thorkild Skjerbæk, 9th ed., Copenhagen: Gyldendal 1992, vol. 2, p. 12.
Henrik Pontoppidans breve, vols. 1–2, ed. and annotated by Carl Erik Bay and Elias Bredsdorff, Copenhagen: Gyldendal 1997, vol. 1, p. 320; vol. 2, p. 17; p. 152.

II. Sources of Pontoppidan's Knowledge of Kierkegaard

Brandes, Georg, *Søren Kierkegaard. En kritisk Fremstilling i Grundrids*, Copenhagen: Gyldendal 1877.
Kierkegaard, Søren, *Frygt og Bæven. Dialektisk Lyrik*, Copenhagen: C.A. Reitzel 1843.
— *Gjentagelsen. Et Forsøg i den experimenterende Psychologi*, Copenhagen: C.A. Reitzel 1843.
— *Forord. Morskabslæsning for enkelte Stænder efter Tid og Leilighed*, Copenhagen: C.A. Reitzel 1844.
— *Philosophiske Smuler eller En Smule Philosophi*, Copenhagen: C.A. Reitzel 1844.
— *Stadier paa Livets Vei. Studier af Forskjellige*, Copenhagen: C.A. Reitzel 1845.
— *Afsluttende uvidenskabelig Efterskrift til de philosophiske Smuler. Mimisk-pathetisk-dialektisk Sammenskrift, Existentielt Indlæg*, Copenhagen: C.A. Reitzel 1846.
— *Kjerlighedens Gjerninger. Nogle christelige Overveielser i Talers Form*, Copenhagen: C.A. Reitzel 1847.
— *Indøvelse i Christendom*, Copenhagen: C.A. Reitzel 1850.
— *Øieblikket*, Copenhagen: C.A. Reitzel 1877.

III. Secondary Literature on Pontoppidan's Relation to Kierkegaard

Benzow, Kristofer, "Det religiösa problemet i Pontoppidans Lykke-Per," in his *Idealitet och religiösitet. Studier kring det moderna religionsproblemet*, Lund: Gleestrup 1921, pp. 90–109.

— "Pontoppidans Lykke-Per. Till belysning av dess religiösa problemställning," *Vår lösen*, 12, no. 1–2, 1921, pp. 4–6; pp. 22–5.

Henriksen, Aage, "Det ubevidste," in his *De ubændige. Om Ibsen, Blixen, hverdagens virkelighed, det ubevidste*, Copenhagen: Gyldendal 1984, pp. 212–20.

Kristiansen, Børge, "Om identitet. Selvet hos Kidde, Pontoppidan og Frisch i lyset af Kierkegaard," *Kritik*, vol. 182, 2006, pp. 128–36.

Villy Sørensen:

A Critical Initiation

Steen Tullberg

I. Life and Art

The author and philosopher Villy Sørensen (1929–2001) is a central figure in post-war Danish intellectual life. He shares features with much of the traditional Danish cultural radicalism in the tradition from Georg Brandes, but constitutes at many points a corrective to it, for example, on the strength of his positive view of the value of religious and mythological symbols as forms of knowledge and on the strength of his far more nuanced view of Søren Kierkegaard.[1]

In an article entitled "Either/Or?" from 1988, he gave a cheery and personal account of the division that occurred early in his life between his poetic and philosophical urges and how *Either/Or* came crashing in to fill that emptiness. The occasion was a series of lectures in 1948 by the literary scholar F.J. Billeskov Jansen (1907–2002), who was the first to point out to Sørensen that Kierkegaard had a great sense of humor. He also relates the story of how he in the winter of 1947–48 had busied himself with writing aphorisms and gives a couple of examples of these youthful attempts, whereupon he remarks, "One might have thought that I had learned something from the aesthete and his diapsalmata, but it was not Søren Kierkegaard who got me to writing aphorisms, it was rather he who got me to stop; it had been done—better before."[2] The meeting with Kierkegaard in the guise of *Either/Or* that both confused and inspired Sørensen did not cause him in the long run to put poetry aside but to supplement it with a thorough study of philosophy. For him, the book left no choice: "There was no getting around philosophy and no getting around Kierkegaard."[3] Sørensen's early diaries—which are very much inspired by Kierkegaard's journal-keeping—bear evidence of this initial impulse and the

---

[1] The article is partly translated by Paul A. Bauer and Jon Stewart. For Villy Sørensen's Kierkegaard reception, see also Peter Fink, "Enten og Eller," in *Både frem og tilbage. Portræt af Villy Sørensens forfatterskab*, ed. by Marianne Barlyng and Jørgen Bonde Jensen, Hellerup: Spring 2002 (*Springs Forfatterskabsportrætter*), pp. 377–87, and "Efterskrift," in *Sørensen om Kierkegaard. Villy Sørensens udvalgte artikler om Søren Kierkegaard*, ed. by Gert Posselt, Copenhagen: Gyldendal 2007, pp. 277–88.

[2] Villy Sørensen, "Enten–Eller?" in *En bog om kunst der forløste. Det danske akademi 1981–1988*, Copenhagen: Gyldendal 1988, p. 45; also in *Sørensen om Kierkegaard*, ed. by Posselt, p. 10.

[3] Sørensen, "Enten–Eller?," p. 52; *Sørensen om Kierkegaard*, ed. by Posselt, p. 19.

inevitability of dealing with Kierkegaard. Kierkegaard is a watermark throughout, albeit an increasingly fading one, and the young Sørensen is particularly interested in the psychological presuppositions for the authorship. He uses Kierkegaard with critical distance in his own struggle to come to terms with the integration of thought and feeling.[4]

In 1988 Sørensen also published a pedagogical introduction to *Either/Or* that was used as an afterword to the Gyldendal edition of the work.[5] Here it is characteristic of Sørensen to interpret the ethical in the direction of mental hygiene. He notes how novel Kierkegaard's use of the word "energy" was at the time, especially in its psychological sense, and the high degree to which Kierkegaard anticipated psychoanalysis' dynamic conception of the life of the soul. When it comes to "choice" in B's (or Judge William's) version, Sørensen points out that the degree to which one can choose oneself is still debatable. One can scarcely choose oneself once and for all, not even according to B's conception: rather it is a process, and his "inner teleology" has a certain kinship with what C.G. Jung called the "process of individuation," a striving toward a psychical wholeness. Either one is allied with oneself or one is pitted against oneself—or as it says in the Bible, "He who does not gather, scatters."[6] It is a matter of either ethical gathering or aesthetic dissipation.

Sørensen is of the opinion that the aesthete's essay contains an original aesthetic theory. He notes that the aesthete has far more affinity with the religious than the ethical. These are not one and the same thing for the aesthete, as is nearly the case for the ethicist. Additionally, Sørensen contextualizes *Either/Or* with concrete examples by pointing out how Kierkegaard's aesthetes rise above the flock of depressives and nihilists typical of the day and how B's letters to A in their criticism of this type of person also contain a criticism of the period, the spirit of the time or precisely the time's lack thereof. The "modern development" that B speaks of has, according to Sørensen, later intensified the problem of the individual's lack of a foundation in a community of faith, and that is the reason why Kierkegaard's works only became widely known in the twentieth century: what in his time was a problem for the individual became in the age of the welfare state a problem for the many. Finally, Sørensen calls *Either/Or* the greatest erotic work in Danish literature: in its two parts a multiplicity of erotic moods stands opposite the one erotic passion that gives life meaning, "history." Even though Kierkegaard gradually pushed the poetical more and more off to the side, he never did it completely: it is impossible to imagine Kierkegaard's thought and its effects without the supreme poetic form of presentation. This may indicate, according to Sørensen, that the poetical is not just "aesthetic," even though the aesthetic part of the authorship is also the most poetic.

Sørensen's criticism of Kierkegaard's sharp distinction between the ethical and the aesthetic (between realizing oneself and formulating oneself) is present from the very beginning in his authorship. It forms the basis of the comprehensive aesthetic,

---

[4]   Villy Sørensen, *Tilløb. Dagbøger 1949–53*, Copenhagen: Gyldendal 1988; see *Sørensen om Kierkegaard*, ed. by Posselt, pp. 20–53.
[5]   Villy Sørensen, "Efterskrift," *Enten–Eller*, vols. 1–2, Copenhagen: Gyldendal 1988, vol. 2, pp. 343–58; also in *Sørensen om Kierkegaard*, ed. by Posselt, pp. 57–84.
[6]   Matthew 12:30; Luke 11:23.

philosophical, and cultural analyses in his pioneering philosophical aesthetics *Poets and Demons* from 1959,[7] and it is a guiding thread that runs through Sørensen's authorship. In *Poets and Demons*, Sørensen refutes Aage Henriksen's description of the epic lines in Kierkegaard's work as constituting novels. He writes:

> A work of art is, according to its essence, a fictional creation of symbols—and the external difficulties which arise in such an endeavor can very well be symbols of internal difficulties; Kierkegaard's "novels" are conceptual poetry: their "idea" is not derived from the artistic sequence but determines it, such that they do not display an artistic structure, but a philosophical system of concepts. This distinction does not constitute an evaluation; it is beyond discussion that Kierkegaard's poetic creations of thought are more significant works than the great majority of novels of his time—but one owes it to Kierkegaard to keep the categories distinct from one another.[8]

The epic lines are, according to Sørensen, illustrations of the philosophical evolution of concepts, and his book distinguishes itself from both Billeskov Jansen's[9] and Aage Henriksen's[10] contemporary books on Kierkegaard by using Kierkegaard to formulate his own aesthetics rather than expounding on Kierkegaard's. The book interprets and applies central Kierkegaardian categories to modern novels, for "Kierkegaard's abstract categories are visible in every major work of art, most clearly in the abstract work of art. Art confirms the Kierkegaardian philosophy and thereby reconciles the aesthetic with the 'dogmatic,' the accidental with the essential. And this reconciliation is another name for 'repetition.' "[11] In Sørensen's interpretation, the Danish poet Harald Kidde (1878–1918) is presented as the "poet of recollection," Thomas Mann (1875–1955) as the "poet of the fall," while the Austrian Hermann Broch (1886–1951) is interpreted and evaluated as the "poet of repetition."

In one of the most penetrating of the contemporary reviews of *Poets and Demons*, the theologian Jørgen K. Bukdahl (1936–79) saw that one of the book's main presuppositions is Kierkegaard's (or Vigilius Haufniensis') *The Concept of Anxiety* (which Sørensen also published with an introduction the following year, 1960).[12] Bukdahl saw how its basic concept is a special fusion of dogmatics and psychology:

---

7   Villy Sørensen, *Digtere og dæmoner*, Copenhagen: Gyldendal 1959.

8   Cf. ibid., p. 25.

9   F.J. Billeskov Jansen, *Studier i Søren Kierkegaards litterære Kunst*, Copenhagen: Rosenkilde og Bagger 1951.

10   Aage Henriksen, *Kierkegaards Romaner*, Copenhagen: Gyldendal 1954.

11   Sørensen, *Digtere og dæmoner*, p. 35; *Sørensen om Kierkegaard*, ed. by Posselt, p. 126. Kierkegaard's concept of repetition is of constant interest and inspiration to Sørensen, and in 1976 he wrote an extensive introduction to the book of that name (published in 1979), see *Sørensen om Kierkegaard*, ed. by Posselt, pp. 92–109. This introduction was published in English as "Søren Kierkegaard," in *The Nordic Mind: Current Trends in Scandinavian Literary Criticism*, ed. by Frank Egholm Andersen and John Weinstock, Lanham et al.: University Press of America 1986, pp. 7–16.

12   Villy Sørensen, "Introduktion," *Begrebet Angest*, Copenhagen: Gyldendals Uglebøger 1960, pp. 7–24; *Sørensen om Kierkegaard*, ed. by Posselt, pp. 128–52. At the beginning of the 1960s Niels Thulstrup (1924–88) and Villy Sørensen were asked by the publishing house Gyldendal if they would take it upon themselves to publish a third edition of the *Samlede*

The philosopher Villy Sørensen has learned from dogmatics to speak about "the fall" and from psychology to speak about "the trauma." These two ways of speaking are blended together in one special Sørensenesque, dogmatic-psychological manner of speaking, when the original sin in *Poets and Demons* is called "the eternal trauma"... Villy Sørensen's entire book builds on the identification of biology and ontology—of the original sin and trauma.[13]

In his second non-fictional book, a collection of essays called *Neither— Nor* (1961),[14] Sørensen unfolds his understanding of art and its opposition to Kierkegaard's in an essay entitled "Søren Kierkegaard and the Magic Flute." Here he deals with the essay on Don Giovanni, "The Immediate Erotic Stages or the Musical-Erotic," beginning, again, by expressing his fundamental wonderment at Kierkegaard's opposition of the aesthetic and the ethical. Because Kierkegaard does not regard the aesthetic attitude to life as being the most valuable, one could assume, according to Sørensen, that Kierkegaard himself would have reservations about the philosophy of music in aesthete A's essay. But there is much evidence that Kierkegaard in fact agrees with A, because art is for Kierkegaard a matter for aesthetics in the sense that the object of its meditations is "the beautiful," which stimulates pleasure and as such an aesthete would presumably be the most suited to write about it. A work of art cannot capture an ethical development, in Kierkegaard's opinion, and attempts to do this fail—aesthetically. Stated differently, Sørensen continues, art cannot then—especially the most immediate of the arts, music—express, according to Kierkegaard, the ethical and the spiritual, but must be content with the aesthetic and the sensible (as in *Don Juan*).

But this is where A errs, according to Sørensen—or Kierkegaard does, in as much as he himself is an aesthete in his view of art. In order to experience that ethical love can well be expressed in music, one needs only, according to Sørensen, to listen to *The Magic Flute*, which Kierkegaard sets lower than *Don Giovanni*, precisely because it expresses human development. The high priest Sarastro, for example, first shows himself to be a scoundrel only to become a particularly good person, and the Queen of the Night, who in her first aria expresses sorrow because her daughter Pamina has been abducted by Sarastro, then goes on in her second aria to express unjust indignation at Pamina's evasion of her authority. The figures of Papageno and Tamino develop likewise, and, according to Sørensen, if one wishes to use Kierkegaardian categories, then Papageno represents the aesthetic love, which does not admit of any development proper, while Tamino represents the ethical— and the latter is, Sørensen claims, expressed just as well in music as the former.

Værker, a request which was motivated by the 150-year anniversary of Kierkegaard's birth in 1963. The conditions were, however, unsatisfactory since the publishing house wanted to publish one volume per month, and the project was instead taken over by the author, Peter P. Rohde (1902–78). See Villy Sørensen, *Perioder. Dagbøger 1961–74*, Copenhagen: Gyldendal 1993, p. 15.

[13]   Cf. Jørgen K. Bukdahl, "Om ontologi og biologi," in his *Frihed og frigørelse. Filosofi—Teologi—Kulturdebat. Artikler og essays 1956–1979*, Århus: Aros 1980, pp. 37–41.

[14]   Villy Sørensen, *Hverken–Eller*, Copenhagen: Gyldendal 1961.

Sørensen finishes by offering his own ideas on art's potential, in that art, he believes, is able to express the development that each human being goes through, namely, the striving to become entirely oneself, which only few are able to achieve. In *The Magic Flute*, the fundamental conflict in human nature is traced through all its perilous phases to a happy ending. If only Schikaneder's text were available, one would not, Sørensen admits, have any confidence in it, but one can easily put one's trust in Mozart. Thus, based on his philosophy of art, Kierkegaard's aesthete, who placed Mozart higher than all other artists, paradoxically enough came to place Mozart too low.[15]

II. Kierkegaard Compared

It is characteristic of Villy Sørensen when dealing with other thinkers and authors that he almost invariably draws Kierkegaard into the picture. This is particularly evident in his work from the 1960s where he writes articles, introductions, and monographs on people like Hans Christian Andersen, Karl Marx, Friedrich Nietzsche, Arthur Schopenhauer, and Franz Kafka.[16]

Poets and Demons is introduced with a characterization of the relation between (the poet) Hans Christian Andersen and (the philosopher) Søren Kierkegaard, and the main point of interest for Sørensen is the difference in the nature of the two authors' recollection and connection to their childhood. The division in the philosophers' soul seems to be of a more radical nature than in the case of the poet, who effortlessly finds a rich material for production in his childhood memories. Sørensen dwells on the strange fact that the first book ever written *about* H.C. Andersen was also the first book *by* Kierkegaard (*From the Papers of One Still Living*, 1838), and he argues that though neither of the two realized it, the existential problems that Kierkegaard expressed in thoughts were very similar to the issues that Andersen brought to expression in his stories and adventures.

Sørensen finds a common denominator for the great "negative" thinkers of the nineteenth century (Marx, Nietzsche, Kierkegaard) in their polemical style of writing.[17] The important relation between Kierkegaard and Karl Marx is treated in several places by Sørensen, who initiated a renewed interest in Marx in Denmark in the early 1960s. The essence of his viewpoint is that the two in all their brilliant one-sidedness supplement one another: the philosopher of existence, Kierkegaard, *must* be supplemented with the critic of society, Marx, if one wishes to understand the modern age in its entirety. The necessity of dealing with Marx is also present chronologically: after publishing *The Concept of Anxiety* (in 1960), Sørensen

---

[15]   In *Neither–Nor* Sørensen also writes about the comical with special reference to Kierkegaard, cf. *Hverken–Eller*, pp. 196–211; *Sørensen om Kierkegaard*, ed. by Posselt, pp. 165–86. See also Tonny Aagaard Olesen, "The Painless Contradiction: A Note on the Reception of the Theory of the Comic in *Postscript*," in *Kierkegaard Studies Yearbook*, 2005, pp. 339–50, see p. 348.

[16]   See *Sørensen om Kierkegaard*, ed. by Posselt, pp. 227–73.

[17]   Cf. Sørensen, *Perioder. Dagbøger 1961–74*, pp. 20–1.

published and wrote an introduction to a collection of Marx's early writings (1962).[18] Immediately thereafter he wrote a book on Nietzsche (1963),[19] where Kierkegaard only sporadically appears. In a diary entry from January 12, 1963, Sørensen expresses a fascination for *On the Genealogy of Morals*, which he considers to be Nietzsche's equivalent to *The Concept of Anxiety*.[20]

When dealing with Schopenhauer, Sørensen's approach is somewhat different in that Kierkegaard actually had read Schopenhauer (in 1854) and is brought on stage more as a competitor and direct adversary than as someone supplementing the protagonist. And the comparison is not necessarily to Kierkegaard's advantage. Sørensen states the difference between them by saying that Kierkegaard speaks ethically about the psychological, while Schopenhauer speaks psychologically about the ethical, and in this context he holds the pre-psychoanalytical elements in Schopenhauer in higher esteem than the pre-existentialist ones in Kierkegaard.[21]

In the book *Kafka's Poetry* (1968) Kierkegaard is introduced in a fairly straightforward way given the fact that Kafka himself had read and felt a certain kinship to Kierkegaard and tried to come to terms with him in his diaries and letters. But on a deeper level the book also unfolds the aesthetics inherent in *Poets and Demons*, where a main point was that Kierkegaard's abstract categories are visible in modern art such as Kafka's stories.

Central to the Kierkegaard discussion in the book is the figure of Abraham and how one is to understand the relationship between Kierkegaard's *Fear and Trembling* and Kafka's *The Castle*. At the end of his analysis Sørensen writes:

> Kafka, who could not accept the principle distinction between the inner and the outer made by Kierkegaard, also could not accept that the inner—the divine—should position itself against the world, against powers and kingdoms, in order for it to come to expression; his castle adventure is indeed about a rebel, but also about the impossibility of rebellion. If there is only a goal and no means [Kafka's main viewpoint], then there is no way out other than redemption [*forløsning*]...[that is, the belief] that the world is transformed by itself.[22]

Thus, Sørensen concludes, while Kierkegaard's faith by virtue of the absurd at the end of his life turned out to hold the belief that the world could be different, Kafka maintained a by no means less absurd belief that the world already *is* different than it is.

[18]   Villy Sørensen, *Karl Marx. Økonomi og filosofi. Ungdomsskrifter*, introduction and selection by Villy Sørensen, Danish translation by Ulrich Horst Petersen, Copenhagen: Gyldendal 1962.
[19]   Villy Sørensen, *Nietzsche*, Copenhagen: Gads Forlag 1963.
[20]   Cf. Sørensen, *Perioder. Dagbøger 1961–74*, p. 60.
[21]   Cf. Villy Sørensen, *Schopenhauer*, Copenhagen: Gad 1969, pp. 91–5; *Sørensen om Kierkegaard*, ed. by Posselt, pp. 253–8.
[22]   See Villy Sørensen, *Kafkas digtning*, Copenhagen: Gyldendal 1968, p. 189; *Sørensen om Kierkegaard*, ed. by Posselt, pp. 272–3.

III. Politics

In addition to his role as an influential literary critic, Villy Sørensen also stands out as one of the post-war period's foremost spokesmen for (the idea behind) the welfare state and, on the whole, as one of the most important thinkers of democracy in Denmark, and precisely when the issue concerns the relation to democracy and its possible content, he has substantial objections to a particular Kierkegaardian tradition.

In 1990 the editor Henning Fonsmark (1926–2006) published his grand critical analysis of the Danish welfare model, *The History of the Danish Utopia*.[23] The book is a fierce analysis of the construction—and exaggeration—of the Danes' highly praised welfare democracy, whose "utopia," according to Fonsmark, consists in the fact that it is encumbered by the economic disadvantage that it can only be sustained by the uninterrupted incurring of debts. In Fonsmark's interpretation the patronizing Danish welfare state is an ideological fusion of Grundtvig and Marx, but in the book's postscript Kierkegaard is introduced into the discussion. This takes place against the background of Johannes Sløk's *This Society!* (1989),[24] which seeks to explicate and make topical Kierkegaard's criticism of democracy from the perspective of an express dissatisfaction with the obviousness and self-satisfaction with which democracy today is made into the sole sacred form of government. According to Sløk, Kierkegaard is, from a certain perspective, in an eminent sense a political thinker. When Kierkegaard/ Sløk reject democracy as a form of government, it is because of the "human fear" and the leveling of differences, which, according to them, is attached to the very essence of democracy, and which, by making the individuals into "masses," gives them fewer and fewer possibilities to be "private" or "themselves" as individuals. Sløk's alternative to democracy is not dictatorship but enlightened despotism or preferably an anarchic community, where the concept of power is done away with. He is aware that Kierkegaard himself did not use the word "anarchy," but he nonetheless interprets Kierkegaard's attack on the church in this direction and ascribes to him a view of the Christian Church in the original Lutheran sense as an anarchic model.

When Henning Fonsmark, from his side, uses Sløk/Kierkegaard, it is not to reject democracy but to sharpen his own criticism of the negative effects of democratic government. In addition, there is a polemic against a "qualitative" conception of democracy, which in its time was carried out by Hal Koch in a discussion with the legal positivist Alf Ross (compare the books *What is Democracy?* from 1945, *Why Democracy?* from 1946, and *Nordic Democracy* from 1949)[25] along with Villy Sørensen's conception of democracy which is related to Koch's and, among other things, is based on a criticism of Kierkegaard's view that all people (in spite of all outward differences) are equal with respect to the most important things in life. Sørensen sometimes expresses his criticism of Kierkegaard on this point in a very

---

[23]   Henning Fonsmark, *Historien om den danske utopi*, Copenhagen: Gyldendal 1990.

[24]   Johannes Sløk, *Det her samfund!*, Viby J.: Centrum 1989.

[25]   Hal Koch, *Hvad er Demokrati?*, Copenhagen: Gyldendal 1945; Alf Ross, *Hvorfor Demokrati?*, Copenhagen: Munksgaard 1946; and *Nordisk Demokrati*, ed. by Hal Koch and Alf Ross, Copenhagen: Westermann 1949.

strong manner and, for example (in a comment to *Tidehverv*'s Børge Diderichsen in 1963) juxtaposes "Søren Kierkegaard and the children who worked themselves to death in the English factories at the same time as he was writing *Works of Love*."²⁶

The point here is that, according to Sørensen, it does not make sense to demand a Kierkegaardian struggle for existence of a human being, unless certain social and material presuppositions have been fulfilled. Sørensen can thus, on the one hand, recognize Jørgen Bukdahl's (1896–1982) indication of the social view in Kierkegaard's attack on the church (in *Søren Kierkegaard and the Common Man*),²⁷ but at the same time criticize the fact that the social in Kierkegaard is exclusively regarded as an "external spectacle": if the social is the goal, then "it is strange that the existentially concerned person is worried so little about it along the way—especially when the goal is never really achieved!"²⁸ For Sørensen, the point of the welfare state (in its correct form) is that the person is to be liberated for a spiritual life, the kind of life Kierkegaard is interested in, and the fact that Kierkegaard's works have enjoyed such great currency in our time (and only in our time, that is, after World War II) suggests, according to Sørensen, that precisely the social development has made the existential issue more urgent. Put differently:

> when Kierkegaard is understood better in our time than in his own, the reason is that the development has proven him correct—and proven him incorrect in his view of the development. Only when society no longer places substantial obstacles in the way of the individual's free unfolding, is it possible for the individual to regard the entire social sphere as something inessential—and to conceive it with the same indifference as Kierkegaard himself did.²⁹

Later on, Sørensen carries this criticism further in a negative interpretation of the 1990s' great interest in Kierkegaard since, according to him, it suggests a spirit of the age which refuses to recognize the both/and of reality, its aggregate nature and compromises. The self-realizing individual in the market-based society imagines—just like Kierkegaard's esthete and ultimately like Kierkegaard himself—that he can take a short-cut from the personal reality to the religious sphere of existence (Sørensen calls it "the source of values" or "the force") by evading the common social-ethical reality—which is left to the market. When one in this manner runs across the social and does not want to know about its conflicts and compromises, it is, according to Sørensen, only logical that one ends up, like Kierkegaard, with "a rather cramped form of Christianity: the cultivation of the paradox."³⁰ Here, again,

---

²⁶   Cf. *Vindrosen*, no. 6, 1963, p. 501.
²⁷   Jørgen Bukdahl, *Søren Kierkegaard og den menige mand*, Copenhagen: Munksgaard 1961.
²⁸   Villy Sørensen, "Den abstrakte eksistens," in *Mellem fortid og fremtid. Kronikker og kommentarer*, Copenhagen: Gyldendal 1969, p. 115; *Sørensen om Kierkegaard*, ed. by Posselt, p. 207.
²⁹   Sørensen, "Den abstrakte eksistens," pp. 114–15; *Sørensen om Kierkegaard*, ed. by Posselt, pp. 206–7.
³⁰   Cf. *Med Villy i midten—28 vidnesbyrd om Villy Sørensen*, ed. by Suzanne Brøgger, Erling Groth et al., Copenhagen: Gyldendal 2004, pp. 314–15.

one recognizes a criticism in the tradition from Georg Brandes and Harald Høffding, for whom Kierkegaard in reality neglected the ethical stage.[31]

IV. Theology

One might say that Sørensen in his late authorship shifts his focus when dealing with Kierkegaard from the relationship between the aesthetic and the ethical to the relationship between the ethical and the religious. Apart from the discussion of the political implications of Kierkegaard's thinking mentioned above, this is expressed most clearly in the postscript to the second edition of Sørensen's big analysis of the historical Jesus from 1993,[32] where he gives his own account of the relation between the ethical and the religious in a criticism of Kierkegaard's *Fear and Trembling*. Sørensen writes in his conclusion:

> If Jesus—as the gospels imply—broke with his family in order to follow his calling, it is an example of what in Kierkegaard is called an absolute duty towards God—and a better example than Kierkegaard's own in *Fear and Trembling*: Abraham who receives the command from Yahweh to sacrifice his son and obeys. The two examples show precisely the distance between the god of power, who demands blind obedience, and a god who is a "father" to all human beings so that one's duties are not limited to one's closest family. Jesus' religiosity was not a "suspension of the ethical," but a sharpening of it, so that the difference between the ethical and the special religious is—that the religious is the special ethical.[33]

With his focus on the historical Jesus and the ethics that can be read out of the gospels Sørensen in many ways shares viewpoints with the Danish theologian K.E. Løgstrup (1905–81). He was sympathetic to Løgstrup's *Confrontation with Kierkegaard* (1968),[34] which was the culmination of a long controversy on the right understanding of Kierkegaard between K. Olesen Larsen (1899–1964) and Løgstrup. More generally, this conflict was between a religious experiential line and a paradoxical line in Danish theology, and Løgstrup argued that the Christian message in Kierkegaard is strictly derived from the paradoxical without reference to what Jesus' earthly and historical life consisted of. Løgstrup's own view was summed up in a much quoted phrase, where he claims that "the only non-paradoxical life is the life of Jesus of Nazareth. Everything is here straightforward and obvious. What is paradoxical is how the life that everyone else lives could come about."[35] Villy

[31]   Villy Sørensen's double criticism of contemporary society and Kierkegaard points to another example of a political neoliberal use of Kierkegaard in the wake of the collapse of communism, namely the Venstre politician and former prime minister (2001–2009) Anders Fogh Rasmussen's *Fra socialstat til minimalstat*, Copenhagen: Samleren 1993, which likewise uses Kierkegaard (in Sløk's version) in his criticism of the welfare state's "slave morality" and flight from responsibility.
[32]   Villy Sørensen, *Jesus og Kristus*, 2nd ed., Copenhagen: Gyldendal 1993 [1992].
[33]   Ibid., p. 256.
[34]   Løgstrup, *Opgør med Kierkegaard*, Copenhagen: Gyldendal 1968.
[35]   Ibid., p. 22.

Sørensen expresses this by saying that "precisely the Kierkegaardian basic ideas about God's human existence are used by Løgstrup about human beings' human existence,"[36] and he writes with admiration about Løgstrup's discovery of the so-called sovereign life-utterances: "Løgstrup's talk of the sovereign life-utterances is a strikingly simple objection to all the common talk about becoming oneself, becoming real [*egentlig*], becoming free."[37] Sørensen, however, also has objections to Løgstrup's interpretation of Kierkegaard, a main point being that Løgstrup neglects the importance of Kierkegaard's battle with the church. With his attack on the Danish State Church, Kierkegaard demonstrated that he was able to transform his reflection into action (regardless of how one might evaluate this action).

Furthermore, Sørensen would never fully subscribe to Løgstrup's Christendom, and he is generally skeptical towards most of the theological tradition and way of thinking. In Sørensen's eyes all theologians, from Paul and Augustine to Luther, Kierkegaard, Nygren, and Løgstrup have a tendency to ignore the fundamental capacity of human beings for liberating themselves from (psychological) bindings. Consequently "grace" is, in his view, not a concept totally independent or void of human psychology, and he points to the fact that theologians traditionally have emphasized that the good is not within human beings' own capacity or dependent on their effort and that they are at the same time guilty of and responsible for evil. Those who, like Pelagius and Erasmus, have challenged this and claimed that the human will is not totally captive have been fiercely attacked by Augustine and Luther.[38]

According to Sørensen, religion is an expression of a collective interpretation, which is formed by the individual experience of its founder (Jesus, Buddha, Muhammad, etc.)—and distorted by theologians, who have not had that same experience. In his general criticism of theology Sørensen draws on the well-documented experiences of religious mystics of all times, and he uses this against Kierkegaard: "In the religious founder's god experience (a word that is of course abominable to theological ears) there is no difference between subject and object, between immanence and transcendence, the humane and the divine—Kierkegaard never had such an original god experience."[39]

---

[36]   Cf. Villy Sørensen, "Løgstrups opgør med Kierkegaard," in *Mellem Fortid og Fremtid—kronikker og kommentarer*, pp. 122–3. Cf. *Sørensen om Kierkegaard*, ed. by Posselt, p. 218.

[37]   Sørensen, "Løgstrups opgør med Kierkegaard," p. 122; *Sørensen om Kierkegaard*, ed. by Posselt, p. 217.

[38]   Cf. Sørensen, *Jesus og Kristus*, p. 197.

[39]   Sørensen, "Løgstrups opgør med Kierkegaard," p. 124; *Sørensen om Kierkegaard*, ed. by Posselt, p. 220.

Bibliography

I. References to or Uses of Kierkegaard in Sørensen's Corpus

"Digteren, Filosoffen og Barndommen," *Berlingske Tidende*, September 13, 1955.
Digtere og dæmoner. Fortolkninger og vurderinger, Copenhagen: Gyldendal 1959, pp. 10–36.
"Introduktion," *Begrebet Angest*, Copenhagen: Gyldendals Uglebøger 1960, pp. 7–24.
"Om det komiske. Fra ironi til humor," *Information*, March 22–23, 1961.
"Om det komiske. Med stadigt hensyn til Søren Kierkegaard," *Hverken–Eller. Kritiske betragtninger*, Copenhagen: Gyldendal 1961, pp. 196–211.
"Søren Kierkegaard og Tryllefløjten," *Hverken–Eller. Kritiske betragtninger*, Copenhagen: Gyldendal 1961, pp. 191–5. (Originally in *Politiken*, November 28, 1959).
"Søren Kierkegaard og det folkelige" (review of *Søren Kierkegaard: Dagbøger*, ed. by Peter P. Rohde, vol. 1, Copenhagen: Thaning & Appels Forlag 1961, and Jørgen Bukdahl, *Søren Kierkegaard og den menige mand*, in *Søren Kierkegaard Selskabets populære skrifter*, vols. 9–10, Copenhagen: Munksgaard 1961), *Berlingske Tidende*, January 6, 1962 (reprinted in *Mellem fortid og fremtid. Kronikker og kommentarer*, Copenhagen: Gyldendal 1969, pp. 98–103).
"Søren Kierkegaard og det eksistentielle," *Berlingske Tidende,* April 30, 1963; also in *Ord och Bild*, vol. 72, 1963, pp. 466–8 (reprinted in *Mellem fortid og fremtid. Kronikker og kommentarer,* Copenhagen: Gyldendal 1969, pp. 104–9).
"Den abstrakte eksistens" (review of Johannes Sløk's *Eksistentialisme*, Copenhagen: Berlingske Forlag 1964), *Berlingske Tidende*, November 11, 1964 (reprinted in *Mellem fortid og fremtid. Kronikker og kommentarer*, Copenhagen: Gyldendal 1969, pp. 110–16).
"Søren Kierkegaard og Karl Marx," *Aarhuus Stiftstidende* and *Aalborg Stiftstidende*, May 7, 1965.
"Kafka og filosofien," in his *Kafkas digtning*, Copenhagen: Gyldendal 1968, pp. 179–89.
"Løgstrups opgør med Kierkegaard," *Mellem fortid og fremtid. Kronikker og kommentarer*, Copenhagen: Gyldendal 1969, pp. 117–26.
"Schopenhauer og Kierkegaard," in his *Schopenhauer*, Copenhagen: Gad 1969, pp. 91–5.
"Forord," in Søren Kierkegaard, *Gjentagelsen*, Copenhagen: Co'libri 1979.
"Andersen and Kierkegaard," *Denmarkings. Danish Literature Today*, ed. by Torben Brostrøm, Copenhagen: Danish Government Committee for Cultural Exchange 1982, p. 20.

"Søren Kierkegaard," in *The Nordic Mind: Current Trends in Scandinavian Literary Criticism*, ed. by Frank Egholm Andersen and John Weinstock, Lanham et al.: University Press of America 1986, pp. 7–16. (Danish version published in 1979 as the preface to Søren Kierkegaard, *Gjentagelsen*, Copenhagen: Co'libri 1979).

"Efterskrift," in Søren Kierkegaard, *Enten–Eller*, vols. 1–2, Copenhagen: Gyldendal 1988, vol. 2, pp. 343–58.

"Enten–Eller?" in *En bog om kunst der forløste. Det danske akademi 1981–1988*, Copenhagen: Gyldendal 1988, pp. 44–52.

Tilløb. Dagbøger 1949–53, Copenhagen: Gyldendal 1988, pp. 8–10; pp. 14–15; pp. 18–21; pp. 29–36; pp. 116–17; p. 148; pp. 151–2.

Forløb. Dagbøger 1953–1961, Copenhagen: Gyldendal 1990, pp. 63–4; p. 147; pp. 173–4; pp. 206–8; p. 210.

Jesus og Kristus, 2nd ed., Copenhagen: Gyldendal 1993 [1992], p. 256.

Perioder. Dagbøger 1961–74, Copenhagen: Gyldendal 1993, pp. 136–7.

Sørensen om Kierkegaard. Villy Sørensens udvalgte artikler om Søren Kierkegaard, ed. by Gert Posselt, Copenhagen: Gyldendal 2007.

II. Sources of Sørensen's Knowledge of Kierkegaard

Adorno, Theodor W., *Kierkegaard. Konstruktion des Ästhetischen*, Tübingen: Mohr 1933.

Bohlin, Torsten, *Sören Kierkegaard*, Uppsala: Svenska Kyrkans Diakonistyrelses Bokförlag 1918.

Brandes, Georg, *Søren Kierkegaard. En kritisk Fremstilling i Grundrids*, Copenhagen: Gyldendal 1877.

Brandt, Frithiof, *Den unge Søren Kierkegaard. En Række nye Bidrag*, Copenhagen: Levins & Munksgaards Forlag 1929.

Bredsdorff, Elias, *Corsaren, Goldschmidt og Kierkegaard*, Copenhagen: Corsarens Forlag 1977.

Brøchner, Hans, *Problemet om Tro og Viden. En historisk-kritisk afhandling*, Copenhagen: P.G. Philipsens Forlag 1868.

— *Erindringer om Søren Kierkegaard. Udgivet med Indledning og Oplysninger af Steen Johansen*, Copenhagen: Gyldendal 1953.

Bukdahl, Jørgen, "Kierkegaard-narkomani. Omkring den psykologiske Kierkegaard-forskning," *Dansk Udsyn*, no. 6, Kolding: Askov Højskole 1959, pp. 360–76.

— *Søren Kierkegaard. Hans fader og slægten i Sædding*, Ribe: Dansk hjemstavns forlag 1960.

— *Søren Kierkegaard og den menige mand*, in *Søren Kierkegaard Selskabets populære skrifter*, vols. 9–10, Copenhagen: Munksgaard 1961.

Cappelørn, Niels Jørgen, Joakim Garff, and Johnny Kondrup, *Skriftbilleder. Søren Kierkegaards journaler, notesbøger, hæfter, ark, lapper og strimler*, Copenhagen: Gad 1996.

Christensen, Villads, *Søren Kierkegaard i Lys af Shakespeares Hamlet*, Copenhagen: Rosenkilde & Bagger 1960.

Fischer, Friedrich Carl, *Die Nullpunkt-Existenz. Dargestellt an der Lebensform Sören Kierkegaards*, Munich: Beck 1933.

[Gude, L.], *Magister S. Kierkegaards Forfattervirksomhed. Iagttagelser af en Landsbypræst*, Copenhagen: C.A. Reitzel 1851.

Harris, Edward, *The Formation of the Soul: A Study of the Process of Adult Religious Learning with Special Reference to Søren Kierkegaard's Philosophical Religious Anthropology*, Stockholm: [Edward Harris] 1995.

Hauberg Mortensen, Finn, *Kierkegaard Made in Japan*, Odense: Odense University Press 1996 (*Odense University Literary and Cultural Studies*, no. 5).

Hejll, Richard, *Kierkegaard och mystiken. En förberedande undersökning, Edda*, Oslo 1938.

Henriksen, Aage, *Kierkegaards Romaner*, Copenhagen: Gyldendal 1954.

Himmelstrup, Jens, *International Bibliografi*, Copenhagen: Nyt Nordisk Forlag/ Arnold Busck 1962.

Høffding, Harald, *Søren Kierkegaard som Filosof*, Copenhagen: Philipsen 1892.

Ibsen, A. and Jens Himmelstrup, *Søren Kierkegaard-Register. Sag- og Forfatterregister*, Copenhagen: Gyldendal 1936.

Jolivet, Régis, *Introduction à Kierkegaard*, Paris, Abbaye Saint-Wandrille: Éditions de Fontenelle 1946.

Jørgensen, Carl, *Søren Kierkegaard. En biografi med særligt henblik paa hans personlige etik*, vols. 1–5, Copenhagen: Nyt Nordisk Forlag 1964.

— *Søren Kierkegaards skuffelser*, Copenhagen: Nyt Nordisk Forlag 1967.

Jørgensen, Merete, *Kierkegaard som kritiker. En undersøgelse af forholdet mellem det æstetiske og det etiske i Kierkegaards litterære kritik*, Copenhagen: Gyldendal 1978.

Koch, Carl, "Søren Kierkegaard og Eventyret," in *Dansk Tidsskrift*, Copenhagen: Jac. Appel & L. Moltesen 1899, pp. 146–60.

— *Søren Kierkegaard og Emil Boesen. Breve og Indledning. Med et Tillæg*, Copenhagen: Karl Schønbergs Forlag 1901.

Kühle, Sejer, *Søren Kierkegaards Barndom og Ungdom*, Copenhagen: Aschehoug Dansk Forlag 1950.

Ljungdahl, Arnold, *Problemet Søren Kierkegaard*, Stockholm: Nordstedts 1964.

Lund, Henriette, *"Mit Forhold til Hende." Af Søren Kierkegaards efterladte Papirer*, Copenhagen: Gyldendal 1904.

McKinnon, Alastair, *Dating Kierkegaard's Battle with Fate*, Copenhagen: Det Kgl. Danske Videnskabernes Selskab/Historisk-filosofisk Meddelelser 1986.

Malantschuk, Gregor, *Fra Individ til den Enkelte. Problemer omkring friheden og det etiske hos Søren Kierkegaard*, Copenhagen: C.A. Reitzel 1978.

Næsgård, Sigurd, *En Psykoanalyse af Søren Kierkegaard*, Odense: Psykoanalytisk Forlag 1950.

Parkov, Peter and Gert Posselt, *Troskab—og Tilgivelse. Regine—Regina. Et påskud for nogle rekapitulerende punktnedslag i Regine Olsens liv efter Kierkegaard*, Copenhagen: Danmarks Nationalleksikon 1992.

Plougmann, Vera, *Søren Kierkegaards kristendomsforståelse*, Copenhagen: Gyldendal 1975.

Przywara, Erich, *Das Geheimnis Kierkegaards*, Munich: Oldenburg 1929.

Rehm, Walter, *Kierkegaard und der Verführer*, Munich: Rinn 1947.

Rohde, Peter P., *Søren Kierkegaard. Et Geni i en Købstad*, Copenhagen: Gyldendal 1962.

Scopetéa, Sophia, "Søren Kierkegaard," *Epopteia*, no. 79, 1983, pp. 379–487.

— *Kierkegaard og græciteten. En kamp med ironi*, Copenhagen: C.A. Reitzel 1995.

Sløk, Johannes, *Die Anthropologie Kierkegaards*, Copenhagen: Rosenkilde & Bagger 1954.

— *Eksistentialisme*, Copenhagen: Berlingske Forlag 1964.

— *Da Kierkegaard tav. Fra forfatterskab til kirkestorm*, Copenhagen: Hans Reitzel 1980.

— *Kierkegaards univers. En ny guide til geniet*, Copenhagen: Centrum 1983.

Thielst, Peter, *Søren og Regine. Kierkegaard, kærlighed og kønspolitik*, Copenhagen: Gyldendal 1980.

— *Kierkegaards filosofi og psykologi. En introduktion*, Copenhagen: Hans Reitzel 1992.

— *Livet forstås baglæns—men må leves forlæns. Historien om Søren Kierkegaard*, Copenhagen: Gyldendal 1994.

Thulstrup, Niels, *Kierkegaard forhold til Hegel—og til den spekulative idealisme indtil 1846*, Copenhagen: Gyldendal 1967.

Thust, Martin, *Sören Kierkegaard. Der Dichter des Religiösen. Grundlagen eines Systems der Subjektivität*, Munich: Beck 1931.

Toftdahl, Hellmut, *Kierkegaard først—og Grundtvig så. Sammenligning og vurdering*, Copenhagen: Nyt Nordisk Forlag/Arnold Busck 1969.

III. Secondary Literature on Sørensen's Relation to Kierkegaard

Bukdahl, Jørgen K., "Om ontologi og biologi," in his *Frihed og frigørelse. Filosofi—Teologi—Kulturdebat. Artikler og essays 1956–1979*, Århus: Aros 1980, pp. 37–41.

Fink, Peter, "Enten og Eller," in *Både frem og tilbage. Portræt af Villy Sørensens forfatterskab*, ed. by Marianne Barlyng and Jørgen Bonde Jensen, Hellerup: Spring 2002 (*Springs Forfatterskabsportrætter*), pp. 377–87.

Kramer, Nathaniel Todd, *Between Kierkegaard and Freud. Villy Sørensen, Danish Modernism, and the Concept of Trauma*, Ph.D. Thesis, University of California, Los Angeles 2006.

Petersen, Carl Steen, *Midtens vovestykke. Om Villy Sørensens essayistiske forfatterskab*, Copenhagen: Gyldendal 2000, p. 52; pp. 89–9.

Posselt, Gert, "Efterskrift," in *Sørensen om Kierkegaard. Villy Sørensens udvalgte artikler om Søren Kierkegaard*, Copenhagen: Gyldendal 2007, pp. 277–88.

Støvring, Kasper, *Det etiske kunstværk. Villy Sørensens poetik og litterære kritik*, Copenhagen: Gyldendal and Odense: Syddansk Universitets forlag 2006, pp. 124ff.; p. 139; pp. 202–3; pp. 255–68.

Tullberg, Steen, *Søren Kierkegaard i Danmark. En receptionshistorie*, Copenhagen: C.A. Reitzel 2006, see pp. 84–5; pp. 105ff.

— "*Either/Or* in Denmark," *Kierkegaard Studies Yearbook*, 2008, pp. 237–96; see pp. 269–72.

— "Denmark: The Permanent Reception—150 Years of Reading Kierkegaard," in *Kierkegaard's International Reception*, Tome I, *Northern and Western Europe*, ed. by Jon Stewart, Aldershot: Ashgate 2009 (*Kierkegaard Research: Sources, Reception and Resources*, vol. 8), pp. 3–120; see pp. 84–6.

Vergote, Henri-Bernard, "Un lecteur danois de Kierkegaard: Villy Sørensen," *Les Études Philosophiques*, 1971, pp. 461–76; see especially pp. 461–4.

Index of Persons

Index of Subjects

absurd, absurdity, 146.
aesthetics, 55.
anguish, see "anxiety."
anti-Semitism, 25.
anxiety, 60, 61, 70, 72, 90, 94, 159.
appropriation, 8.
atheism, 22, 27, 105, 109, 113, 115, 116.
attack on Christendom, see "attack on the church."
attack on the church, 18, 28, 30, 35, 128, 129, 158, 160, 162, 173, 174, 176.
authority, 84–6.

Bible, 109, 168.
James, 127.
Job, 83, 145.
Matthew, 143.
New Testament, 52–4, 81, 82, 122, 138.

Catholicism, 27.
choice, 71.
Christendom, 32, 53, 82, 102, 117, 126, 129, 131, 158, 176.
Christianity, 5, 17, 22, 26, 27, 30, 32, 52–4, 73, 82, 87, 88, 92–4, 102, 105, 108, 109, 111, 114, 127, 128, 130, 138, 141, 145, 149, 153–63 passim, 174.
New Testament, 160, 162.
official, 53, 61, 126, 129, 131, 137.
comic, 80.
communication, 65–99.
indirect, 8, 30, 72–4, 94.
conscience, 151.
contemporaneity, 5.
Corsair, The, 25, 32, 34, 36, 50.

Darwinism, 103, 112

decision, see "choice."
demonic, the, 5, 11, 81, 94, 111.
depression, 140.
despair, 11, 79, 92, 94, 110, 111, 116, 128, 155, 156, 159.
double movement, 155.
doubt, 144.
dying from the world, 127.

earnestness, 80.
eroticism, see "love, erotic."
eternal happiness, 162.
ethics, teleological suspension of, 115, 148, 175.
existence, spheres of, 26, 32.
existentialism, 19, 115.

faith, 4, 90, 91, 93, 94, 126, 144, 146, 154, 155, 162.
Fall, the, 170.
fascism, 25.
freedom, 23, 28, 79, 80, 90, 111, 125.

genius, 84, 85.
God, death of, 102.
God-man, 7, 161.
grace, 130, 153, 154, 176.
Grundtvigianism, 66, 138, 144.

Hegelianism, 32.
hiin Enkelte, see "single individual, the."
history, 168.
humanism, 18, 23, 30.

idealism, 28.
imitation, 4, 126, 127, 130, 149, 154, 161.
incarnation, 4, 7.